Thomas Fenwick

Archbishop Lynch's answers to questions and objections concerning Catholic doctrine and practices

With appendices

Thomas Fenwick

Archbishop Lynch's answers to questions and objections concerning Catholic doctrine and practices
With appendices

ISBN/EAN: 9783743305496

Manufactured in Europe, USA, Canada, Australia, Japa

Cover: Foto ©Lupo / pixelio.de

Manufactured and distributed by brebook publishing software (www.brebook.com)

Thomas Fenwick

Archbishop Lynch's answers to questions and objections concerning Catholic doctrine and practices

ARCHBISHOP LYNCH'S

"ANSWERS

TO

Questions and Objections concerning Catholic Doctrine and Practices."

REVIEWED BY

REV. T. FENWICK,
ELDER'S MILLS, ONT.

WITH APPENDICES.

TORONTO:
PRESBYTERIAN PRINTING AND PUBLISHING COMPANY, Ltd.
1890.

Entered, according to Act of Parliament of Canada, in the year Eighteen Hundred and Ninety, by the REV. THOMAS FENWICK, in the office of the Minister of Agriculture.

AS AN EXPRESSION
OF THE WARM AFFECTION
WITH WHICH
I, HIS ONLY CHILD,
STILL REMEMBER HIM,
I INSCRIBE THE FOLLOWING WORK
TO THE MEMORY OF

My Father.

———o———

"A son honoureth his father."—*Malachi i. 6.*

———o———

THOMAS FENWICK.

CONTENTS.

	PAGE
DEDICATION.	5a
CONTENTS.........	7a
PREFACE	11a
DEVICE OF THE WALDENSIAN CHURCH.................	13a
REMARKS ON ADDRESS TO ROMAN CATHOLICS..........................	15a

REVIEW.

CHAPTER 1.—Review of Contents and the Archbishop's Dedication 1

CHAPTER 2.—*Questions*—(1) Why do the Catholics believe in what they do not understand?—(2) Why do Catholics not make the Bible their rule of faith, as the Protestants do?................ 9

CHAPTER 3.—*Questions*—(3) Must there not be many men of many minds?—(4) What, therefore, is the true rule of faith?—(5) Which is the more reasonable rule?—(6) Are Catholics prohibited to read the Bible? 20

CHAPTER 4.—*Questions*—(7) Did not Christ command His disciples to search the Scriptures?—(8) By what marks and signs can the true Church be known?............................. 31

CHAPTER 5.—*Questions*—(9) Why is the Catholic Church called Roman Catholic?—(10) Why do so many poor belong to the Catholic Church?—(11) Is it true that no matter what Church a man belongs to, etc., he will be saved?—(12) Can a man be honest in all respects, etc.?—(13) Why is the Catholic Church not progressive?—(14) What is the difference between the Catholic and Protestant religions?. 42

CHAPTER 6. -*Questions*—(15) Did not the Catholic Church fall into error?—(16) Are not all denominations branches of the true Church of Christ?—(17) Do Catholics believe that all who die outside of their communion are lost? *Objection*—(1) As there are many roads leading to a city, etc. Q. (18) What is the meaning of Councils?........... 53

CHAPTER 7.—*Questions*—(19) What is meant by the Infallibility of the Pope?—(20) What is the meaning of Papal Supremacy? *Objection*—(2) Is not the Pope only a Bishop? Q.—(21) What means the Hierarchy of the Church?—(22) Who are the Cardinals?—(23) How are the Popes elected?—(24) Why do not Catholics attend Protestant meetings?—(25) Why do Catholics hold so strongly to tradition?............... 62

CHAPTER 8.—*Questions*—(26) Whom do the Catholics worship?—(27) Do Catholics worship the Virgin Mary and the Saints?—(28) Was not the Virgin Mary a mere ordinary woman?—(29) Do not the Catholics give her too much honour?—(30) What means the Immaculate Conception?—(31) Is there Scripture for this?... 72

CHAPTER 9.—*Question*—(32) Do Catholics worship images of Christ and His saints?.. 83

CHAPTER 10. — *Questions* — (33) Does it not insult Christ to pray to the saints?—(34) How can the Saints hear our prayers?—(35) Does not the Catholic Church suppress the Second Commandment?... 93

CHAPTER 11.—*Questions*—(36) What is the meaning of the "communion of saints"?—(37) Do Catholics worship relics of saints?—(38) Do we read anything in the Bible about relics?........... 108

CHAPTER 12.—*Questions*—(39) Are the religious orders sects in the Church?—(40) Why do monks and nuns make vows?—(41) What do Catholics believe respecting good works?—(42) Have miracles ceased in the Church?—(43) Do Catholics place any faith in holy wells?.................................. 117

CHAPTER 13.—*Questions*—(44) What do Catholics believe concerning purgatory?—(45) Why do Catholics fast?—(46) Why do not Catholics eat meat on Fridays?—(47) Did not Christ say: "It is not that which goeth into the mouth," etc.?....... 127

CHAPTER 14.—*Questions*—(48) What is the meaning of rosaries?—(49) What are scapulars?—(50) Why do Catholics make the sign of the cross?—(51) Why have Catholics their children baptized?—(52) Is baptism absolutely necessary for salvation?—(53) What becomes of children who die unbaptized?—(54) Will merely pouring the water suffice for baptism?—(55) Is immersion necessary for baptism?—(56) What is the meaning of confirmation?... 136

CHAPTER 15.—*Questions*—(57) Why do Catholics confess their sins to the priest?—(58) Can the priest, as man, by his own power forgive sins?—(59) Does not confession encourage the sinner, etc.?—(60) Is confession always necessary?—(61) Are there any exceptions to the law of confession?—*Objection* (3) But do we not read in Scripture, etc. (Luke v. 21)? Q.—(62) Can a priest forgive the sins of any one he pleases?—(63) Is it blasphemy to say that a man can forgive sins?—(64)

CONTENTS. 9a

	PAGE.
Is the Catholic mode of obtaining forgiveness more difficult than the Protestant? *Obj.*—(4) But do not we read, "If we confess our sins?" etc. *Q.*—(65) Did the first Christians confess?—(66) Was confession continued in the Church? *Obj.*—(5) But was it not introduced by the Council of Lateran? *Q.*—(67) Is not confession practised in some Protestant Churches?—(68) Do the married clergy of the Greek Church hear confessions?............................	146

CHAPTER 16.—*Questions*—(69) What is the meaning of Indulgences? *Objection*—(6) Protestants say that when the sin is forgiven there is no temporal punishment due. *Q.*—(70) By what authority does the Church grant Indulgences?—(71) What is the Mass?—(72) If Christ was once offered on the cross, why offered every day in the Mass? *Obj.*—(7) Is it not contrary to common sense to say that bread could be the body of Christ? *Obj.*—(8) How could Christ hold His body in His own hands?... 158

CHAPTER 17.—*Questions*—(73) Why are the Mass, etc., performed in Latin?—(74) Why does the priest use such strange vestments?—(75) Why so many colours in the vestments?—(76) Why are candles used on the altar during Mass?—(77) Why is incense used in the Church?—(78) Why does the Church use so many ceremonies?—(79) Did Christ use ceremonies? 170

CHAPTER 18.—*Questions*—(80) Why do Catholics genuflect when they enter their churches?—(81) Why use holy water?—(82) Why do Catholics communicate under one kind? *Objection*—(9) But did not Christ say: "Except you eat the flesh of the Son of Man, and drink His blood," etc.? *Q.*—(83) What do Catholics mean by the sacred ministry, or the priesthood?—(84) Why do not priests marry?—(85) Can men and women live chastely without being married?—(86) Why are the priests called Fathers?........................... 178

CHAPTER 19.—*Questions*—(87) What do the Catholics believe of Christian marriage?—(88) Why does not the Church permit divorce? *Objection*—(10) But did not Christ permit divorces in certain cases? *Q.*—(89) Why does not the Catholic Church approve of marriages between Protestants and Catholics?—(90) Why are priests sent for to anoint the sick? *Obj.*—(11) Was not this anointing only to cure the body, and to be discontinued? *Q.*—(91) Does belief in one's own predestination ensure salvation?—(92) Has God destined some people for heaven—others for hell?—(93) Will all be saved on account of the death of Christ?—(94) What will become of those who never heard of Christ?—(95) What do you think of those who say, "There is no God"?.................................... 187

APPENDICES 207

PREFACE.

> *The Most Reverend*
> **John Joseph Lynch, D.D.,**
> FIRST ROMAN CATHOLIC ARCHBISHOP
> OF TORONTO.
> *DIED MAY 12, 1888.*
>
> AGED 72 YEARS.

HEN Sir Isaac Brock was first buried,* the United States Commander, as a mark of respect to a fallen foe, gave orders that during the sad ceremony, fighting should cease on his side, and minute guns be fired from Fort Niagara. In a like spirit, I set up the above tablet to the memory of him whose work I review in the following pages. A large part of them was written before his death. I decided that having gone so far, I would go on and finish.

His Grace's work was published in 1877. Soon after, I reviewed it in a series of twenty letters in the *British American Presbyterian*, now the *Canada Presbyterian*. I have used the very same style in the following work that I used in these letters. I looked on the Archbishop as an outspoken person, whose learning was not very extensive, and I have treated him accordingly. Even when I make sport of him—as I now and then do—I do so with the most kindly feelings towards him. Some may think that while it was quite becoming in me so to treat him while he was on

* See Note at the end of the Preface.

earth, it is far otherwise, now when he is in the world of spirits. In reply, I say that, in accordance with a very common figure of speech, I treat him as still living in his book. For example, we say: "Milton says this," and, "Shakespeare says that." Addison makes Cato say: "Plato, thou reasonest well," referring to a work of that philosopher which he has just been reading. I treat His Grace, on the whole, just as I did while he was alive, and as I would have done had he been still alive. In some instances, I have refrained from using a certain form of good-natured banter which I would otherwise have used, just because it would have been unbecoming in circumstances as they are now. I refer, for example, to a part of my remarks on honouring images.

Since writing the letters referred to, I have visited Europe, where I have seen a good deal of Romanism at home. I spent three weeks in what may still, in an ecclesiastical sense, be called the Pope's own city.

As I remark near the close of this work, my object in it is not to discuss everything pertaining to the Romish controversy, but simply review what the Archbishop says in his "Answers to Protestant Questions and Objections."

Those of my readers who do not hold what are commonly called Calvinistic views, will, I am sure, very readily excuse me for giving expression to such, near the close of my Review. When His Grace attacked certain peculiar doctrines of my Church, I, of course, could not let it pass unnoticed. Had he let them alone, I would have let him alone.

Of course, when the Archbishop quotes Scripture, he does so from the Douay Bible. I may remark that Psalm ix. in it, is Psalms ix. and x. in the Protestant Bible. Psalm x. in the former is, therefore, Psalm xi. in the latter, and so on to the end. When I quote Scripture, I do so from the Authorized Version, except when I mention another.

Some of my readers may think that I am very "disorderly," because, instead of finishing one subject before taking up another, I often leave one unfinished, take up several others, and then come back to the first, in the case of some, several times. In my defence, I have to say that I simply follow the order in which His Grace has arranged the "Questions and Objections" which he tries to answer. Order, in the sense of proper arrangement, was, certainly, not *his* first law.

The reader will find the style of the following work, in some respects, quite new, also some of the views on certain doctrines of the Romish Church which I express.

His Grace's work reached a sixth edition during his lifetime. The first time that he visited the present Pope, he gave him, among other things, a copy of one.

PREFACE.

NOTE.

A friend who read the MS. of the following work, remarked to me that the words "first buried" sounded strange to him. As they may do so to others, I shall here explain why I use them :—

Sir Isaac Brock has been buried more than once. Soon after the close of the war, a monument in his honour was set up on Queenston Heights, where he fell. If I be not mistaken, his remains, and those of his aide-de-camp Macdonnell, who fell in the same battle, were put within it. A few years after, some malicious persons shattered it with gunpowder. At once, an effort was made towards getting a new one. Many years, however, passed away, during which, the matter was allowed to rest. But, at last, the new monument became a reality. As yet, no harm has befallen it. The remains of the British general and his aide-de-camp now rest in stone coffins within it.

The old inhabitants of Toronto will remember an undertaker named John Ross, who was often familiarly called "John Ross the coffin maker." Several years ago, a "brother of the trade" did to him what the latter had himself done to hundreds. John, who was himself in the battle, made the first coffins for Sir Isaac and his aide-de-camp.

ELDER'S MILLS, ONT., *October*, 1890.   T. FENWICK.

DEVICE OF THE WALDENSIAN CHURCH.

REMARKS

On the Archbishop's Address to His Catholic Friends.

WHEN I wrote the following Review, I used a copy of the first edition of His Grace's work. The first time I was in Toronto after I finished it, I bought a copy of the last one. I wished to do His Grace full justice. I very naturally supposed that the glaring blunders in the first would not be found in it, and I meant, should such be the case, to give him the benefit thereof. The last edition is the sixth. It is marked "86th thousand," and was published in 1879. There is not the very slightest difference between it and the first. But there is added to it a short address from the author to his "Catholic Friends," which is not in the first. On that I shall now make a few remarks.

He is not so respectful to them as he is to his Protestant friends. He does not say to *them*, "My Dear Friends," but simply, "To our Catholic Friends. A few months ago, we dedicated to our Protestant friends," etc.

"Our good Lord has mercifully blessed this unpretending work."

The word "mercifully" is not a correct one here. According to present use, "mercy" means kindness to one who deserves punishment. That, of course, is not what His Grace means. He should have used the word "graciously," or one of the same meaning. "Grace" means kindness shown by a superior to an inferior who, simply, does not deserve it. Such is plainly what his Grace means.

"It has been found very useful and instructive to many."

What distinction is there between "useful" and "instructive," as here used?

"We have been informed that many Catholics bought several of these books to distribute, and to lend to their Protestant neighbours, who became far less bigotted, in fact, more friendly in their intercourse, and were not afraid to enter a Catholic Church, and listen to the sermons which they had been erroneously informed were delivered in Latin."

Is not "lending to," just a form of "distributing"? "Less bigotted" and "far more friendly in their intercourse. Either of these expressions is sufficient. These Protestants, it seems, were afraid of a Latin sermon. It could have done them as little bodily harm, as it could have spiritual. We speak of delivering a lecture, and of preaching a sermon. The Protestants whom His Grace's work would favourably incline towards Romanism, are not very intelligent ones.

"It was to give a ready answer to Catholics, as well as to inform Protestants, in search of true faith that this little book was composed."

"Love is blind." The "learned prelate," poor body! does not know that this child of his brain will be of little help to intelligent, anxious enquirers, either among his own people, or among Protestants. By "true faith," he means "the true faith," that is, the true religion. The two expressions are quite different in meaning.

"We exhort all Catholics to a greater zeal in propagating the truth wherever they can."

The principle on which this exhortation is founded is a most excellent one. If we believe a certain doctrine to be true, we should, in proportion to its importance, strive to get others to do the same, using, however, lawful means for that end. Of course, when Romanists believe that all knowingly and wilfully out of their Church shall go to hell, they should be zealous in seeking to bring them into it. Had the Archbishop stated his exhortation as fully as his Church teaches is the duty of her members in the case, he would have added, "and by whatever means they can." Let us hope that he omitted that, just because he thought that he had said enough.

"Those who convert others from the error of their ways will have gained their neighbours' and their own salvation."

Bad English here, Your Grace. Say "shall gain." You plainly refer to James v. 20. The Apostle there says that "he who converteth the sinner from the error of his way *shall* save a soul from death, and *shall* hide a multitude of sins." Bad theology here, also, Your Grace. If the converter be already a believer in Christ, he is already saved. Consequently, he cannot be saved again. But let that pass. Well, your Church considers it enough for a man's salvation that he profess to belong to her, and do whatsoever she commands him — especially that he pay her well. But we are saved by grace, through faith, not by belonging to any particular part of the visible Church, or by leading others to connect themselves with it. The multitude of sins which James says shall be hidden are not those of the converter, but of the converted. The *Greek* verb in the middle voice, requires this. "Though this hiding of sins was included in the previous 'shall save,' St. James expresses it to mark in detail the greatness of the blessings conferred on the penitent through the converter's instrumentality, and to incite others to the same good deed."

His Grace, in connection with his exhortation, refers to one passage of Scripture, the one which we have just been considering. In connection with it, I shall quote two. "They be blind leaders of the blind. And if the blind lead the blind, both shall fall into the ditch." (Matthew xv. 14.) "Ye compass sea and land to make one proselyte, and when he is made, ye make him twofold more the child of hell than yourselves." (xxiii. 15.)

"We have most earnestly recommended this humble work to the merciful power of our dear Lord, the great High Priest and Pastor of souls,"—

"Earnestly recommended." A very old fashioned expression, in the sense here used. In this enlightened age, we speak of recommending Mike O'Hoolahan to Mr. Jones as a first-class shoemaker, and Smith's Balm of a Million of Flowers to those who have "no hair on the top of their head, on the place where the hair ought to grow." "Merciful power." Another odd expression. To prove that power can be merciful, is beyond any one's power. Here, as in a sentence which we lately noticed, "merciful" is wrongly used.

"that the fire of truth and charity, which He came to cast on earth, may be more and more enkindled."

His Grace here refers to Luke xii. 49. What is meant by the "fire" there spoken of, is a question on which there is a difference of opinion among even the writers of his own Church. I shall not discuss it, but I would make a remark on the word "enkindled" at the close of the sentence just quoted. It is a poetical one, but, as here used, a ridiculous one. When a fire kindles, it begins to burn. It can then become greater, or spread. But it cannot more and more *begin* to burn. After a human being has received life, he begins to grow. But he cannot continue beginning to grow. It is the same with fire. What the Archbishop plainly means, is the increase or spreading of the fire of which he speaks. Had he prayed that that fire may spread till, to use another figure,

"—— like a sea of glory,
It spread from pole to pole,"

that would have been quite proper. But to pray that it may be more and more kindled, is ridiculous.

"May He bless all who join us in diffusing the true doctrine revealed by Him, preserved and preached to the whole world by the Catholic Church."

Whoever carefully compares the whole system of doctrine of the Romish Church with the word of God, will see clearly that the most of it was not revealed by Christ, and, therefore, it is not true. His Grace should have said " and preserved." He has just spoken of what has been, as he believes, done by Christ. Then he proceeds to speak of what his Church—that is, the Archbishop's—has done, and is still doing.

He closes by addressing his Catholic friends, as he does his "Dear" Protestant ones :—

" Your faithful servant in Christ,
" † JOHN JOSEPH LYNCH,
" *Archbishop of Toronto.*
"St. Michael's Palace, Feast of the Annunciation, 1878."

Of course, those addressed need not be afraid of the dagger-looking object which he here displays.

ERRATUM.

On page 61 of Review, 6th line from the top, for "only Councils can," read "Councils can only."

Review

OF

ARCHBISHOP LYNCH'S

"Answers to Questions and Objections Concerning Catholic Doctrine and Practices."

Chapter 1.

Review of the Contents and Dedication.

BEFORE the work which I am about to review, there is a Table of Contents, at the close whereof is the following :—

†

"TO THE GREATER HONOUR AND GLORY OF GOD."

Ha! what stands above these words? As Macbeth says: "Is this a dagger which I see before me?" It is very like one. What means this sign? Means it, "'War to the knife' against Protestants?" And the words beneath—what mean they? How often His Grace's Church has used the dagger in slaughtering heretics,[1] professing, and that, no doubt, in all sincerity, to do so for the end which they express! But let us judge him charitably. Let us believe that the seeming dagger is a cross, and that the only dagger which the Archbishop desires

(1) See Appendix I.

to use against Protestants is his "little book," with which he hopes to kill them by turning them into "good Catholics," which shall, in his sight and that of his Church, be "to the greater honour and glory of God." Let us now pass on to

THE DEDICATION,

which is to Protestants. It is like the forest spoken of in I. Samuel xiv. 26, where—as the Hebrew means—"behold! there was a stream of honey." His Grace's Church calls Protestants "accursed heretics." *He* calls them, in the title, his "Protestant Friends." Yea, more, he begins his address to them by calling them his "Dear Friends." This, certainly, is very *friendly* language. If it come from his heart, he is not a good son of his Church. But he is one, though he should speak "with flattering lip, and with a double heart," if he do so for what—according to her—is "to the greater honour and glory of God." Let us now consider some of the things which he says to his "Dear Protestant Friends." I shall state them in his own words.

ARCHBISHOP.—"During a missionary career of over thirty years, ... we have met with many estimable persons, who were most anxious to acquire the knowledge of truth which would lead them most securely to eternal life."

These "estimable persons"—as we are afterwards told—were Protestants. They must have been Protestants of a very poor kind, else they would have known that "the Word of God which is contained in the Scriptures of the Old and New Testaments, is the only rule to direct us how we may glorify and enjoy Him."[1] Mere knowledge of the truth will not save any one. The Holy Scriptures are able to make men wise unto salvation *through faith which is in Christ Jesus*. (II. Tim. iii. 15.)

ARCHB.—"They believed in our Lord Jesus Christ as their Redeemer, but were afraid to join any of the modern religious denominations, lest they might not find in them all that Christ taught."

(1) Shorter Catechism of the Presbyterian Church, Question 2.

Of course, they never for a moment thought of joining any of the *ancient* religious denominations. They did not believe in Christ in the sense in which the Scriptures represent doing so as connected with salvation (See, for example, John iii. 36), else they would have joined some religious body. We know that no Church on earth is perfect, but some appear to us more scriptural than others. We should connect ourselves with the one which appears to us most so. The faith in Christ which those had of whom His Grace speaks, was, plainly, but an exercise of the understanding.

ARCHB.—" They respected all, believing that they contained many pious people, yet, distrusting their own powers of examining and pronouncing which was the true, or which was the false, they hesitated to join any."

They were, certainly, persons of "broad sympathies." They held in equal esteem denominations of utterly opposite views on the most important doctrines. According to their representation of themselves, they were very humble. They wished to find some human being who would do their thinking about religion for them, so that they would need only to join the Church which he would bid them join. The Scriptures say: "If any man lack wisdom, let him ask of God." (James i. 5.) But they had never made the matter of church membership a matter of prayer. Their modesty was, in fact, laziness arising from carelessness.

ARCHB.—" We asked those persons if they ever examined the doctrines of the Catholic Church, acknowledged by all to be the first."

Och! shure, an' Yir Lardship's Rivirince is the by to knock the Prahtestants into smithereens. Ye've done it now. You say that the docthrines uv the Cahthlic Church are acknowledged by ahll to be the first. What can bate that? Hooraw! Yes, all make the acknowledgement of which His Grace here speaks—except those who do not. The number of the latter is many millions. It is larger than that of the former. The simple statement which we are now considering, is not enough. The speaker must prove the truth of it by proving that these doctrines are according to the Word of God. The peculiar doctrines of his Church he cannot prove to be so. The cool, unhesitating manner in which the Archbishop makes this unqualified statement concerning his Church is most amusing. The thought of it is almost about enough to refresh one when the thermometer rises to near 100 degrees above zero. "Had ever examined" would be a more correct expression than "ever examined," "The Archbishop's English"—as we shall often see hereafter—is not of the best quality.

"They ('those estimable persons') said, No; they were taught and believed from their infancy that that Church was most corrupt in its doctrines and practices, . . . (and) that they had never spoken to a Catholic Priest before, or read a Catholic book. Then, we replied, would you not like, as a just man, before pronouncing judgment, to give fair play, and hear the other side of the question?"

"The learned prelate" does not express himself here very elegantly. His meaning is, however, plain enough. He bids "those pious people" who "distrust their own powers of examining and pronouncing which is the true Church or which is the false," exercise their "private judgment," as Paul bids the Corinthians do when he says to them, "I speak as to wise men; judge ye what I say." (I. Corinth. x. 15.) So far, the principle which His Grace here lays down is a most excellent one. But does he grant the same privilege to his own people? Does he allow them to hear "the Protestant side of the question"? Nay, verily. With *them*, "the case is altered." They must turn a deaf ear to "the other side." They bring down on themselves the wrath of " Mother Church " if they reason that if His Grace's advice, which we have just been considering, be good for Protestants, it cannot be bad for "Catholics," and act accordingly. In his Answer to Question 24—which we shall at another time consider—he states the reasons "why Catholics do not attend Protestant worship," and he, of course, approves of them. The freedom of thought which his Church gives her children is akin to the freedom of speech of which we have the following instance recorded in *Punch*: A person, pointing to a picture, says to a friend: "I'll knock any fellow down who says that is not an original. Now, sir, let me have your candid opinion on the subject."[1]

ARCHB.—"We further remarked that there were a great many respectable and good living Catholics who would leave that Church if it were so corrupt as they supposed. We certainly would not belong to it."

The most that this proves is that those spoken of are sincere in their profession. But may not their eyes be "darkened that they do not see"? We know what a powerful effect on the mind early impressions have. How many who have left the Romish Church have said that, at one time, they walked in darkness! The sinnner is blind to his folly and danger. Hence, Christ came "to preach recovering of sight to the blind," and He commissioned Paul to "open the eyes of sinners, and to turn them from darkness to light." Peter says that God has "called His people out of darkness into His marvellous light." I have not the least doubt that many in the Church of Rome see no fault in it. But the true test of a Church is the Word of God. Have those of whom the Archbishop speaks ever tried their Church carefully and prayerfully by it? All that I need do, at present, is simply to point out the weakness of the Archbishop's argument.

ARCHB.—"We considered it due to truth and honour to explain, 1st. What was *not* the faith of Catholic; and, 2nd, What they do actually believe."

Bad composition, Your Grace. You should have said either "1st. What was (or is) not the faith of Catholics; and, 2nd. What was (or is) their faith," or, "1st. What Catholics do not believe; and, 2nd. What they do believe."

(1) See Appendix II.

Archb.—"'Thou shalt not bear false witness against thy neighbour' is one of the commands of a just God, who wills that we be respected, not only in our property, but also in our reputation. Many bear false witness (we hope unwittingly) to the faith and practices of the Catholic Church."

We shall often find while we are examining his "Answers," that His Grace bears false witness ("let us hope unwittingly") against the faith and practices of Protestants. Instead of saying, "bearing false witness to," he should have said, "bearing false witness against."

Archb.—"Our Protestant friends who know us, we think, can bear testimony of our kindly feelings towards persons of all denominations. We acknowledge that the precept of loving our neighbour as ourselves extends beyond our relations and Church associates. Christ has made no distinction, neither should we."

This is "as a very lovely song," but whether the speaker "thinks it in his heart" or not, we cannot tell. Only God "searches the hearts and tries the reins of the children of men." The Archbishop's language here is in direct opposition to that of the standards of his Church. According to *them*, heretics are to be put to death, if that can be done without harm to her interests. A boy once gave it as a reason for letting alone another who had called him bad names, that the latter was "bigger" than he. When the Romish Church does not persecute heretics, it is only for a reason of the same kind. Putting a tiger into a strong cage does not change his nature. When we look at one in a menagerie, we do so with all the more pleasure when we consider that he is "confined to his room." If Archbishop Lynch's Church were to get again the power which she once had, she would show no mercy to heretics; and if he did not obey her commands, he would not be a good son of hers. I have no doubt that many of her members —yea, even of her priesthood—have the most friendly feelings towards Protestants, but such are better than their Church. We have great reason to thank God that we live in a land where the Romish Church has not full power, though she has all the freedom which she can reasonably desire, if not a little more. Regarding the manner in which she teaches that heretics should be treated, I shall speak more fully hereafter.[1]

ARCHB.—"We put the questions and objections concerning the Catholic Church, as nearly as we could recollect, in the very words used by our Protestant interrogators."

Your Grace, would not "can," in this sentence, be more "illigant" than "could"?

ARCHB.—"The true faith is spreading and gaining ground in many places; it is also combatting with increasing success the indifferentism and infidelity which appear to gain the ascendancy among a certain class of would-be philosophers."

The latter part of this passage is contained in the first. By "the true faith," the speaker, of course, means his Church. It is not, on the whole, spreading. It is losing far more than it is gaining. But the true faith—properly so called—is spreading. Do not "spreading," "gaining ground," and "combatting with increasing success," all mean the same thing? "Indifference" is a more common word than "indifferentism," and just as good. The same is true of "among," as compared with "amongst." Would it not be better to call these philosophers "self-styled" than "would-be"? They believe that they *are* philosophers.

ARCHB.—"Christianity has been on its trial since its founder was judged by the world and condemned; but Christianity, like its author, reigns from the cross. It conquers in great humiliations and public calamities."

The "learned prelate's" composition here is very like a school-boy's. But we can readily assent to what he says.

He then goes on to say that "Our Lord has His elect everywhere, and is continually bringing them together." In

(1) See Appendix I.

support of this, he quotes John x. 16, "And other sheep I have," etc., and John xvii. 21, "That they all may be one," etc. He adds that "there are trials and tribulations in store for those who embrace and follow the truth, but St. Paul consoles them when he says, 'For that which is at present momentary and light of our tribulations,' etc. (II. Cor. iv. 17.)" Here His Grace and we are in full accord, though his views of Christ's elect, and of those who embrace and follow the truth, are, most probably, not precisely the same as ours.

The Archbishop closes his Dedication in the following words:—

"With an earnest prayer to our divine Saviour for the glory of His Kingdom, and 'for peace on earth to men of good will' (Luke ii. 14).
"We are, yours faithfully in Christ,
"† JOHN JOSEPH LYNCH,
"Archbishop of Toronto."

In this prayer, also, we can heartily unite with the author, though the expression "prayer for the glory of Christ's Kingdom" sounds somewhat strange, and he and we may not have the same belief as to what forms that glory. Whether he would be "ours faithfully in Christ," if his Church were to have full power in Canada, we, of course, cannot tell. It is far better that he is not put to the proof. A dagger-looking object, like the one already spoken of, stands before his name. Of course, after listening to the loving words which have just fallen from his lips, we must not put a bad meaning on it. We must not suppose that it means that these words are like his of whom David thus speaks: "His mouth was smooth as butter, but his heart was war; his words were softer than oil, yet were they *drawn swords*," (†) (Psalm lv. 21, *Rev. Ver.*)

Here I shall close my remarks on His Grace's Dedication, and, at the same time, my first chapter.

Chapter 2.

Questions—(1) Why do the Catholics believe in what they do not understand? (2) Why do Catholics not make the Bible their rule of faith, as the Protestants do?

E come now to "the learned prelate's"

"ANSWERS," ETC.

In my review of them, I shall give his own words as often as I can do so without taking up too much space. When I find it necessary to give only the substance of them, I shall state his arguments with all the force which really belongs to them. I wish to do so. Mis-stating an opponent's arguments is one form of bearing false witness against our neighbour. No real advantage is gained thereby. I proceed now to my task.

At the beginning, we find the words "CHAPTER I." We, therefore, very naturally expect to meet with, at least, one chapter more. But the whole work is contained in "CHAPTER I." It is absurd to speak of the first of a thing of which there is only one. Who ever speaks of the first wheel of a new wheelbarrow? His Grace would never think of saying "The First Book of Genesis," "The First Epistle to the Romans," "The First Chapter of the Book of Obadiah," or "The First Chapter of the Epistle of Jude." Och! me darlint, a good scholar loike Yir Lardship's Rivirince should spake corrictly.

QUESTION 1.—"Why do Catholics believe in what they do not understand?"

Protestants do the same, but "let that pass." His Grace answers: "Because God requires of them (Catholics) to do so." What he further says on this point is very true, though somewhat confused. He says: "Faith is to believe that which we cannot understand, relying on the authority of God who reveals." "Faith" is a noun; "to believe," a verb in the infinitive mood. Would it not, therefore, Your Grace, be more elegant English to say here : " Faith is belief in that which we cannot understand," etc., or, "believing that which we cannot understand," etc.? As we can have faith in the word of a fellow-being, the author should have said that he here speaks of faith in relation to the word of God. He tells the story of St. Augustine once seeing a child scooping out with its hand a hole in the sand of the sea-shore. He asked it why it was doing so. The child replied that it was going to put the sea there. According to the Archbishop, the Saint said, "That is impossible." The child answered : " It is just as impossible for this hole to contain the ocean as for your head to contain the thought that now occupies it—God." His Grace should have made the child say: " as possible." According to the common form of this story, St. Augustine, when the child told him for what purpose it was making the hole in the sand, smiled and walked on. But soon after, he said to himself: " I am as foolish as that child, for I am trying to understand matters which I can no more understand than the hole which he has made in the sand can hold the sea." This seems to be the correct form of the story. According to the Archbishop's, the child spoke to the Saint in an impudent manner. Further, how did he know what was in the Saint's mind at the time ? The "learned prelate" further says : "People believe on the word of learned men what they do not understand. They believe that the sun stands still, though to the eye it appears to move." Your Grace, if you had lived in the days of Galileo, and had believed that about the sun, you would have had to keep it to yourself, else the " Holy " Inquisition would have put you into the " Kill ease," and if you had " stood still " in your heresy, have, by and by, " lynched " you. The Archbishop's Answer to Question 1 is—as the boarder said to his landlady about his coffee—" very good—such as it is."

Q. 2.—"Why do Catholics not make the Bible their rule of faith as the Protestants do?"

This question may be understood in two senses: (1) "Why do 'Catholics' not make the Bible their rule of faith? The Protestants do so." (2) "Why do 'Catholics' not make the Bible their rule of faith in the same manner as the Protestants do?" In answer to another question, His Grace says that the true rule of faith is the word of Jesus Christ. He, therefore, does not understand the one under consideration in the first sense. Further, his Answers apply to it in the second. Cardinal Wiseman says truly that "the fundamental principle of Protestantism is this, that the Word of God alone is the true standard and rule of faith;" and, again, that "the principle that whatsoever is not in that book, cannot be true in religion, or an article of faith; is the principle of Protestantism."[1] Protestants also believe "that, when anything is offered as necessary to be believed in order to salvation, every Christian hath a right and liberty of judging whether it can be proved by the Scripture to be necessary or not."[2]

Our friend, the Archbishop, does not agree with his "Dear Protestant Friends" on these points. What his views thereon are, we shall see as we go on through the galleries of his "little book" before us. His answers to Question 2 are as follows:—

1. "Because the Bible nowhere tells them to do so, and yet St. Paul says, 'Without faith it is impossible to please God,'" (Heb. xi. 6).

His Grace argues that because the Bible nowhere says that it is our only rule of faith, or—to express it otherwise—nowhere forbids us to add anything to it as our rule of faith, therefore we may add tradition to it as such. Well, granting for the present, that his statement is correct, I maintain that if the Bible says that we are to take it as our rule of faith, that is enough. We cannot add anything to it, unless it gives us

---
(1) Wiseman's Lectures on the Catholic Church, pp. 8, 19.
(2) Protestantism Contrasted with Romanism, Vol. I., p. 5.

authority to do so. Now, we find no mention in the Bible of anything but itself as our rule of faith. Of many passages which prove this, I can quote only one or two: "If they hear not Moses and the Prophets, neither will they be persuaded though one rose from the dead;" "Beginning at Moses and all the Prophets, He expounded unto them in all the Scriptures the things concerning himself. . . . All things must be fulfilled which were written in the law of Moses, and in the Prophets, and in the Psalms, concerning Me" (Luke xvi. 31; xxiv. 27, 44.); "The Holy Scriptures are able to make thee wise unto salvation" (II. Timothy iii. 15.) Suppose the Archbishop should take a Breviary to a bookbinder to have it bound again. When it comes back to him, he finds Kirwan's Letters to Archbishop Hughes bound up with it. To this union, he is, of course, strongly opposed. Accordingly, he goes to the craftsman referred to, and expresses his views of it with great animation. The latter, in self-defence, says: "Your Grace did not say that I was to bind only the Breviary." The Church dignitary addressed would look on that as "a moity wake argymint." He would say in reply, something like this: "When I told you to bind the Breviary, that was enough. You had no right whatever to bind up anything with it, unless you had my consent to your doing so." In this case, his reasoning would be quite correct; but his argument against the Bible as the only rule of faith, which we are now considering, is as false as that of the bookbinder in the case supposed. Take another illustration. His Grace calls some day on one of his flock whom he finds suffering from a "cruel bad cowld." He advises him to take a good drink of warm skilligalee just before going to bed. Accordingly, Pat has the prescribed medicine ready at the time appointed. Believing that "union is strength," he adds thereto "a good drap uv the craythur," to make it more "howlesome," then sends it down "Red Lane," smacking his lips after "all is over." He reasons about the skilligalee, precisely as "His Lardship's Rivirince" does about the rule of faith. "Ye see that His Grace didn't say wan word agin putting a shillelah in it; naythur he did."

But we are distinctly forbidden to add to the Word of God. "Add thou not unto His words" (Proverbs xxx. 6.) "If any man shall add unto these things, God shall add unto him the plagues that are written in this book" (Revelation xxii. 18.)

Let us now look at one or two proofs that it is the right and the duty of all Christians to read and study the Scriptures. The Israelites were commanded to teach them diligently to their children (Deut. vi. 7-9.) The Scriptures were read before all Israel—men, women and children, and strangers—that they might hear, and learn, and fear the Lord, and observe to do all the words of the law (xxxi. 11-13.) In answer to the question, "Wherewithal shall a young man cleanse his way?" the Psalmist answers, "By taking heed thereto according to Thy word" (Psalm cxix. 9.) The Bereans did not believe what even Paul preached to them, till after they had compared it with the Scriptures and found that the two agreed (Acts xvii. 11, 12.) Paul says to the Corinthians: "I speak as to wise men; judge ye what I say" (I. Corinth. x. 15.) Timothy knew the Scriptures from his infancy—for so the original means (II. Timothy iii. 15.) He was taught them by his mother Eunice, perhaps also, by his grandmother Lois (i. 5.) (See also Acts xvi. 1.) Now, all those spoken to, or of, in the passages which I have mentioned or quoted, were what is commonly called "lay persons." It is true that Timothy was a preacher of the Gospel, but he was taught the Scriptures as soon as he could understand anything. We cannot for a moment suppose that less has been given to, and is required of us than was given to, and required of Israel of old, or even the early Christians. I have not made use of John v. 39, which, according to the Authorized Version, contains a command to search the Scriptures. I prefer the rendering of it in the Revised one, which makes it a statement. As such, the verse seems to me to connect more naturally with the next verse (40), than it does as a command. Still, taken even as a statement, it is not in the least opposed to the point which I have endeavoured to prove.

Let us now turn to the other Answers which our "Dear Roman Catholic Friend" (we are his "Dear Protestant Friends") gives to this question (p. 1).

2. "Because such a rule would be impossible to the generality of Christians."

How it would, we can only guess, as His Grace does not tell us. This Answer is really no answer at all. It seems to be contained in his fourth Answer. If it be so, it is an utter waste of words.

3. "Because it would be changeable according to the interpretation that each individual would choose to put on the text, as his learning, prejudice, ignorance or previous training would induce him."

The interpretation of words does not in the least affect the words themselves. His Grace must mean that if every one were allowed to read the Bible and to judge for himself, there would be, owing to the different causes mentioned, an immense variety of interpretations put on it. No other interpretation, which any one can understand, can be put on the words before us. Do not "learning" and "previous training" here amount to the same thing? Is not "prejudice" a result of "previous training"? Och! me darlint, sure an' it's mesilf that's shacked at an archbishop exprissin' his oidayahs in sich a clumsy way.

4. This Answer is in substance as follows :—

"(a) There could be no rule of faith till the Bible was all written and in the hands of every one who could read and rightly interpret it. But before A.D. 63, when the last of the New Testament was written, the true faith was spread throughout the whole world. (b) The Scriptures were not separated from the Apocrypha till A.D. 494. (c) Till the invention of printing in 1440 but few had Bibles. Even at the present day a very large part of the people are unlearned."

(a) The Old Testament, as we see from passages already quoted, and many others, was the rule of faith before the New

Testament was written. (b) The Jews and the early Christians never acknowledged the Apocrypha of the Old Testament to be divinely inspired. At the third Council of Carthage, A.D. 397, nearly one hundred years before that of Rome, a list of books forming the Scriptures of the New Testament was adopted, which is precisely the same as our own. The early Christians never received the Apocrypha of the New Testament as of divine inspiration. Admitting that the Council of Rome, the one to which His Grace refers, rejected the Apocrypha of the Old Testament, which is doubtful, the Council of Trent, A.D. 1546, received it as of equal authority with the Old and New Testaments. Therefore, Council opposed Council; and, if the Council of Trent was in the right, the Church was for fifteen hundred years without a large part of the Word of God. (c) Those who could not read were commanded to listen to the reading of the Word as they had opportunity. Under the Old Testament, and in the early ages of the Christian Church, there were few who were learned. The great mass of the people had, therefore, to get their knowledge of the Scriptures in the latter way. This is why the expression "hearing," instead of "reading," the law, or the word, is so often used in both Testaments.

I once attended a public meeting in Toronto, at which a Roman Catholic Jew gave an account of what he called his conversion to Christianity. It was, chiefly, a pointing out the agreement between Judaism and Romanism. In the course of his remarks he said, with reference to every one reading the Scriptures, "Suppose I were blind, how could I read them?" As almost all present were Romanists, this question, of course, caused a "roar of laughter." I did not on that occasion "speak out in meetin'," but—as the song says—"said I to myself, said I." I said in this way, "Your Church commands every one of her members to confess to a priest, at least once a year, all his sins which he remembers. Now, suppose one is dumb. He cannot write, neither can he speak with his fingers. How can he make his confession?"

5. "Protestants themselves do not take the Bible alone as their rule of faith, as each denomination has its peculiar creed. . . . If any member of the various denominations should interpret the Bible in a different sense from that recognised by the whole body, he would be told to retire from the Church. If the words of Christ, 'This is My body,' be taken in their literal sense by a Protestant, he would be charged with Romanizing, or believing Catholic doctrine. These words of Christ have been interpreted in a hundred different ways by Protestant writers."

There we have a beautiful specimen of—confusion. This is one of the Answers which the "learned prelate" gives to the question, "Why do Catholics not make the Bible their rule of faith as the Protestants do?" Therefore, according to him, they do not, because Protestants themselves do not. In this instance, then, they follow the Protestants. Admitting that what His Grace here says about the latter is correct, that does not justify the former. If I do wrong, "You're another," or —to use the language of His Grace's Church, "*Tu quoque*"— is no argument in my favour. "Two blacks do not make a white." But he confounds two things which in their nature are quite distinct from each other. My rule of faith teaches me what I *must* believe. My creed is a statement to the world of what I *do* believe. Och! but it's astanished oi am that an intilligint gintleman loike Yir Lardship's Rivirince doesn't persave the dufference betwane them. The Archbishop is quite correct in what he says about a member of any of the other Churches holding doctrines opposed to the creed of his Church, if he means a minister thereof teaching them. That Church would act only on the principle on which every society has to. Of course, it would allow more freedom to a private member. But if it should cut off a minister or a private member, it would not curse him up and down, through and through, and all around, as the Romish Church does in a case of that kind. His Grace is quite correct in what he says about a Protestant literally interpreting the words of Christ, "This is My body." No true Protestant so interprets them. But our

"Dear Roman Catholic Friend" "draws the long bow" when he speaks of the hundred different ways in which Protestant writers have interpreted these words. A small boy once told his mother that a thousand cats were fighting in the back yard. But after she had cross-questioned him a little, he admitted that, at any rate, there were two. If His Grace were treated in like manner, he, too, would have to lessen his first statement very considerably. Well, striking out the words "a hundred," as merely "a flourish of trumpets," and reading "several different ways," or merely "different ways," and, instead of "Protestant writers," "Roman Catholic writers," the statement would be quite true. Even the most eminent writers in His Grace's Church are very much divided in their views of the words which he quotes.

6. "The Bible interpreted by individuals has given rise to over five hundred sects and denominations, and new ones are forming every day, all disagreeing in their views and beliefs of various texts of the Scriptures, and yet making the Bible the corner-stone of their religion, 'and are tossed about by every wind of doctrine'" (Ephes. iv. 14.)

His Grace's "little book" was first published in 1877— ten years ago.[1] Well, according to him, 3,650 sects of the kind which he describes have been formed during that time. To these add the "over five hundred" in being when he wrote. This makes, in all, say 4,200. But I shall not criticize him too severely. No doubt, in "the heat of the moment," he leaped before looking. What is the difference between "sects" and "denominations," and between "views" and "beliefs"? The several interpretations of the Bible of which His Grace here speaks are not said to change it. But he speaks very differently in Answer 3, of which this one is just a repetition.

All professing Christians outside the Church of Rome are not Protestants. Still, there are many denominations among the Protestants. They are, however, in perfect harmony on essential doctrines. But there is an immense variety of

(1) This was written in 1887.

opinions on essential doctrines among Roman Catholic writers, some of whom are Doctors, others Popes, and others Saints. The best educated Roman Catholic is not allowed to judge for himself in matters of religion. He must believe just what the Church teaches. If anything which a Roman Catholic believes be according to the word of God, that Roman Catholic believes it, not because it is according to the word of God, but because his Church bids him believe it. Every one should have full liberty to read God's word, and judge for himself. If any one wilfully misinterpret it, he shall have to give account to God for that. Whoever reads that word with reverence, with love, with readiness to believe what it teaches and to do what it commands, and with prayer for the help of the Holy Spirit to enable him to understand it, shall learn therefrom what it is necessary for him to know while he is in the world. What he knows not now, he shall know hereafter, as far as a created mind can understand it. When "the day breaks, the shadows shall flee away." God has promised it, and "faithful is He who hath promised, who also will do it." Where there is political freedom there are political sects.

7. "A rule of faith being so necessary ought to be easily understood, but St. Peter says, speaking of the Epistles of St. Paul, 'That certain things are hard to be understood which the unlearned and unstable wrest, as they do also the other Scriptures, to their own destruction'" (2 Peter iii. 16).

His Grace thinks that a rule of faith ought to be easily understood. A rule of faith from God must, in the nature of things, teach some doctrines "too high for us to attain thereto." But even the Romish rule of faith contains "things hard to be understood," many of which are believed by Protestants. Among these are the following: God never had a beginning. He has no form. He is everywhere present. He knows all things. He can do all things. He never changes. There are three distinct persons, yet one God, "the same in substance, equal in power and glory." One is the Father, another the Son, yet each is Eternal. Christ is God and Man in two distinct natures and one person. There are some things in the Romish rule of faith which, to Protestants, are utter nonsense. Admitting them to be true, they are, at least, hard to be understood. Roman Catholics acknowledge them to be so. I shall mention only one—the doctrine of Transubstantiation. This they term a mystery. His Grace, in his answer to Question 1, says that "Catholics believe in what they do not understand, because God requires of them to do so." Further on in the same Answer, he says, "People believe on the word of learned men what they do not understand . . . yet refuse to believe truths on the Word of God, because, forsooth, they do not understand them." This is not consistent with his 7th Answer to Question 2. What we need to know for our salvation, is taught so plainly in Scripture that "babes" (Matt. xi. 25), can understand it.

Regarding the "wresting" of the Scriptures spoken of by Peter in the passage quoted by His Grace, Dr. Littledale very justly remarks: "There is not a hint of withdrawing the Scriptures from circulation because of this abuse on the part of a few, nor in the case of these few is there any distinction drawn between clergy and laity; while, as a fact, most of the ancient heresies have had a clerical, not a lay origin."[1]

I may add that the Fathers advocated the right and the duty of every one to study the Scriptures. As Dr. Littledale says: "The ancient Church was to the full as much vexed by manifold sects and heresies, often appealing to the Bible, as modern Christianity, perhaps even more so, and therefore the same reason might have been pleaded then as is urged by the Roman Church now for keeping the Bible a sealed book."[2]

(1) Plain Reasons Against Joining the Church of Rome, p. 94.
(2) Plain Reasons Against Joining the Church of Rome, p. 94.

Chapter 3.

Questions—(3) Must there not be many men of many minds?—(4) What, therefore, is the true rule of faith?—(5) Which is the more reasonable rule?—(6) Are Catholics prohibited to read the Bible?

QUESTION 3.—" Must there not be many men of many minds?"
ANSWER.—" Yes ; but not in matters of faith and morality."

ROMAN CATHOLICS make great use of the divisions among Protestants as an argument against their religion. We say in reply that Protestants disagree only on questions of secondary importance, but are in perfect harmony on those of primary importance. The Archbishop makes here the same distinction. His Church makes the same. According to her, there are questions of *faith* (which includes morality), and questions of *discipline*. She regards the former as essential, the latter as non-essential. For example, she allows the Maronite priests who belong to her communion to marry, but forbids the rest of her priesthood to do so.

Q. 4.—" What, therefore, is the true rule of faith, or by whose authority are articles of faith to be defined?"

To the view of a Protestant, these are two perfectly separate questions. "Defining articles of faith," he considers as simply drawing up a Confession of Faith. The difference between a Rule of Faith, and a Confession of Faith, I have pointed out in my review of His Grace's 5th answer to Question 2. In his Answers to the question before us (4), he first takes up the second part.

He says that "Presbyterians and Methodists say (that articles of faith are to be defined) by the authority of their General Assembly or Conference. The Church of England has to acknowledge that the royal authority must settle its rule of faith." These denominations and all other Protestant ones, declare to the world what they believe are certain doctrines taught in the Word of God. Of course, they cannot allow to remain in their communion, any who preach contrary to them. No society can safely keep within it, any who act against it. But no Protestant denomination curses any who withdraw from it, or whom it puts out, as the Romish Church does in such cases. Here is what the Church of England says about the rule of faith: "Holy Scripture containeth all things necessary to salvation; so that whatsoever is not read therein, nor may be proved thereby, is not to be required of any man, that it should be believed as an article of Faith, or be thought requisite or necessary to salvation."[1] Whatever civil courts may decide concerning the worship or government of that Church, they cannot set aside the article which I have just quoted. All Protestant churches believe the doctrine which it expresses.

His Grace adds: "None (of these three denominations) claim infallibility for these authorities, therefore they have no infallible rule of faith, and all are liable to error, according to themselves." In one of his Answers to Question 7, he says: "Protestants do not pretend to infallibility, and consequently are liable to lead their followers astray." According to His Grace:—

(I.) "He who does not pretend to infallibility is fallible. Protestants do not pretend to infallibility. Therefore, they are fallible."

(II.) "He who pretends to infallibility is infallible. The Church of Rome pretends to infallibility. Therefore, she is infallible."

Therefore, those medicines which, according to the newspapers and like publications, can cure almost anything, have really the virtues ascribed to them. A show said to be "the biggest show on earth" must, therefore, be so. Excuse me,

(1) Thirty-nine Articles; Article VI.

Yir Grace's Rivirince, fur giving ye a good pat on the back. Let me shake hands wid ye. Ye've sittled the Prahtestants, so ye have. Oi'm proud uv ye. Ye're an aner to the owld sod. Erin go bragh! The shamrock fur ivir!

In his Answer to the first part of this question (4), His Grace says:—

"The true rule of faith ordained by Jesus Christ is His Word, interpreted by His infallible Church, which He established to act in His stead."

In support of this, he quotes three passages. The first is, "Hear the Church; and he that will not hear the Church let him be considered as a heathen and publican" (Matt. xviii. 17). This passage has not the very slightest reference to a rule of faith. In the 15th verse of the chapter, our Lord supposes one professing follower of His to have wronged another. He bids the latter go to the former, and talk over the matter with him by himself. Perhaps the wrong-doer will acknowledge his fault, and the two become as good friends as they were before. If this effort prove unsuccessful, let the injured one put forth another. Let him go to the wrong-doer with two or three of the brethren. It may be that he will listen to *them* (v. 16). If that fail, let the other lay his case before the Church. If the wrong-doer continue obstinate, then let the wronged one, while he has no ill feelings towards him, keep aloof from him—for such is the meaning of our Lord's counsel in the 17th verse. His Grace has either never read the three verses, or he has utterly misinterpreted the one which he quotes, I shall charitably suppose, owing to want of attention. He can plead guilty to whichever of these charges he likes. One or other is true. The next proof is: "He that hears you hears Me, and he that despiseth you despiseth Me, and he that despiseth Me despiseth Him who sent Me" (Luke x. 16). The seventy disciples to whom our Lord addressed these words, were to receive the same honour as Himself when they preached the preaching which He bade them. Christ said of His teaching, "It is not Mine, but His that sent Me" (John vii. 17.) The same was true of theirs. Protestants believe that, for the same reason, ministers of the Gospel now should receive the same honour when they speak according to the Word of Christ in the Scriptures, but only when they do so (Isaiah viii. 20). The Bereans tried even Paul's teaching by the Scriptures. The Archbishop's last proof in support of this point is, " Behold, I am with you all days to the consummation of the world" (Matt. xxviii. 20). This—as one expresses it—"vouches for nothing more than that Christ will always preserve some one branch of his Church as a living witness of the truth, so that it shall never wholly and entirely fall into error."[1] And, as Dr. Littledale says: "There is in Scripture no promise of infallibility to the Church at any given time. . . . The Church of one generation may err, and that grievously, but there will be always enough truth mixed with the error to bring things right again. That is to say, the Church is *indefectible* in the long run, though the teaching voice may be fallible at any given time."[2] Even in the days of the Apostles, there were divisions in the Church. I may here remark that the Apostles were to the Church like what the twelve Patriarchs were to ancient Israel. Each was the head of a tribe, yet the twelve tribes together formed one people. But there is this difference between the Apostles and the Patriarchs. One of the latter was the head of the kingly tribe, another of the priestly. But in the promise which we are considering, our Lord does not say one word about any therein addressed having power over the rest. He puts all on a perfect level. But let us hear what the highest Roman Catholic priest in Toronto has further to say on this subject.

"The Church is an infallible guide. Christ could not tell us to obey any other. He promised infallibility to His Church. 'And He said to Peter, Thou art a rock, and upon this rock I will build my Church, and the gates of hell shall not prevail against it'" (Matt. xvi. 18.)

(1) Protestantism Contrasted with Romanism, etc., Vol. I., p. 190.
(2) Plain Reasons Against Joining the Church of Rome, pp. 146-7.

Of course, by "The Church," His Grace never means any other than his own. The Church is not an infallible guide. Cardinal Newman himself, in the *Rambler* for July, 1859, shows that the laity have sometimes saved the Faith betrayed by Popes or Bishops, when, in St. Hilary's words, "the ears of the people were holier than the hearts of the priests," so that, the Cardinal observes, "the *Ecclesia Docens* is not at every time the active instrument of the Church's infallibility." Of course, Christ could not tell us to obey any but an infallible guide. But He does not command us to obey the Church. He says: "Call no man your father upon the earth: for one is your Father, which is in heaven" (Matt. xxiii. 9.) We are to obey Himself speaking to us in His word. We have just seen that He did not promise infallibility to His Church in the sense in which His Grace uses the expression. His Church, as we shall see hereafter, from time to time, has grievously erred from the faith. As I have so many of His Grace's Answers yet to examine, I cannot, without making this work too bulky, examine this favourite passage of his Church with anything like fulness. I shall just say that our Lord gave Peter no superiority—the other Apostles gave him none—and he claimed none. The Romish Church countenances four different interpretations of "the Rock." All the Apostles and the Prophets are, together, "the Church's one foundation," "and the corner stone is Christ" (Ephes. ii. 20.) Christ Himself is said to be the only foundation (1 Corinth. iii. 11.) Both passages are in perfect harmony with each other. All the Apostles received power to bind and loose (John xx. 23.) "The gates of hell" are not the power of Satan, but of Hades, the invisible state. This promise seems, therefore, to be one of protection from utter destruction, like the one, "No weapon that is formed against thee shall prosper" (Isaiah liv. 17), and the other, "I will be unto her a wall of fire round about" (Zech. ii. 5.)

Q. 5.—"Which is the more reasonable rule—the word of God interpreted by an infallible Church, or the same word by a body of men who are fallible, and whose creeds may be formed or reformed by other men?"

A.—"Certainly the word of God, interpreted by an infallible Church—the Church of Christ."

What I have said in answer to His Grace's Answer to Question 4, makes it unnecessary for me to review at length his words which I have just quoted. Christ has not appointed any particular company of men as the only keepers of the truth. The Romish Church is not infallible. She is not the Church of Christ. The Westminster Confession of Faith very truly says: "The infallible rule of interpretation of Scripture is the Scripture itself. . . . The supreme Judge, by which all controversies of religion are to be determined, and all decrees of councils, opinions of ancient writers, doctrines of men, and private spirits are to be examined, and in whose sentence we are to rest, can be no other but the Holy Spirit speaking in the Scripture."[1] Dr. Littledale "reasons well" when he says: "God gave a revelation to the Jews fifteen hundred years before Christ, but no one pretends that they ever had an infallible living voice to keep them from all error regarding the law of Moses. And yet, as they had not Christ's example and teaching, nor the indwelling of the Holy Spirit in the Jewish Church, they needed such an infallible guide more than Christians do."[2]

Q. 6. "Are Catholics prohibited to read the Bible?"

A. "No; Bibles are sold in all Catholic book stores, and there are few Catholics, who are able to procure the Bible, that have not one. It is an old calumny, having for its foundation, that Catholics are prohibited from interpreting the Bible according to individual fancies."

The fourth Rule of the Congregation of Prohibited Books, approved by Pius IV., says: "It is manifest by experience that if the Holy Bible in the vulgar tongue be suffered to be

(1) West. Con. of Faith, Chap. I., Sect's 9, 10.
(2) Plain Reasons Against Joining the Church of Rome, p. 148.

read everywhere without distinction, more evil than good arises." Clement XI., in his Bull *Unigenitus*, in 1713, condemned as "false, scandalous, pernicious, seditious, impious, blasphemous and heretical" the 101 Propositions of Quesnel, of which five relate to the reading of the Scriptures. The following are three of them. "It is useful and necessary at all times, in all places, and for all kinds of people, to study and learn the spirit, holiness and mysteries of the sacred Scripture." "The reading of Holy Scripture is for all." "The Lord's Day ought to be hallowed by Christians with pious reading, and above all of Holy Scripture. It is dangerous to attempt dissuading Christians from this reading." The other two are to the same effect. The Romish Church continues to affirm that "if the sacred Scriptures be everywhere indiscriminately published, more evil than advantage will arise thence, because of the rashness of men." Is not this, to all intents and purposes, forbidding Roman Catholics to read the Scriptures? If I say to a person, regarding some particular object: "If you touch it, you will hurt yourself very severely," is it not the same as saying to him: "Do not touch it"? If people believe that their reading the Scriptures is like one handling nitro-glycerine who does not know how it should be handled, will they not, very naturally, let them alone? No Roman Catholic is allowed to read, without permission from his priest, a translation of the Scriptures, even one by a member of his own Church. Roman Catholics often burn copies of Protestant translations of the Scriptures. Protestants never burn Roman Catholic ones. The difference between the two translations is very slight. If those who burn copies of Protestant ones do not know it, they are very ignorant. If they do, it is plain that they hate the Bible. When His Grace says that "Bibles are sold in all Catholic book stores," he says what is not true. I do not deny that it is true of such places in Protestant countries where the Romish Church does many things against her will. But it is far otherwise in countries where she has full power. There we see her in her true colours.

Even in the large cities in those countries, it is very difficult to find any copies of translations of the Scriptures in the common tongue. Those which are met with, are so costly that few can buy them, which is really forbidding others to read them. Even in Protestant countries, no Roman Catholic Bibles are sold as cheap as Protestant ones. His Grace says that few Catholics, who are able to buy the Bible, are without one. Many of that class have none. Many who have one, do not read it. They keep it as a piece of ornamental furniture, and an argument against Protestants when the latter say that the Church of Rome forbids the reading of the Scriptures. I have conversed with some of the best educated laymen in Rimouski, in the Province of Quebec, and I found them to be utterly ignorant of the Scriptures. If they had a Bible, they did not read it. In Roman Catholic countries, few even of the highest classes have a Bible. I fear that Archbishop Lynch himself does not study his Bible as diligently as a minister of religion should. But let us hear what he further says on this subject.

"Interpreting the Bible by individuals has been the source of a multitude of errors, false doctrines, and so-called religions."

Our attention has already been directed to a statement of the same nature. I would just say that there is an immense variety of opinions, even on essential points, among the writers whom the Romish Church holds in honour. Every Romish priest solemnly swears that he will never "take or interpret the Holy Scriptures otherwise than according to the unanimous consent of the Fathers."[1] That consent is just as much a reality as the man in the moon is. The Pagans made the same objection to the early Christians which the Romanists now bring against the Protestants,—"We know not which to choose of your sects." The test which Chrysostom bade them use, was the word of God. What is the difference between "errors" and "false doctrines" here?

(1) Creed of Pope Pius IV.

"A respectable Protestant publisher in this city informs us that in one year he sold one thousand Catholic Bibles."

What His Grace has just said about Bibles being sold in all Roman Catholic book stores, makes me take what he here says, as some say we should eat nuts—with a little salt. I would like to ask that publisher a question or two. A Bible, strictly speaking, contains both the Old and the New Testaments. It is quite likely that most of these "Catholic Bibles" were only New Testaments. Many Protestants call the New Testament "the Bible," as if it were the whole of the Bible. That publisher may have called both Bibles and New Testaments "Bibles." He may have said that he had sold one thousand, meaning that he had done so while he had been in business, and His Grace may have misunderstood him. Many Protestants who sell Romish books of devotion, take no interest whatever in them. They sell them just as they sell photographic albums, fancy soap, and walking sticks—to "turn a penny" by them. Hence, they are apt to call all these books "Catholic Bibles." Even a Roman Catholic once showed me a book which he called a Bible, but which was only a prayer book. I do not contradict His Grace, but if I knew who that "respectable Protestant publisher in Toronto" is, I would, "for further particulars, apply to" him.

"Every Sunday, at Mass, throughout the entire world, Catholic priests read and explain the Gospel and Epistle of the day to the people."

They do not *read* the Gospel and Epistle to the *people*. The Breviary Lessons are in Latin. Besides, they are part of an office which is never said in any parish church whatever, namely, the Nocturns or Night Hours. An explanation of the Gospel at Mass *may* be given, but is not obligatory. There is nothing in Roman Catholic churches corresponding to the reading of the Scriptures in Protestant ones. Preaching is a very unusual thing in St. Peter's at Rome. There is no pulpit there. When Pius IX. preached his first sermon, which, I think, was also his last, after he became Pope, it was the first by a Pope during three hundred years. The late Rev. Dr. Murray ("Kirwan") of Elizabethtown, N.J., was brought up a Roman Catholic. He was a true Christian, though, of course, Your Grace speaks most bitterly against him. Well, hear what he says: "For years together I sat daily at table with a Catholic priest, who was a member of the family, and the curate of the parish, and I never saw a Bible used in the family. I never heard at table, or in the morning, or in the evening, a religious service. The numbers of the Douay Bible published by subscription in folio, were taken in the family, but never read. And not only so, but I never heard a sermon preached in a Catholic chapel in Ireland; nor a word of explanation on a single Christian topic, doctrine, or duty." "I venture the assertion that there are multitudes of Catholic churches in Catholic countries where a sermon would be as great a rarity as would be the saying of mass in a Scottish kirk!"[1]

Before closing this Answer, I would notice the Brief of Pius VI. prefixed to Archbishop Martini's Italian version pubblished in 1778. This is the only argument of any weight in proof that the Romish Church approves of the circulation of the Scriptures in the mother tongue of the readers. But it is an illustration of the truth of the saying: "All is not gold that glitters." The edition to which that brief applies is in *twenty-three* volumes. Such a work is, of course, a very costly one, and, therefore, it is virtually a prohibited one to most persons. In 1818, an edition of it without any notes was published, but it was immediately put on the Index—treated the very same as if it had been an infidel book. Leo XII., in his Encyclical of 1824, terms translations of the Bible into the mother tongue of the readers, "poisonous pastures." He makes no mention of Pius VI.'s commendation of Martini's.

We see, then, that the Church of Rome discourages her

1) See Appendix IV.

people to read the Scriptures,[1] that she dares not publish translations in the mother tongue of their readers without notes designed to make them interpret the Scriptures as she does, that in countries under her sway, she approves only of such copies of these as are too costly for most persons to get, and that none of her members is allowed to read even translations which she approves, without permission from his priest, which permission the latter is very apt to refuse if he thinks that the applicant really desires to know the truth. There are priests who exhort their people to the diligent and prayerful study of the Scriptures, yea, do not forbid them to read Protestant translations. Such, however, are "few and far between," and better than their Church.

(1) See Appendix III.

Chapter 4.

Questions—(7) Did not Christ command His disciples to search the Scriptures?
(8) By what marks and signs can the true Church be known?

QUESTION 7.—"Did not Christ command His disciples to search the Scriptures?"

HIS GRACE says that He did not. The New Testament was not written, and the Old was in the hands of the priests and a few of the laity. But He did not forbid them to do so. This kind of argument, we have already seen, has great weight with the Archbishop. Further, Christ's disciples heard Him repeatedly speaking of what Moses and the Prophets had said. Was not this really an exhortation to them to search the Scriptures? His Grace adds:—

"Christ said to the Scribes, 'You search the Scriptures; they give testimony of Me.'"

How this proves that He did not command His disciples to search the Scriptures, I must say that I need something more powerful than the Most Rev. J. J. Lynch's spectacles to enable me to see. The Archbishop next says:—

"Before Protestantism commenced, there were upwards of twenty versions of the Scriptures into all the modern languages."

What connection this has with the "Answer" to which it belongs, is another riddle which I must "give up." If His Grace mean by "modern languages" those now spoken, his use of the word "all" here, is like what he says about the hundred ways in which Protestant writers have interpreted Christ's words, "This is My body." If he mean the languages now spoken in Europe, he says what also is incorrect, though not on such a large scale as in the other instance. Before the

Reformation—the time to which His Grace refers—the Scriptures were not translated into, for example, the Gaelic, Irish, Welsh, Norwegian, Swedish, Danish and Breton languages. I am not aware that since then, a Roman Catholic translation of them into any new language has been made. If it be otherwise, the number of languages of that kind into which such translations have been made is very small. On the other hand, Protestants at the present day publish the Bible wholly, or in part, in three hundred languages.

His Grace next says:—

"The first use printing was put to was to publish Catholic Bibles. First at Mentz, in 1462," etc.

Very good; but that was of no benefit to the mass of the people. These Bibles were copies of the Vulgate, which is in Latin. Only scholars, therefore, could understand them. Besides, they were bulky, and, therefore, expensive. The printed Roman Catholic translations which the Archbishop mentions, had so many notes connected with them that they, also, were too costly for most persons. The Church of Rome has never sought to put the Word of God within the reach of the common people, save in Protestant countries. But the Reformers acted altogether differently as soon as they could make use of the printing press.

The "learned prelate" closes his "Answer" to this Question (7) with a list of early printed Roman Catholic and Protestant versions, and one of early Roman Catholic manuscript versions. His object is to show that his Church was before the Protestant one in seeking to spread abroad the Word of God. What I say in the last paragraph, shows that he "has not whereof to glory," as regards, at least, the printed ones. The latest which he mentions is a Roman Catholic one, printed in 1578. His list is very defective. He mentions Bruccioli's, in Italian, printed at Venice in 1532. In his preface, the translator waxes indignant at all prohibitions of the Bible, and every hindrance to its widest spread among the people. His work, however, seems to have had scarcely any circulation in Italy outside of Venice, and was indeed put in the first class of prohibited books. Probably, His Grace was not aware of these facts when he wrote his "Answers." The first Protestant version of the Bible was published in 1530. Luther's version of the New Testament first appeared in 1522—not 1552, as His Grace says. Taverner's Old Testament firstappeared in 1551, the Great Bible in 1539, the Genevan in 1560, and the Bishops' in 1568. Of these English versions, the Archbishop says nothing. The only Roman Catholic version in English, consists of the New Testament published at Rheims in 1582, and of the Old Testament published at Douay in 1609. It is from the Vulgate, but the translators, notwithstanding their constant abuse of heretics in the notes, are greatly indebted to Protestant versions. The English of it is most wretched. In modern editions, the English is better, and the notes are less furious. Still, there is great room for improvement in both. Wycliffe's version in MS. appeared about 1380. He was anxious to have the Word of God widely spread among his countrymen. But I must here bring my remarks on this subject to a close.

Q. 8.—" By what marks and signs can the true Church be known from the numerous churches that spring into existence?"

In answer to this, His Grace mentions five, which we shall presently consider. What is the difference between "marks" and "signs"? But, "let that pass." He says that his Church has all these, but outside it, we do not find them. They are described as follows:—

1. "The true Church must have been instituted by Christ and continued by His apostles and their lawful successors, under the presidency of St. Peter and his successors in office."

The apostles, as such, could not have successors. Further, many of those in the so-called line of succession did not obtain their office lawfully. Once more, the doctrine of intention makes it utterly uncertain that any one was rightly ordained.

But if only one was not rightly ordained, the line referred to, must end at him. We have seen that Peter had no authority over his fellow apostles. We have no clear proof that he ever set his foot in Rome. Even if he did, it was utterly impossible for him to be bishop there for twenty-five years. He could not, therefore, have successors in office there. But even granting all that the Romish Church says about Peter's connection with Rome, Papal succession is a matter of the greatest uncertainty. Where it begins—who was the first Pope after Peter?—is a question which has not yet been fully settled. Several of the Popes obtained office by unlawful, in some instances, by abominable, means. During 500 years, the highest Romish authorities, among whom were Popes and Saints, maintained that the story of Popess Joan was true. Several of the Popes were ambitious, several of grossly vile lives, several both.[1] The doctrine of intention makes it utterly uncertain that any of the Popes was rightly baptized, and rightly ordained. Sometimes two, sometimes three, claimed to be each the true Pope, cursing each other and declaring each other's acts to be of no force. Sometimes, most bloody fights took place between the followers of one, and those of another. Sometimes, a Council put both or all out of office, and appointed a different one. The others were not satisfied with this, so the strife continued. Even the highest Romish authorities confess their utter inability at times to tell who was the rightful claimant. Och! me honey, Yir Grace's Rivirence, many's the scrimmage that's been at Donnybrook Fair. Toimes wur thin purty loively, I tell ye. Oo! how the bys made their blackthorns play whack on ache other's heads loike paypul batin carpits! The words they'd be spakin wor purty sthrang wid foire and brimstone. But there nivir wuz a scrimmage at Donnybrook Fair to aykwil those betwane the contindin Papes and those who follyd thim. Och! me jewel, oi intrate ye not to attimpt to foind out the loines uv Apostalical and Papal succishun, or ye'll be afther settin yer vinirable

(1) See Appendix V.

fut on a bog that'll swally ye up intoirely, an' our beloved Archbishop 'll nivir be sane again. There's nivir a bog in ould Oireland that kin aykwil it.

2. "It must be Catholic as to time as well as to place; spread throughout the entire world from the apostolic times."

His Grace's Church is not Catholic as to *time*. It is not apostolic, for it has widely departed from apostolic doctrines. Additions have been made, from time to time, to its doctrines and ceremonies. For example, before December 8, 1854, the Immaculate Conception of the Virgin, and before July 18, 1870, that of Papal Infallibility, were open questions.[1] It is not Catholic as to *place*. From the days of the Apostles, there have been Churches holding the leading doctrines of Protestantism and rejecting the peculiarities of Romanism. There can be no doubt that the Greek Church is as old as the Romish. The former has never submitted to the latter, but, on the contrary, has excommunicated the Pope and all the Romish priesthood. It makes no account of Romish baptism. It is said that in the East, where the Greek Church is the ruling one, a Roman Catholic, if you say to him: "Are you a Catholic?" answers: "No, I am a Papalist." It is only the Greeks who there call themselves Catholics. An inquisitor of the 13th century, says: "Waldensianism is the most ancient heresy; and existed, . . . according to some, from the days of the Apostles." According to many Romish authorities, the Waldenses rejected all the peculiarities of Romanism, were remarkable for the purity of their lives, and their love of learning, and were spread almost throughout the whole Latin world.[2] I could give the names of several other Churches of the class already described, but I must pass on.

3. "It must teach the same doctrines."

It could very easily be shown that the greatest variety of

(1) See Appendix VI.
(2) See Appendix VII., and end of Preface.

opinion, even on essential points, is expressed by Romish writers, among whom are Doctors, Cardinals, Popes and Saints.[1]

4. "It must be holy in its doctrines, sacraments, and in the large number of its members, though some may be so only in name."

The Romish Church teaches doctrines which are most unholy. One is that some sins are venial. Another is that one can do works of supererogation—that is, be better than God requires him to be. A third is that a sinner can have the merits of these works put to his account to make up what he lacks. On this, indulgences are founded. A fourth is that the Church can give one liberty to do what would otherwise be a mortal sin. Such permission is called a dispensation. A fifth is that of Purgatory, according to which, one can go almost any length in sin, yet, at last, be received to glory. A sixth is that oaths contrary to the interests of the Church are not binding. Many others of the same kind could be mentioned. The Romish Church is unholy in its sacraments. Take the two Scriptural ones. According to her, Baptism takes away original sin. The Mass—her form of the Lord's Supper—makes the death of Christ insufficient to take away sin. Take two of her five additional sacraments. Penance makes self-inflicted suffering atone for sin. Extreme Unction prepares one for Heaven by a little holy oil put on certain parts of the body in the hour of death. His Grace is even more unfortunate in saying that his Church is holy in the large number of its members. Very many of the Popes were guilty of the grossest sins. Several of the Councils were composed of persons of the vilest character. In past ages, when the Church of Rome thought that she could safely disregard public opinion, the great mass of priests, monks and nuns lived most shamefully and shamelessly. The exceptions were like only a star here and there in a cloudy sky. These statements are made on the

---

(1) Look, for example, at the fierce controversies between the Dominicans and Franciscans, the Jansenists and Jesuits, the Scotists and Thomists, the Canonists and Schoolmen, and the Nominalists and Realists. On the question of Infallibility there are several parties.

authority of Roman Catholic writers. Even at the present day, the more "Catholicism" there is, the more crime there is. For example, in Vienna, the capital of Catholic Austria, more than half of the children born there, are bastards. During the reign of the Pope, licentiousness, robbery and murder abounded in Rome—his own city. Many other facts could be given showing how much more fruitful in crime Romanism is than Protestantism.

5. "It must be infallible; that is, it never can teach error."

The Archbishop's Church has not this mark. I have shown that she is unholy in her doctrines and sacraments. She, therefore, teaches error. We shall have many another proof of this before we reach the end of "the learned prelate's" work. Let us now hear what he says about Protestants.

"Other Churches did not commence in the times of the Apostles. . . . They are not universal, as regards time."

What difference is there, Your Grace, between these two sentences in meaning? Well, your Church did not commence in the times of the Apostles, unless one of the sects which then appeared, was the beginning of it.

"Their founders are well known in different times and countries. Luther, Calvin, Lollard, Knox, Wesley, Irving, Swedenborg, etc."

Those who removed the soil under which the houses in Pompeii were buried, did not build these houses. They merely brought them again to the light. Luther, Calvin, and Knox merely removed the mass of error under which the Romish Church had buried the Gospel. Wesley did not seek to change the creed or the forms of the Church of England, but to arouse it to a more lively concern for the salvation of the ungodly. Protestants do not acknowledge the Irvingites and Swedenborgians as belonging to them. Sects arose in the earliest ages of the Christian Church which the Christians opposed. The Protestants have firmly withstood the different forms of error which have sprung up among them.

"Other churches do not possess unity of faith, disagreeing among themselves on essential points : witness the various articles and Confessions of Faith, and their attempts to improve on them,[1] and the divisions in their respective bodies. There are many sects among the Methodists, Presbyterians, and also parties in the Church of England."

His Grace here bears false witness against his "Dear Protestant Friends," "let us hope unwittingly,"—to use his own language. Protestants agree fully among themselves on essential points. Witness the various "Articles and Confessions of Faith" of all the Reformed Churches. Even the Romish Church professes to give her members liberty of opinion on non-essential points. The "attempts to improve" were directed only to stating essential doctrines in plainer language, not in removing them altogether, and to removing articles concerning non-essential ones, on which there was a variety of opinion. His Grace's Church has many a time "attempted to improve" her creed, but the improvements which she has made on it, need very much to be improved. Several Popes—"heads of the Church on earth, under Christ the great Head," as the Archbishop calls them—professed different creeds. Vigilius professed four.[2] Marcellinus was an idolater. One drank to the health of the Arch-Fiend. The Archbishop does not see many divisions among the Methodists and Presbyterians in Canada. He should put the word "and" between the names of these bodies. The different parties among them agree on essential points. Those ministers in the Church of England who preach contrary to her creed, and act contrary to her rules, some of whom are really infidels, and others Papists,[3] are liars, yea perjured persons. They have most solemnly professed to believe her creed, and promised to preach according to it, and act according to her rules. If they were honourable men, they would "go out of the midst of her." A quack once said to his clown before a crowd which he was haranguing : "Andrew, did we come here for want?" "No, indeed," said the latter : "we had too

---

(1) See Appendix VIII.   (2) See Appendix V.   (3) See Appendix IX.

much of that at home." His Grace does not need to leave his own Church to find one in which there is an abundance of parties.

"Other churches fail in the sanctity of doctrine, allowing divorces against the command of our Lord Himself, who said: 'Whom God hath joined together let not man put asunder.' (Matt. xix. 6.) Divorces open the doors to numerous sins and scandals."

When I come to the question, "Why does not the Church permit divorces?" I shall show that the word of God permits them in certain cases. The granting of divorces is a favourite argument with His Grace against Protestant Churches. Approving of the enforced celibacy of the clergy, monks, and nuns, and condemning divorces such as those allowed by Protestant Churches, is "swallowing a camel and straining out a gnat."

"The Protestant Churches deny the necessity of good works, affirming that faith alone is all sufficient, consequently a man may live all his life without any works of charity."

These statements are glaring misrepresentations. The only favourable view that can be taken of His Grace here is that he is utterly ignorant of that whereof he affirms. By good works, Protestants understand "only such as God hath commanded in His Holy Word." They deny the necessity of good works to merit for us eternal life. "We cannot, by our best works, merit pardon of sin, or eternal life at the hand of God." This is the teaching of Scripture. "He that believeth on the Son hath everlasting life. (John iii. 36.) "By grace are ye saved through faith, and that not of yourselves: it is the gift of God; not of works lest any man should boast." (Ephes. ii. 8, 9.) "Not by works of righteousness which we have done, but according to His mercy He saved us." (Titus iii. 5.) We can make peace with God only by taking hold of His strength—believing in the strong One on whom He has laid help. (Isaiah xxvii. 5, Psalm lxxxix. 19.) At the same time, Protestants believe good works to be of very great value, and that it is, therefore, our duty to be "careful to maintain good works. (Titus iii. 8.) They believe that "without holiness no man shall see the Lord. (Hebrews xii. 14.) The Westminster Confession of Faith expresses the views of all Protestants on good works when it says: "These good works done in obedience to God's commandments, are the fruits and evidences of a true and lively faith, and by them believers manifest their thankfulness, strengthen their assurance, edify their brethren, adorn the profession of the Gospel, stop the mouths of the adversaries, and glorify God, whose workmanship they are, created in Christ Jesus thereunto; that having their fruit unto holiness, they may have the end eternal life."[1] Protestants believe that faith without works is dead, therefore, useless, and that while, on the one hand, we must trust wholly in Christ for salvation, we must, on the other, be as diligent in doing good works as if we could by them merit salvation. Protestants, therefore, while they look on good works as utterly worthless in one respect, look on them as of very great value in another. A thing may be of great value for one purpose, yet be of none whatever for another. A steamboat would be utterly worthless on the land, a railway train would be the same on the water. Protestants put good works in their proper place, which the Archbishop's Church does not.'

"Other Churches do not furnish the great means of sanctification instituted by Christ, viz.: the Sacraments, especially Penance, and the true body of Christ."

Penance is not a sacrament. Transubstantiation—as we shall afterwards see—is a doctrine utterly opposed to the word of God. The Romish Church teaches that it is infinitely more important to have Christ in the stomach, than to have Him in the heart.

"Other Churches do not pretend to infallibility, and consequently are liable to lead their followers astray."

---

(1) Confession of Faith, Ch. xvi., Sect. ii.

As I have already observed, according to this, a Church which pretends to infallibility, is not liable to lead its followers astray. "Pretence" or "assurance," or—to use a homely phrase—"cheek," has great power, it seems. Such a Church as the one just mentioned, *may*, however, lead its followers astray. His Grace's has led hers far astray. Her "pretensions" to infallibility are only a "pretence."

"To pronounce which Scriptures are to be received as the Word of God, and which are Apocryphal, requires infallibility, otherwise the true may be pronounced false."

The Romish Church, the only one which "pretends" to infallibility, has declared the Apocrypha of the Old Testament to be a part of the word of God. It has, therefore, while not pronouncing the true to be false, pronounced the false to be true.

Chapter 5.

Questions—(9) Why is the Catholic Church called Roman Catholic?—(10) Why do so many poor belong to the Catholic Church?—(11) Is it true that no matter what Church a man belongs to, etc., he will be saved?—(12) Can a man be honest in all respects, etc.?—(13) Why is the Catholic Church not progressive?—(14) What is the difference between the Catholic and Protestant religions?

QUESTION 9.—"Why is the Catholic Church called Roman Catholic?"

ANSWER.—"Because the head of the Church on earth under Christ is the Bishop of Rome, successor of Peter in that See."

THAT Peter was Bishop of Rome has yet to be proved. It cannot be proved. It was impossible for Peter to be Bishop of Rome as he was an apostle—the Apostle of the Circumcision. We have seen that neither Christ, nor his fellow-apostles gave him any superiority over the latter, and that he himself never claimed it. In his Epistle to the Romans, Paul sends no greeting to Peter. He would, certainly, have sent one, had Peter been Bishop of Rome, which Peter must have been when Paul wrote it, if he ever was. In that epistle, Paul expresses a strong desire to preach the Gospel in Rome. (Romans i. 9-11; xv. 23.) But he says also that he has "striven to preach the Gospel, not where Christ was named, lest he should build on another man's foundation." (xv. 20.) He would not have used such language had Peter been, at the time of his writing it, Bishop of Rome. The see of Rome in which Peter was bishop is a *sea* too stormy for any Romanist to venture his bark on it. The title "Roman" has a limited meaning, "Catholic" an unlimited one.

"The Episcopal Church is called the English Church because its head is the Queen of England, and so with the Russian Church."

The English Church is so called, not because the "Queen of England" is its head, that is, its temporal head, but because it is the Church established in England by law. The expression, "Queen of England," is not correct. It should be, "Queen of Great Britain and Ireland." The Church which is established in Russia, and of which the Emperor is the temporal head, is called the Greek Church.[1] That Church is, of course, not so called because its temporal head is the King of Greece. The Church of Scotland is so called, because it is the Established Church of that country, not because the Queen of Scotland is its temporal head. That Church owns no one as such. The learned prelate—"poor body!"—has a very limited knowledge of other churches than his own.

"The Wesleyans, Congregational, etc., take their names from their founders, or from some peculiarity in their faith or discipline."

"Wesleyans" here should be "Wesleyan Methodists." "Congregational" should be "Congregationalists." These professing Christians can prove their right to the names by which they call themselves. His Grace's Church is neither "Holy," "Catholic," "Apostolic," nor "Roman," as descended from the church at Rome to which Paul wrote one of his epistles.

Q. 10.—"Why do so many poor belong to the Catholic Church?"

This is a very interesting question. Let us hear how His Grace answers it, and accounts for the fact to which it refers.

"Christ came to evangelize the poor, (Luke iv. 18) 'The Spirit of the Lord . . . hath anointed Me to preach the Gospel to the poor.' And He said, 'The poor you will always have with you.'"

His Grace here reasons well—to those who can understand him. His proofs are as clear as charcoal.

"The early Christians were nearly all poor; the generality of the rich were too fond of ease and the honours of the world to embrace

(1) See Appendix X.

the religion of Jesus Christ, and too many at the present day are following their example."

Other proofs of the kind above described, of the connection between Popery and so much poverty can be given. I have no doubt that many of the early Christians were poor, but I am inclined to believe that the number of such was smaller than His Grace represents. Poor persons do not own lands or houses. The language of Luke seems to mean that several who owned the one or the other, joined themselves to the early Christian Church. (See Acts ii. 44, 45; iv. 32, 34-37.) Still, after all, His Grace is quite correct in what he here says of the rich. What he says of multitudes at the present day is as true.

"Riches form no sign of the true faith, for Jesus has said, 'Woe to you that are filled: for you shall hunger' (Luke vi. 25). 'Amen, I say to you that a rich man shall hardly enter into the kingdom of heaven.'"

What the Archbishop here says of riches, is just as true of poverty. The fact of a man's having very little of this world's goods, does not necessarily prove that he is a true Christian. It is infinitely more important to have true faith in the heart, than in the head. "He is not a Jew who is one outwardly; neither is that circumcision which is outward in the flesh: But he is a Jew who is one inwardly; and circumcision is that of the heart, in the spirit, and not in the letter; whose praise is not of men, but of God." So says Paul in his Epistle to the early Church of Rome (ii. 28, 29.) "The Pope's a very wealthy man, which nobody can deny." Consequently—according to the learned prelate's reasoning—he shall hardly enter into the kingdom of heaven. Some of the Popes, we have great reason to fear, have not entered into it.

The Archbishop next says that Christ did not promise His followers riches, but foretold that they would meet with many trials and tribulations, and that the rich must be poor in spirit—"that is humble and lovers of the poor"—else they cannot enter into heaven. In support of what he has said, he quotes the blessing on the poor in spirit in Matt. v. 3, and what James says about God having chosen the poor (James ii. 5.)

Humility or "lowliness of mind" and loving the poor, are closely connected, but they are different graces. The first is poverty of spirit. The second is rather a form of mercy, the grace of which our Lord speaks in Matt. v. 7. His Grace confounds poverty of spirit with poverty of purse, in his two quotations referred to.

Our "Dear Roman Catholic Friend" professess to account for so many poor being in his Church. His attempt to do so is, certainly, not a success. If he proves anything at all, it is that there are so many poor in his Church, because there are so many godly persons there. This is not complimentary to wealthy Roman Catholics, though their Church has a special favour to the gold ring and goodly apparel (James ii. 2.) If an empty purse be a proof of a renewed heart, tramps and anarchists have strong claims on us to rank them among the excellent of the earth.

Here is *my* answer to this Question. Because their Church makes them pay her so much. She makes money by everything she does for her members from their birth, till they are let out of Purgatory. When Chiniquy's father died, the priest took the cow which was very much the support of the family, as payment for masses for the repose of his soul. Again, Roman Catholics have such a great number of holidays, especially where she has great power. In her sight, it is a far less heinous sin to work on the Lord's Day than on these. This, of course, takes away so much from the time required for needed worldly work. While the word of God commands us to be fervent in spirit, serving the Lord, it also commands us to be diligent in business. (Romans xii. 11.) The same commandment which bids us give one day in seven to God, bids us labour and do all our work on the other six. (Exodus xx. 9.)

Papal countries are countries without the Bible. Even the Roman Catholic Bishop of Birmingham has to admit that a familiarity with the Bible does more for the intellectual culture of mankind than all mere literary study put together. He claims for "Catholic" children, "so far as they may do so with propriety," the same advantages that Protestants have in this respect. Of all means for the moral culture of mankind, we can truly say of the reading of the Bible, "with care, and reverence, and with prayer for the grace and blessing of God," as David said of the sword of Goliath, "There is none like it."

Bishop Ryle very truly says: "The nations which enjoy most moral light, are nations in which the Bible is most known. The parishes in our land where there is most true religion are those in which the Bible is most studied. The godliest families are Bible-reading families. The holiest men and women are Bible-reading people. These are simple facts which can not be denied." Have we not good reason to believe that the Lord will bestow His blessings on such, even in temporal things, and withhold it from those who do not prize His Word.[1]

Q. 11.—"Is it true to say that no matter what Church a man belongs to, if he is honest and well conducted he will be saved?"

The substance of His Grace's "Answer" is "No." Protestants say the same. His Grace says: "Persons who care very little about any religion, and those holding ridiculous doctrines sometimes say, 'It is.'" A somewhat ridiculous piece of English composition. He considers that it would be "of no use for Christ to establish a Church on earth if people were not obliged to belong to it, or were left to make up a religion of their own fancy." The Church here spoken of is, of course, the Archbishop's. The last part of the sentence is, of course, a "hit" at Protestantism—one which the writer often uses.

(1) See Appendix XI.

REVIEW OF "ANSWERS" TO QUESTIONS 12-14. 47

Q. 12.—"Can a man be honest in all respects without practising the religion which our Lord came on earth to establish," etc.? "Again, is a man honests in all respects when he merely pays his debts and is just to his neighbour, and most unjust to God?"

"To earth" would be better English here than "on earth." The religion of which His Grace speaks is, of course, the "Catholic." The composition of his "Answer" to this Question is of the schoolboy kind, but no one who believes in God can find fault with its theology.

Q. 13.—"Why is the Catholic Church not progressive?"

A.—"Because the Catholic Church was founded by Christ Himself, who, with infinite wisdom, gave it laws and doctrines; therefore there can be no improvement made. The Catholic Church has been always the same from the beginning, and will be the same to the end of time." Etc.

We have already see that she was not founded by Christ. Therefore, she did not receive her laws and doctrines from Him. Some of these, as we have seen, He could not give her, as light cannot give darkness. There is abundance of room for improvement in her. She has not always been the same from the beginning. Her peculiar laws, doctrines, and ceremonies have been adopted by her from time to time. For example, the doctrines of the Immaculate Conception of the Virgin Mary, and Papal Infallibility were no part of her creed till Dec. 8, 1854, and July 18, 1870. We have reason to believe that the end of the "Catholic" Church will be before that of time.

Q. 14.—"What is the difference between the Catholic and Protestant religions?"

Answer 1st gives their respective origins. This has already been answered.

2nd. "In the Catholic religion there are seven sacraments, the Protestants have only two, and some denominations none. They also deny sacramental grace."

Five of these seven sacraments have no authority in the word of God. Only two have authority there. These the Protestants have. The "some denominations"—even according to His Grace's form of language—are not Protestant. The last sentence, of course, refers to the Protestants. Placing it where it is, is a piece of most wretched composition. Protestants do not deny sacramental grace, but they do not believe that it is necessarily connected with the performance of the mere outward act.

3rd. "The Catholics acknowledge" the Apocrypha.

These books have always been rejected by the Jews as uninspired. They are never referred to in the New Testament. They contain ridiculous statements. They contradict in some places the Old Testament, and reliable profane history. They commend some things forbidden by the word of God. The writers of two practically say that they are not inspired.

4th. "The Catholics acknowledge one head . . . ; the Protestants as many heads as there are denominations, and sections of denominations. The English and Russian Churches acknowledge the sovereign as head, though Christ did not appoint kings to rule His Church."

What His Grace here says about "one head" has already been answered. What he says about the Protestants is utterly untrue. All Protestants believe that Christ is the King and Head of the Church. The English Church believes that the sovereign is only its temporal head. The Greek Church—which the learned prelate calls the Russian—is not Protestant. It is quite true that Christ did not appoint kings to rule in His Church. The Pope, therefore, ought to have no temporal power. The medal which the present one caused to be struck in honour of his jubilee, but which was confiscated by the Italian Government, has on it the words, "Leo XIII., Pontifex Maximus et Rex" (*Leo XIII., Supreme Pontiff and King.*)

Sometimes, popes and bishops could not take office without

the king's or emperor's nomination or consent. Sometimes, they took it without any other authority than his nomination. For example, Otho of Saxony in 963, deposed Pope John XII., and put Leo VIII. into his place. Henry the Black chose three popes in succession, who took office without any other ceremony than his nomination.

If Christ "did not appoint *kings* to rule His Church," much less did He appoint *courtezans* to do so. Yet the latter have often ruled in His Grace's. Cardinal Baronius says that "at one period, shameless women, all powerful at Rome, disposed of sees at their will, named the bishops, and enthroned their lovers in the chair of St. Peter," and asks : " Who would dare to give the names of Roman pontiffs to intruders forced in by the vilest women?"

5th. "Protestants say they can interpret the Bible as they please."

This I most distinctly deny. I challenge His Grace to prove his statement from the creed of any Protestant Church.

"Catholics receive the interpretation of the Bible from the Church, *i.e.*, from the body of the Bishops in conjunction with the Pope's teaching."

If the Pope be personally infallible, he has no need of the bishops to give infallibility to his teaching. If he need them for that purpose, how can he be personally infallible?

6th. "The priests of the Catholic Church are ordained by a sacrament instituted by Christ."

Christ did not institute any such sacrament.

"They are commissioned to preach and dispense the sacraments by proper authority."

So are Protestant ministers.

"Protestants do not acknowledge the sacrament of Holy Orders."

Of course they do not, as they do not believe that Christ instituted it.

"They do not consider a divine mission necessary."

They do. They believe that no one should enter into the Gospel ministry whom the Lord does not call thereto.

"Hence their ministers are looked on as not differing, by any sacerdotal character from the laymen of their church."

Protestants believe that the only priest whom we need is Christ, who has "put away sin by the sacrifice of Himself." Yet, they look on their ministers as, under Him, their spiritual guides, and "esteem them very highly in love for their works' sake."

"They are married and attend to their wives and families as well as to their congregations."

Though they may find certain disadvantages in having wives and families, may they not also find certain advantages therein? If they have Scriptural authority for it should they be condemned? But more on this matter, by and by, Your Grace.

7th. "Protestants admit women to preach contrary, to the order of St. Paul."

Only some do. These, however, do not admit them into the pastoral office.

"The Catholic Church does not permit divorces, the Protestant Churches do."

The latter have reason and Scripture on their side for doing so.

8th. The Catholic Church obliges her children to fast after the example of Christ and His Apostles, and obliges the priests and those who receive Holy Communion to fast before receiving it."

Christ fasted forty days and forty nights, which none of His Apostles ever did. We have not the slightest proof that His Apostles kept Lent, and abstained from eating flesh on

Fridays. They did not fast before receiving the Communion. Christ instituted that ordinance as He and they were eating the Passover.

"Protestants do not enjoin any fasting except perhaps one day in the year, holding that it is at any rate pleasing to God."

Though they do not enjoin fasting, they do not forbid it, that is what is properly so called, in certain circumstances. This, His Grace here seems to admit, though he expresses himself in a very awkward manner. To what particular day in the year does he refer?

9th. Catholics profess to have the true body of Christ and a true sacrifice to God in the Blessed Eucharist."

We shall afterwards see that in this they are utterly mistaken.

"Protestants have only the symbol of it, mere bread and wine, and no sacrifice."

They believe in Christ's real, but spiritual, presence with His people in the Lord's Supper. They believe that such have there more than a symbol of His body and blood, more than mere bread and wine, and that, though they have no sacrifice, they have a feast on one. All Protestants agree with the following language of the Westminster Confession of Faith, Chapter XXIX., Section VII. :—"Worthy receivers, outwardly partaking of the visible elements in this sacrament, do then also inwardly by faith, really and indeed, yet not carnally and corporally, but spiritually, receive and feed upon Christ crucified, and all benefits of His death: the body and blood of Christ being then not corporally or carnally in, with, or under the bread and wine; yet as really, but spiritually, present to the faith of believers in that ordinance, as the elements themselves are to their outward senses."

10th. "Catholics venerate the saints and pray to them; Protestants do neither."

The saints here spoken of, are those in the other world. Protestants believe that there are saints on earth as well as in heaven. They reverence the memories of the latter, and delight in fellowship with the former, but they pray to neither. They believe that many of the saints in the Romish calendar were—to express it mildly—not saints, and that some never had a being. This point we shall afterwards more fully consider.

11th. Here His Grace speaks of the unity of his Church, and the diversities in the Protestant one. These points we have already more than once reviewed.

Chapter 6.

Questions.—(15) Did not the Catholic Church fall into error?—(16) Are not all denominations branches of the true Church of Christ?—(17) Do Catholics believe that all who die outside of their communion are lost? *Objection.*—(1) As there are many roads leading to a city, etc. Q. (18) What is the meaning of Councils?

QUESTION 15.—"Did not the Catholic Church fall into error?"

OF course, His Grace denies that his Church has done so. He says that if she has, then "the promises of Christ unconditionally made on several occasions have not been fulfilled, which would make Christ out a false teacher, and consequently not the Son of God or our Redeemer, which no Christian will say." He, however, admits that some in her have "erred from the faith." He says: "Bad churchmen and their followers fell into error, and were cut off from the very times of the Apostles. . . . 'In the last time some shall depart from the faith, giving heed to the spirits of error and doctrines of devils speaking lies in hypocrisy.'" (I. Tim. iv. 1, 2.) His Grace believes that, notwithstanding these facts, the promises of Christ have not been broken. Well, then, may not His Church be a descendant of one of the parties holding false doctrine which arose in the Apostolic Church? The true way to find out whether she has, or has not, fallen into error is to try her by the word of God. Alas! "weighed in the balances" thereof, she is "found wanting"—sadly so. The Archbishop should have made his quotation which I have just given, at least, a few words longer. In the 3rd verse, the Apostle says: "Forbidding to marry, and commanding to abstain from meats," which is perfectly true of the Romish Church.

"There was a large defection from the Church in the times of the so-called Reformation, but the conversions in other countries largely made up for the loss in Europe."

This "defection" is constantly increasing. "The house of David is waxing stronger and stronger, but that of Saul is waxing weaker and weaker." According to Père Huguet, there was, from 1840 to 1874, an increase of 15,000,000 among the Roman Catholics throughout the world. Had it been fully one-half per cent. in the year—which is less than half the yearly increase of population in Britain—it would have been 32,300,000. There was, therefore a loss of 17,300,000. In the United States of America, where the Celtic element is fully one-fourth of the population, and the Spanish one is very strong in those parts which formerly belonged to Mexico, there should be to-day 22,000,000 Roman Catholics, instead of which there are not more than 9,000,000 or 10,000,000. The late Pope used to say that the true Catholic Church is but a "little flock" when Liberals, indifferents, and non-practising members are not reckoned as belonging to it. I shall show elsewhere that the increase of Protestants is remarkably greater.

"The Catholics of the world number, according to the best authority (*Scientific Miscellany*), 225,000,000; Protestants of all denominations taken collectively, 65,000,000, less than one-fifth of all calling themselves Christians; Schismatics, Greek and Russian, are 60,000,000. Those never assume or receive the title of Catholics, though they say in their creed: 'I believe in the Holy Catholic Church.'"

Père Huguet, already referred to, gives in a work published two years before His Grace's, the number of Roman Catholics throughout the world as scarcely 204,500,000. Other authorities, at least, as good as the *Scientific Miscellany*, give tables of population less favourable to the Roman Catholics, and more favourable to other denominations. But for the sake of convenience, I shall take up this question more fully elsewhere."[1]

(1) See Appendix XII.

REVIEW OF "ANSWER" TO QUESTION 16.

Q. 16.—"Are not all denominations branches of the true Church of Christ?"

A.—"There is no foundation for this assertion in the Bible."

Taking these words as they stand, I fully agree with the "learned prelate." Of course, our views regarding the "true Church" are not the same. Almost the whole of the rest of his answer is a confused mass of statements which we have already considered. He says in it:—

"The various sects and denominations"——

What difference, Your Grace, is there between "sects" and "denominations?"

"Differ from one another as the kingdom of England differs from that of the United States."

There is "the United Kingdom of Great Britain and Ireland," but no "Kingdom of England." According to His Grace, the United States are a kingdom, the same as "England." This is a perfectly fair interpretation of his words "that of the United States." I fancy I see an old-fashioned "Yankee" sitting whittling a stick. He is told that he is a subject—ruled over by a king who wears a crown and royal robes, holds a sceptre in his hand, sits on a throne, and so forth. At once he stops whittling. His eyebrows are arched like the rainbow. His eyes almost start out like a lobster's. His hair almost lifts up his old beaver hat. After a while, he heaves a deep sigh. Then he gives a long whistle. I need not go on with my description. Yir Grace, shure an' it makes me face like a rid hot coal to hear an archbishop spakin sitch monsthrus bad grammar as ye be doin here.

"The Holy Spirit cannot be the author of contradictory doctrines held by the several denominations, consequently Christ cannot be their author."

This is a piece of rather clumsy English. However, what it expresses is quite orthodox. "The contradictory doctrines" would be better English. The Archbishop's Church is one of "the several denominations." She tolerates several contradictory doctrines among her members.

"Many persons join religious denominations with far less thought and care than they take to buy a horse. The affair of salvation is the most serious business of earth. 'What will it profit a man to gain the whole world and lose his own soul?'"

Here, His Grace is most orthodox, though he expresses himself in a not remarkably elegant manner.

"Many have grave doubts concerning their church and its doctrine, but dismiss them carelessly lest they might lose friendship or some worldly advantage by a change of religion. Those people are not safe in conscience."

The first of these sentences is perfectly true. We have very good reason to believe that many of those described in it are to be found in the Archbishop's own Church. The second is—Och! its intoirely beyant me comprehinshun. Shure Yir Grace is the by to confound the sinses uv the Prahtestants.

"A friend of mine heard a gentleman say, 'I must have some religion. I think I will join Rev. ——'s church. It is a fashionable church; and very little is required to be a member of it beyond paying a heavy pew rent.'"

Perhaps, if this story were truly told, it would be very different from what it is here. The Vicar-General of Rimouski heard that I refused to marry a Roman Catholic couple who asked me to marry them, unless they would promise to be Protestants for three months. A most ridiculous story. If a person only pays "a heavy pew rent" to the Romish Church, she will allow him a very great liberty in sinning.

Q. 17.—"Do Catholics believe that all who die outside of their communion are lost?"

A.—"Catholics believe that all are not Protestants who are considered so. They believe that all who live and die protesting against the truths revealed by our Lord, which they could have known by using ordinary diligence, and who live disobeying His commandments are lost."

It is quite true that all are not Protestants who are considered so. "All are not Israel who are of Israel." True Protestants do not "live and die protesting against the truths revealed by our Lord." Why not say "live and die disobeying," as well as "live and die protesting against?"

"From this category are excluded: 1st. All baptized children who die before they embrace error and are free from other sins."

Why not simply say, "have not committed sin?" What are the "other sins?" Are they only mortal ones, or both mortal and venial? Why is embracing error particularly mentioned? Why should unbaptized children who die before they embrace error, etc., be lost? Their being unbaptized was not their fault.

2nd. "All baptized adults, who are in good faith, and free from mortal sin, and who believe in the principal doctrines of Christianity, but through no negligence, indifference, or malice, had not sufficient means of knowing the whole truth, which they would have embraced could they have discovered it."

His Grace plainly considers baptism essential to salvation. But Paul says: "Christ sent me not to baptize, but to preach the Gospel." (1 Corinthians i. 17.) Is a person who dies unbaptized "through no negligence, indifference, or malice," but who believes on the Lord Jesus, lost? What is here meant by being "in good faith"? Even the least heinous sin is "mortal," if it be not forgiven. Even the most heinous is "venial," if forgiveness be sought in God's appointed way. "The principal doctrines of Christianity." Then—according to our "Dear Roman Catholic Friend"—there are doctrines of Christianity which are only of secondary importance. If those persons here spoken of, were trusting in Christ alone for salvation, they would not have joined the Romish Church, even though they could have discovered all her doctrines. These, His Grace says, "in reality belong to the soul of the true Church," a curious expression which plainly means "are really Roman Catholics."

"Persons who through human respect and worldly motives do not embrace the true Church are not of this number."

That is they are not really Roman Catholics. Yis, Yir Lardship's Rivirince, that's a fact. It's jist as thrue as that ye're our beloved Archbishop.

"Many belong merely to the body of the Catholic Church, and are counted as members, but who do not belong to its soul."

Yir Grace has hit it again. Och! but it's yirsilf that's the knowin wan.

"To belong to the soul of the Church one must be, besides being baptized, free from mortal sin, believe implicitly at least all the doctrines of Christ."

By "the Church" is here meant, of course, the Archbishop's. The word "and" should be placed before "believe." "At least all the doctrines" is a very curious expression. In a former sentence, His Grace says that "believing in the principal doctrines" is sufficient.

"When occasions present themselves we exhort all Christians to make an act of faith in all the revealed truths of the Bible, in the meaning intended by the Holy Spirit, and not in the false sense of erring man, and to pray in the language of the Apostles, 'Lord increase our faith' (Luke xvii. 5)."

What is here meant by "an act of faith"? The Spaniards used to make one (*auto da fé*) by burning heretics, but, of course, His Grace does not mean one of that kind. "In all the revealed truths of the Bible." This is not in harmony with his statement which we have just considered, that "belief in the principal doctrines of Christianity" is sufficient. The truths in the Bible are, of course, revealed ones. According to the Romish Church, tradition is of equal authority with the Bible. Why then, does not His Grace exhort all Christians to make, when occasions present themselves, an act of faith in all the revealed truths of tradition, as well as of the Bible? He seems to set more value on the Bible than on tradition.

OBJECTION 1.—"As there are many roads leading to a city so there are many roads leading to heaven."

The "learned prelate's" Answer is not quite to the point. Those who make the objection which he quotes, plainly mean that persons may belong to different churches, yet go to heaven. His Grace says that there are many roads leading by, that is past, a city also, and cross roads leading to many places besides. "Also, and" should be "and also." He then quotes what is said in Scripture about the strait gate and narrow way, and about keeping the commandments to enter into life. "This," he says, "makes the road so narrow." " Here endeth" his "Answer" to the "Objection."

Q. 18.—" What is the meaning of Councils?"

A.—"General or partial assemblies of Bishops for the remedying of abuses, settling disputes, defining matters of faith brought recently into dispute."

The English of this Answer is not very classical, but "let it pass." We shall presently see that His Grace speaks elsewhere, very differently about general and partial Councils from the way he does here. He says that bishops are placed by the Holy Ghost to feed the Church of God, and watch over those who try to bring into it false doctrines. In proof of this, he refers to Acts xx. 28, 29. But those spoken of in these verses, though Scriptural bishops, were not diocesan ones. They were the elders of the Church of Ephesus.

"General Councils alone with the Pope at their head are infallible in their decrees; particular councils of Bishops are not."

The state of the earth described in Genesis i., 2, as "waste and void," is a striking figure of the opinions of the Romish authorities on the subject of Councils. In opposition to His Grace, the Cisalpine party " places infallibility in a General Council; and teaches that it is superior to the Pope, and has authority even to depose him." " The Church of Rome unanimously acknowledges several General Councils with which the Pope had nothing to do." " Councils have contradicted each other ; Popes have contradicted Councils, and papally ratified Councils have contradicted Popes. In none of them, therefore, can infallibility be lodged." "A Pope and papally ratified Council are alike infallible on the Ultramontane theory; and a ratified and unratified Council are alike infallible on that of the Cisalpines."[1] If infallibility belong only to a General Council with the Pope at its head, then it is as much infallible as he is. If he gives it its infallibility, then he only is infallible and there is no need of it.

"Christ would not have said to His Apostles, 'He that heareth you, heareth Me,' etc. (Luke x., 16), if the pastors of the Church, as a body could lead the people into error.

When the Apostles preached the preaching which Christ bade them, Christ in effect spoke. His Grace admits that heresy sprang up in the early Christian Church.

"St. Paul in His Epistle to the Hebrews, chap. xiii., 17, says, 'Obey your Prelates,'" etc.

These "Prelates" were simply what we commonly call pastors.

"Councils cannot invent any new doctrine: they only can define what was the belief of the Church from the beginning, and define it

---

(1) Protestantism and Romanism, Vol. I., pp. 197, 200.

is a dogma of Catholic faith, to be explicitly believed. They make, however, new decrees of discipline according to the exigencies of the times."

"They only" mean that it is only Councils which can define, etc. Then the Pope, by himself, has no infallibility. But the learned prelate plainly means that ~~only~~ Councils can only define, etc. Och! me darlint, is it possible that sitch a well edicated jintleman as yirsilf can't spake betther? Councils have declared as having been believed by the Church from the beginning, dogmas on which, before that time, Romish authorities held widely different views. "Explicitly" plainly should be "implicity." Decrees of discipline are, of course, not decrees of faith. Therefore, according to the Archibishop's Church, they are not binding.

"Councils are held by denominations outside the Catholic Church, but their decrees are not considered even by themselves irreformable or binding in conscience."

This proves nothing in favour of Councils inside His Grace's Church. Many of her members consider certain of the decrees of these Councils as not "irreformable, or binding on the conscience," which is better English than "in. conscience."

Chapter 7.

Questions.—(19) What is meant by the Infallibility of the Pope?—(20) What is the meaning of Papal Supremacy? *Objection.*—(2) Is not the Pope only a Bishop?. *Q.*—(21) What means the Hierarchy of the Church?—(22) Who are the Cardinals?—(23) How are the Popes elected?—(24) Why do not Catholics attend Protestant meetings?—(25) Why do Catholics hold so strongly to tradition?

QUESTION 19.—" What is meant by the Infallibility of the Pope?"

O do His Grace justice, I shall give his Answer in full, though it is somewhat lengthy. He says:—

"It means that the Roman Pontiff when he speaks *ex cathedrâ*—that is, when in discharge of the office of Pastor and Doctor of all Christians by virtue of his supreme Apostolic authority, he defines a doctrine regarding faith or morals to be held by the Universal Church, by the divine assistance promised to him in blessed Peter, is possessed of that infallibility with which the divine Redeemer willed that this Church should be endowed for defining doctrines regarding faith and morals; and that therefor such definitions of the Roman Pontiff are irreformable of themselves and not from the consent of the Church."

This is simply a translation of the definition adopted by the Vatican Council. The language is far from being as clear as it should have been, especially on a point of so much importance. The first part and the last seem to teach the doctrine of the personal infallibility of the Pope. The middle seems to teach that of the infallibility of the Church. The expression, "this Church," is, no doubt, a misprint for "His Church," that is, Christ's.[1] Of course, it does not mean that the Pope himself is the Church. "When does he speak *ex cathedrâ?*" is a question to which Roman Catholics cannot

---

(1) It is in the last edition, as well as in the first.

give a clear answer. We can understand what is meant by his speaking as the Moderator or President of a General Council; but that, they say, is not what *ex cathedrâ* means. The best interpretation of *ex cathedrâ* for them, is just—*ex cathedrâ*. It prevents any troublesome questions from being asked.

His Grace attempts to prove that the Pope is infallible. He says:—

"In every well ordered society or government there must be a final Tribunal at which all disputes must be settled. It is meet that in the Church of God there should be such a tribunal."

What he here says about the State is quite true. The "final Tribunal" in it, is not, however, infallible. Sometimes its decisions are neither wise nor just. In a free country, it is allowed to criticise them. Sometimes disputes are settled by an appeal to the people. In the Church of God, there is a "final Tribunal," but a very different one from that which His Grace has in view. In the Westminster Confession of Faith it is thus described: "The Supreme Judge, by which all controversies of religion are to be determined, and all decrees of councils, opinions of ancient writers, doctrines of men, and private spirits, are to be examined, and in whose sentence we are to rest, can be no other but the Holy Spirit speaking in the Scripture." (Chap. I., Sec. 10.) In Sec. 6, of the same chapter, it is said: "There are some circumstances concerning the worship of God, and government of the Church, common to human actions and societies, which are to be ordered by the light of nature and Christian prudence, according to the general rules of the Word, which are always to be observed." We may sometimes not quite agree with the Church's decisions on these points, but if it be not sinful to comply with them, we should comply for the sake of peace.

"Now as the teaching Church, that is the Bishops of the Church conjoined to the Pope as their head form an infallible council, so the Pope as head of the Church must enjoy that infallibility, but only in certain cases when exercising his prerogatives as universal doctor and teacher."

According to the first part of this quotation, the bishops, when they are in Council, under the presidency of the Pope, are as infallible as he, and he is no more infallible than they. Each separately is fallible. Both together are infallible. We would naturally suppose that one fallible added to one fallible, would make simply two fallibles. But, according to the "learned prelate," they make one infallible. How do they do that? A most remarkable thing! Oh! I see! Light has come into my mind. I cry as Archimedes once did: "Eureka, I have found it!" Strike sulphur and chlorate of potash with a hammer, separately, and each remains quiet. Mix them, and strike. Then you have a loud "crack." A liquid acid and a liquid alkali, separate, are quite still. Put them together, and you have a "fizz." So, put a fallible head—the Pope—and fallible members—a Council—together, and you have an infallible body. I think that the Pope, if he knew of this way of silencing a heretical cavil, might do worse than send me the decoration of the Order of Gregory the Great. Though he would thereby acknowledge his fallibility apart from a Council, that would be nothing. Popes have often acted and spoken inconsistently. If the Pope be personally infallible, he can himself settle disputes. It is, therefore, only a farce to call Councils to do so. Of course, if the Pope and the bishops together form an infallible council, he, as the head of that Council, must be infallible. We would, therefore, naturally expect the learned prelate to say so. But he says, "so the Pope as head of the Church must enjoy that infallibility." Does he mean that the Council of which he speaks, is the Church? If he do, then, according to him, the Pope is not always head of the Church for a General Council is not always sitting. Och! Yir Lardship's Rivirince, shure an' oi foind mesilf here in as grate darkniss as that in Agypt on a cirtin mimorable occashun. His Grace adds that the Pope is infallible "only in certain cases when exercising his prerogatives as universal doctor and teacher." According to this, the Pope is personally infallible. "When does he act in the manner just described?" is a question to which—as I have already said—Roman Catholics never can give but an extremely misty answer.

"That infallibility Christ has conferred on Peter and his successors for the proper direction of His Church."

To prove this, he, of course, quotes the passage about the rock in Matt. xvi. 18. He adds: "But I have prayed for thee that thy faith fail not; and thou being once converted confirm thy brethren" (Luke xxii. 32.) But about twenty years after Christ uttered the words in the last of these passages, Paul withstood Peter to the face, because he was to be blamed. Peter dissembled on a certain occasion. "The other Jews dissembled likewise with him; insomuch that Barnabas also was carried away with their dissimulation." "They walked not uprightly according to the truth of the Gospel." (Galatians ii. 11-14.) Peter, certainly, did not then confirm his brethren. Where was his infallibility? His Grace says that "the Bishops of the Church conjoined to the Pope as their head form an infallible council." But, according to the Romish Church, it is only the Popes who are the successors of Peter, and, therefore, only they are infallible. It may be said that the bishops receive their authority from the Pope. Then Peter's fellow-apostles are nothing in the Church. But Paul says that the Church is built "upon the foundation of the apostles (not Peter only) and prophets." (Ephesians ii. 20.) The bishops must themselves be infallible, if they, with the Pope at their head, form an infallible council. Do they receive their infallibility from the Pope?

"The Pope is not impeachable" (no doubt a misprint for 'impeccable'), "he can commit sin like other people;"——

If he be not impeccable, he can, of course, do what is stated in the last clause. That he can, is most clearly proved by the lives of, among others, John X., John XII., Boniface VII., Gregory VII., John XXIII., Sixtus IV., and Alexander VI. These were among the vilest wretches that ever lived.

"nor is he infallible in his private capacity, in his discourses, or in his governments."

By "his private capacity," the Archbishop must here mean the Pope's private opinion, for he has just spoken of the ability of the latter to sin like other people. Well, if we take away his private opinion, his discourses, and his governments, what is left in which the Pope can be infallible? What is left of a knife after the blade and the handle are taken away? Does not speaking *ex cathedrâ* belong to the "discourses" and "governments" of the Pope?

Q. 20.—"What is the meaning of Papal Supremacy?"
A.—"It means that the Pope as successor of St. Peter, who was made head of the Church by Christ Himself, is supreme Bishop of all the other Catholic Bishops of the Church."

In support of this, His Grace, I need not say, quotes the passage about the rock in Matt. xvi. 18. He adds the charge to Peter in John xxi. 15-18: "Feed My lambs, feed my sheep." He says: "The lambs are the people, and the sheep the pastors." Peter, then, is the chief Pastor or Shepherd. But he himself applies that title to Christ. (I. Peter v. 6.) The Archbishop thinks that Christ made Peter superior to the other apostles by giving him the keys of the kingdom of heaven. "Keys," he says, "denote the master." As the Romish Church makes so much of the promise of Christ to Peter, "I will give unto thee the keys of the kingdom of heaven," (Matt. xvi. 19), let us, for a little, examine it. Immediately after the words just quoted follow these: "and whatsoever thou shalt bind on earth shall be bound in heaven; and whatsoever thou shalt loose on earth shall be loosed in heaven." The power of binding and loosing is, of course, the consequence of receiving the keys, or rather, the same as it. Now, in Matthew xviii. 18, Christ bestows the very same power on all the disciples. He must, therefore, have given them also the keys, though He does not say anything about these. The retaining and remitting of sins spoken of in John

xx. 28, is, most likely, the same as the binding and loosing already referred to. What the "keys," "binding and loosing," and "retaining and remitting of sins" are, we do not here need to enquire. The question for our present consideration is: "Did our Lord set Peter above his fellow disciples?" We see that He did not, for He bestowed the same powers on all alike.[1]

"Feeding the people and the pastors denotes one superior in authority. Feeding here means governing and directing."

In a flock, there are both sheep and lambs. In the flock of God there are, according to His Grace's interpretation, both pastors and people. When Christ said, "Fear not, little flock," and "There shall be one fold," rather "flock," He referred to both. Therefore, when Paul said to the elders of the Church of Ephesus, "Take heed . . . to all the flock over the which the Holy Ghost hath made you overseers, to feed the Church of God," (Acts xx. 28), he meant that they were all chief Pastors, that is, Popes. Hurrah! When Peter says to the elders: "Feed the flock of God which is among you, taking the oversight thereof," (I. Peter v. 1, 2), he makes them all Popes like himself. Hurrah!

When we consider that shortly before our Lord gave Peter the charge under consideration, that Apostle had denied Him three times, at the last with cursing and swearing, we see how lovingly He dealt with him when He gave him it. He, by so doing, signified to him before his fellow disciples that He had restored him to the office from which he had, by his grievous sin, cut himself off. That Peter was the only one addressed, did not in the least set him above the other disciples. In one sense, it was humbling to him. He was the only one of the disciples to whom his Lord said three times: "Lovest thou Me?"

OBJECTION 2.—" Is not the Pope only a Bishop?"
A.—" The Pope is Bishop by ordination,"——

(1) See Appendix XIII.

But if he have not been rightly ordained ? The doctrine of intention gives rise to some very troublesome questions.

"but a universal Bishop respecting jurisdiction."

Which he claims to be, but never was, is not, and never shall be.

Q 21.—" What means the Hierarchy of the Church ? "

His Grace closes his Answer to this by saying: "This is considered the most perfect organization on earth for the maintenance of the true faith, handed down from the Apostles, and the upholding of ecclesiastical discipline." This statement would be perfectly true if the following changes were made in it:—Leave out from "the true faith" to "the Apostles" and put in "error." Leave out "ecclesiastical discipline" and put in "priestcraft."

Q. 22.—"Who are the Cardinals ?"

His Grace says: "Their duties are :—First, to elect the Pope ; second, to assist him in the general government of the Church." In the particular government thereof—whatever that is—he is, of course, "monarch of all he surveys," though, according to the Archbishop, he is not infallible in his "governments." (Q. 19.) One of the duties of the Cardinals as the Pope's assistants, he tells us, is "To revise writings on religious subjects, and to see that no error slips into the composition of Catholic authors; also to condemn anti-Christian works, and that no ecclesiastic holding heretical opinions shall retain office in the Church." Another is " To revise the decrees of particular Councils." A third is "To report on sacred rites, ceremonies, indulgences, and relics ; examination of candidates for the Episcopacy," etc. The composition of the description of the first of these duties needs itself to be revised. But "let that pass." Cardinals revise writings on literary and scientific subjects, as well as those on religious ones. His Grace says in "Answer" 5 to "Question" 8, that one needs infallibility to enable him to know what Scriptures are the word of God and what are not. (p. 9.) Surely, infallibility is equally necessary in revising writings on religious subjects, and the decrees of particular Councils, and in examining candidates for the Episcopacy, to enable one to pronounce what is truth and what is error, "otherwise the true may be pronounced false," and the false true. It would be most useful in judging sacred rites, ceremonies, indulgences and relics. Take, for example, the case of the last mentioned. Without infallibility, the false might be pronounced true, and so a relic of a scoundrel might be honoured as one of a saint. Some years ago, certain holy relics were brought to Montreal from Rome. The faithful duly honoured them, very naturally supposing that they could not but be genuine. By and by it was found that they were a proof of the truth of the proverb, "All is not gold that glitters," of which the bishop, accordingly, gave due notice to all parties concerned.

But if the Pope be himself infallible "as universal doctor and teacher," what need has he of the Cardinals to help him in the cases referred to ? If he and they need to be in partnership to come to infallible decisions, then they are infallible as well as he. If their decisions be not infallible, then they are not "binding in conscience," as His Grace would say.

Q. 23.—" How are the Popes elected ?"

The answer to this question I shall pass by. I look on the election of the Pope as alike absurd and impious.

Q. 24.—" Why do not Catholics attend Protestant meetings and revivals ?"

In reply, the Archbishop says that "Catholics" believe that their Church is the true one, "disbelieve" Protestant doctrines, and, therefore, do not wish to countenance services of which they do not approve. He considers that they would act hypocritically if they did, and, of course, approves of their absenting themselves from these services. Yet, in the Dedication of his work to his "Dear Protestant Friends," he exhorts them "as a just man, before pronouncing judgment, to give fair play, and hear the other side of the question." He wrote his work, hoping that they would. Fair play here seems to be, in his opinion, of what may be called the "jug handle" kind—all on one side. That side is his own Church, as regards getting.

Q. 25.—" Why do Catholics hold so strongly to tradition ?"

His Grace answers: "Because the Holy Scripture orders them to do so." Of course, then, Scripture does not order them to hold to tradition contrary to it. Tradition must, therefore, be tried by Scripture. What need, then, is there of tradition? In support of his statement, the Archbishop quotes the following passages: "Hold the traditions which ye have been taught, whether by word, or our epistle" (2 Thessal. ii. 15), "The tradition which he received of us." (iii. 6.) It is plain from the last of these, that the "word" and "epistle" spoken of in the first, are Paul's preaching to the Thessalonians, and the letter which he had already written to them. The word rendered "tradition" in the passages quoted, simply means something delivered to one. The verb from which it is formed is rendered "delivered" in Luke i. 2, and Acts xxviii. 16. When Paul wrote to the Thessalonians, the Bible was not complete. Therefore, the preaching of the Apostles was to be treated as the word of God. The Thessalonians so treated Paul's. (1 Thessal. ii. 13.) But now we have no warrant to receive anything as from them, save what is contained in the written word.

"Not, however, every tradition, but such as are handed down from the apostolic times, through the constant teaching and councils of the Church, and the approved writings of the Holy Fathers."

The teaching and Councils here spoken of are very variable. Some of the writings ascribed to the Fathers are very doubtful. Others are forgeries. But the Fathers do not always agree even in those ascribed to them, which are genuine. The Jews had traditions which they said God gave Moses besides the law contained in the Old Testament. Many of these were directly opposed to it. The like is true of the traditions of the Church of Rome and the written word.

His Grace says: "Protestants themselves believe in many traditions." He mentions two, as if they were the whole of the "many." 1st. "In the keeping of the Sunday, not the Sabbath, but the first day of the week." Protestants keep it because they believe that they have scriptural warrant for so doing. When they refer to the fact that the early Christians kept it, they do so merely in confirmation of their views, not as an authority for their doing the same. 2nd. "The eating of blood though forbidden in the first council of Jerusalem." (Acts xv. 29.) Very few Protestants who eat blood refer to tradition in favour of their doing so. They eat it, just as most persons drink liquor—because they like it. Taste, not tradition, is what leads them to do so. His Grace would have spoken more correctly if he had said that many Protestants refrain on conscientious grounds, from eating blood. Those who do so, take Scripture, not tradition, as their reason for it.

"All that Christ and His Apostles said and did have not been recorded; were they the world would not contain all the books that should be written." (John xxi. 25.)

According to *Punch*, the most acute man is a Yankee Jew born of Scotch parents. Well, it would utterly baffle him, much more a Philadelphia lawyer, to see how the passage just quoted, proves that there are traditions handed down from Apostolic times which are of equal authority with the written word.

The Holy Spirit has caused only as much to be written as He knew to be necessary for our salvation. The Evangelist John says: "Many other signs truly did Jesus in the presence of His disciples which are not written in this book. But these are written, that ye might believe that Jesus is the Christ, the Son of God; and that believing ye might have life through His name." (xx. 30, 31.) It is dishonouring to the Holy Spirit to say that some things which He has not caused to be written, are of equal authority with those which He has. Why have some been written, and others not?

Chapter 8.

Questions.—(26) Whom do the Catholics worship?—(27) Do Catholics worship the Virgin Mary and the Saints?—(28) Was not the Virgin Mary a mere ordinary woman?—(29) Do not the Catholics give her too much honour?—(30) What means the Immaculate Conception?—(31) Is there Scripture for this?

QUESTION 26.—" Whom do the Catholics worship?"
ANSWER.—"God alone, one God in three Divine persons."

THEN follows a full statement of the doctrine of the Trinity. On this point, His Grace is thoroughly sound.

"It would be damnable sin of idolatry to give to any creature, even to the mother of God, the sovereign worship due to God alone."

By "the mother of God" is here meant, of course, the Virgin Mary. She was the mother of Christ only as man. She could not be His mother as God. It would be better to apply to her the names given her in the Bible. There she is never called "the mother of God." With that exception, the Archbishop here says what is quite true. We shall, however, see by-and-by, that the Romish Church really gives the Virgin Mary "the sovereign worship due to God alone."

He says that the titles, "His Worship the Mayor," or "Her Most Excellent Majesty the Queen," do not mean such worship and majesty as we attribute to God. Here, again, the Archbishop is thoroughly orthodox. It is to me a most pleasing variety to walk with him "in sweet accord." I cannot reasonably expect this to continue to the end of his book. However, it is good in the meantime. My "separated brother" might have mentioned also the title, "His Grace the Archbishop." Many Protestants disapprove of such titles being applied to mere human beings. However, what he here says about them is quite true.

His Grace says that when such expressions as "my life," "my hope," "my all," are addressed to the Virgin, they have only the limited meaning which they have when parents and children use them to express their love to each other. On this I remark—(1) Parents and children often apply such expressions to each other without duly considering their meaning, just as many say: "The sun is so hot that it is like to roast me to death," "I was like to die with laughing," and so on. Any "good Catholic" will say that it would be only mocking the Virgin to address her in that manner. (2) Parents and children often use them towards each other in most unbecoming senses. (3) These expressions, when parents and children use them properly towards each other, refer only to earthly things. But Roman Catholics use them towards the Virgin in a far higher sense, as we shall afterwards see.

Q. 27.— "Do Catholics worship the Virgin Mary and the Saints?"
A.—"No. They pay divine worship only to God. They reverence the Saints as friends of God, and highly honoured by Him."

In support of his second statement, His Grace quotes two passages, (Psalm cxxxix. 17, and John xvii. 22). In the latter, our Lord says: "The glory which Thou gavest Me, I have given them." Therefore, according to the Archbishop, the Virgin Mary and the Saints are equal in dignity. But it is well known that Romanists place the Virgin above the highest angels. For example, they often, in pictures, represent the Father and the Son placing a crown on her head above which a dove is hovering, which is the Holy Spirit. Saints and angels bow before her. Further, they apply to her titles of greater honour than they do to the saints. Once more, the Romish Church teaches that higher honour (*hyperdouleia*) is to be paid the Virgin than that (*douleia*) which is to be paid the Saints.

To say that Romanists do not give divine worship to the Virgin Mary and the Saints, is utterly false. I shall have occasion to refer to this again; but, in the meantime, I shall give one proof in support of what I have just said. In "A Portrait of the Admirable Joseph," by a Romish priest, published in Dublin in 1838, is the following prayer: "O, Jesus, Mary, and Joseph, most blessed Trinity, bless me with the triple benediction of the most holy Lord." Jesus, Mary, and Joseph are often called a trinity. If this be not worshipping the last two as God, language has no meaning.

Q. 28.—"Was not the Virgin Mary a mere ordinary woman?"
A.—"By no means. She was not an ordinary woman, of whom the Scripture says, 'that all nations shall call her blessed.'" (Luke i. 48.)

The Scripture does not say so. It only says that *she* said it. His Grace should quote correctly. According to his reasoning, Leah was not an "ordinary woman," for she once said: "The daughters will call me blessed." (Gen. xxx. 13.) He whom the Lord blesses, is blessed. Now, God, by His servant the Prophet Malachi, said to His ancient people that if they would obey His commands, "all nations should call them blessed." (Malachi iii. 12.) This does not mean that they would be no "ordinary" people in themselves. Christ says: "Blessed are the poor in spirit," "Blessed are they that mourn," etc. Very many other passages to the same effect could be quoted. Yet those to whom they refer, are only "ordinary" persons. The angel Gabriel, and Elizabeth, the mother of John the Baptist, each called the Virgin Mary "blessed *among* women." (Luke i. 28, 42). But Deborah and Barak, in their song of thanksgiving—both in the Authorized and the Revised Versions—call Jael, the wife of Heber the Kenite, "blessed *above* women." (Judges v. 24.) According to His Grace's reasoning, she was greater than the Virgin Mary—more than "no ordinary woman." If, instead of "above," we take the marginal reading in the Revised Version "of,"—that is, "among"—we have the very same language used regarding her which was used by Gabriel and Elizabeth regarding the Virgin Mary. When a certain woman once said to our Lord: "Blessed is the womb that bare Thee," He said: "Yea, rather, blessed are they that hear the word of God and keep it" (Luke xi. 27, 28), thereby placing them above His mother. Yet they are only "ordinary" persons. The only sense in which the Virgin Mary can rightly be said to have been "no ordinary woman," is that of being the mother of the Messiah. But she was not so honoured because she was "no ordinary woman." She was "no ordinary woman" because she was so honoured—that is, the first was not the cause, but the effect, of the second.

It was absolutely necessary for our salvation that Christ should be truly man, as well as truly God. But He could not have been truly man, and, therefore, He could not have been one with us, had He been born of "no ordinary woman." His Grace uses that expression. (Hebrews ii. 11, 14.)

"She alone is called, and is in reality the mother of Jesus Christ, the Son of God." (Luke i. 43.)

The Bible would not call more than one woman His mother. He could not have more than one mother.

"She was no ordinary woman to whom an archangel was sent from heaven and addressed in the most honourable title of 'full of grace,' whom the Son of God obeyed and loved above all other women, as every good son will love his own mother."

There are several mistakes here, Your Grace. (1) Gabriel, who was sent from heaven to tell the Virgin Mary of the high honour which was to be bestowed on her, is not an archangel. In the book of Daniel, he is called a man, because he appeared to that prophet in the form of one (viii. 15, 16; ix. 21). In the Gospel by Luke, he is called an angel (i. 11, 13, 18, 19, 26. 28, 30, 34, 35, 38; ii. 21, connected with i. 31). We never read in the Bible of more than one archangel. "The voice of the archangel." (I. Thessalon. iv. 16.) "Michael the archangel." (Jude 9.) (2) "To whom he was sent and to whom he addressed," etc., is a fair interpretation of your words. Say "and whom he addressed." (3) "In the most honourable title." Say "by the most," etc. (4) "Full of grace." The original of the word so rendered in the Vulgate, means—so to speak—not character, but privilege. The only other passage in which it is found, is Ephesians i. 6, where it clearly describes those there spoken of, as graciously dealt with by God. The translation of the word in Luke in the Authorized Version, is as good as any other. Mary was indeed highly honoured in being made the mother of the long-promised and long-looked-for Messiah. (5) "Obeyed and loved above all other women." Your Grace, does this mean that Christ obeyed, as well as loved, all other women, only not so much as He obeyed and loved His mother? Your words can fairly be so interpreted. Of course, you mean "above" to apply only to "loved." Say, then, "whom the Son of God obeyed, and whom He loved," etc. (6) "As every good son will love His own mother." Why does Your Grace make no mention of obedience here? Will not every good son obey as well as love his mother? Once when Christ was preaching, it was told Him that His mother and His brethren desired to see Him. He answered and said: "My mother and My brethren are these which hear the word of God and do it." They are nearer to Him, and, therefore, dearer to Him, than even His mother and His brethren, considered merely as His kindred according to the flesh, were.

"In fine, God's mother is no ordinary woman."

His Grace thinks that it is vain for any to attempt to disprove it. The arguments which he has brought forward to prove it, are anything but convincing to those properly called free-thinkers. Let us fancy one of Galileo's judges when he was tried before the Inquisition for heresy, arguing as follows: "The earth does not go round the sun. No one ever saw it do so. We see the sun rising and setting. The Scriptures speak of it doing so. Why should the earth go round the sun? This earth is more important than the sun. There is no Holy, Catholic, Apostolic, and Roman Church in the sun. In fine, the earth does not go round the sun." This would have been just as good reasoning as that of His Grace which we are now considering. In the last sentence, he calls the Virgin Mary "God's mother," a favourite name for her with him, as it is with his Church. In the second, he calls her "the mother of Jesus Christ the Son of God." The only passages in Scripture in which titles like that of "the Mother of God" are applied to her, are the following: In Matthew i. 23, she is, in effect, called the mother of Emmanuel, who is "God with us." In Luke i. 35, the angel Gabriel says to her: "that holy thing which shall be born of thee shall be called the Son of God." In the 43rd verse, her cousin Elizabeth, the mother of John the Baptist, calls her "the mother of my Lord." As the divine and human natures are so closely united in Christ, that is sometimes said of the one which is true only of the other, as when it is said that the Lord of glory was crucified. (I. Corinthians ii. 8.) On this ground, these titles are, in these passages, applied to the Virgin Mary. But it is very remarkable that the Holy Spirit when He speaks of her directly, calls her simply "a virgin," "Mary," "the wife of Joseph," and "the mother of Jesus."

Q. 29.—"Do not the Catholics give her too much honour?"

A.—"They would if they adored her, or confided in her more than in Christ their only Redeemer: but when they only beg of her to pray to her Son for them and treat her as a mere creature, yet the most favoured, they do not honour her too much."

In reply to the foregoing, I say that Roman Catholics *do* adore her. We have already seen that they class her with Joseph and Christ as together forming a Trinity. In "The Key of Paradise," she is addressed as follows: "I reverence you, O sacred Virgin Mary! and together with the Holy Trinity, bless and praise you infinitely." Bellarmine says:

"Praise to God and to the Blessed Virgin: *also* to Jesus Christ." They apply to her names and titles which rightly belong only to the Father and the Son. The well known hymn commonly called the *Te Deum*, and the Psalms have been made to apply to her. Roman Catholics *do* confide in her more than in Christ. For example, St. Liguori says: "Mary is our only refuge, help, and asylum." "There is but one city of refuge, and that is Mary." "Our Blessed Lady withholds God's arm until He is pacified." "Often we shall be heard more quickly, and be thus preserved, if we have resource to Mary, and call upon *her* name, than we should be if we called on the name of Jesus our Saviour." "At the command of the Virgin all things obey, even God." "He who is protected by Mary will be saved; he who is not will be lost." Mary has only to speak, and her Son executes all." In Genoa, it has often happened that while scarcely anybody would offer five shillings to be allowed to carry the image of Jesus Christ, the priest was offered 200, and even 300 shillings for allowing the offerer to carry the statue of the Madonna (a heavy one). Sometimes the contenders came to blows about it, and then the church became a boxing school, and everything went topsy-turvy.[1] Roman Catholics often ask blessings from the Virgin Mary personally and directly. For example, they say: "O holy Mother of God! despise not our entreaties in our necessities, but always free us from all dangers." "Drive our sins away." "Protect us from our enemy, and receive us in the hour of death." In the Mass Book, printed at Paris in 1634, we find these words: "By thy authority as a mother, command the Redeemer." A few more proofs of the same kind as the foregoing I shall give elsewhere.[2]

"One embrace or act of obedience from her infant son did her more honour, and pleased her more than the honour paid her by all the angels of heaven or men on earth. You do not please the Son by dishonouring His mother."

(1) Seventeenth Evangelization Report of the Free Italian Church (for 1887).
(2) See Appendix XIV.

How this proves that "the Catholics" do not give the Virgin Mary too much honour, I frankly own that I am utterly unable to see. The Church of Rome grievously dishonours Christ's mother by unduly exalting her as they do. Of course, then, they do not thereby "please the Son."

Q. 30.—" What means the Immaculate Conception of the Blessed Virgin ?" ·

A.—" It means that the Blessed Virgin, when her soul and body were first joined and united was preserved from the sin which all the other children of Adam inherit. This was done by a singular grace and privilege of an omnipotent God, in virtue of the merits of Christ, who for His own honour and glory, saved in advance from sin His future dear mother."

What difference is there between "joined" and "united" ? "First joined and united." Of course, His Grace believes that the Virgin Mary soon after she died, was raised from the dead and received up alive into glory, as His Church teaches. "All the other children of Adam." That is, of course, those descending from him "by ordinary generation." They "sinned in him, and fell with him in his first transgression."[1] Christ, in His humanity, was truly a "child of Adam." (Luke iii. 23-38.) But He was not one in the way just described, else, in Him, there would have been sin. That He might be without sin, He was "conceived by the power of the Holy Ghost." But the Virgin Mary descended from Adam by ordinary generation, for she had both an earthly father and an earthly mother. It happened to her, therefore, as it happened to his "other children" descending from him in the same way. (See Romans v. 12-19.) God could not, "in advance," save her from the consequences of her connection with Adam. Had He done so, He would have acted contrary to His own law, which He cannot do. The merits of Christ are all powerful to deliver men out of a state of sin and misery, and to bring them into a state of salvation. But they

---

(1) Shorter Catechism, Question 16.

are utterly powerless to save men "in advance" from coming into a state of sin and misery. If Christ needed to be born of a sinless mother in order that He Himself should be without spot, there was as much need, for a like reason, that His mother should be born of a sinless mother. And so we can go on till we come to Eve. Further, that the Virgin Mary should be free from sin, it was absolutely necessary that her father should be so too. Of course, then, his father needed to be without sin. And so we can go on, till we come to Adam. Though the Virgin Mary was a sinner like every other member of Adam's natural posterity, Christ received no taint from being born of her. But it would have been far otherwise had He had an earthly father. The Archbishop's Church does not teach that the Virgin Mary was herself conceived by the power of the Holy Ghost. It should, therefore, to be consistent, teach the doctrine of the immaculate conception of her father. In a word, it should teach the doctrine of the immaculate conception of all her progenitors up to the first, that is to say, of all the descendants of the latter. According to the dogma of Papal infallibility, the Pope has but to declare it, and cursed is he who dissents therefrom. We do not know how far he will go in that direction. If a principle be good, carry it out.

Q. 31.—"Is there Scripture for this?" (the doctrine of the "Immaculate Conception," etc.)

A.—"In Genesis iii. 15: 'I will put enmities between thee and the woman, and thy seed and her seed, and she will crush thy head, and thou shalt lie in wait for her heel.' Now, the enmities would not be complete if the mother of God would be stained by original sin."

His Grace believes, and rightly so, that the serpent addressed in the passage which he here quotes, is Satan. It is, however, not she, but her seed who is to crush the serpent's head. The words "she" and "her" mean in the original "he" or "it," "his" or "its." They refer to the seed spoken of. Now, Christ is the seed of the woman. He was formed, "by the agency of the Holy Spirit, of the substance of the Virgin." In Galatians iv. 4, He is said to have been "made of a woman." Speaking according to the figurative language of the passage quoted by His Grace, Satan bruised only the heel of Christ, but Christ bruised Satan's head. It was not necessary for our salvation that the mother of Christ should be sinless. Though He was "made of a woman," yet as He was not one of Adam's natural posterity, He was "holy, harmless, undefiled, and separate from sinners."[1]

The Archbishop quotes only one passage to prove that the mother of Jesus was not shapen in iniquity; and her mother did not in sin conceive her. (Psalm li. 5.) If it stated that doctrine quite distinctly, it would be enough. But we have seen that it has really no bearing whatever on that doctrine. On the other hand, we find the Virgin speaking of herself as a sinner saved by grace. In Luke i. 47, she says: "My spirit hath rejoiced in God my Saviour." Strange language from the lips of one who, according to the Church of Rome, needed no Saviour! "They that be whole need not a physician, but they that are sick." (Matthew ix. 12.) I once had some conversation with the late Vicar-General Bruyère. In the course of it, I asked him how he explained the words of the Virgin which I have just quoted. I had no doubt that he would interpret them in harmony with the doctrine of the Immaculate Conception, and I wished to hear how he would. He answered: "God was her Saviour, for He saved her from the taint of original sin." This was taking for granted the very thing to be proved. I said: "Admitting that what you say about her is true, is it not very strange that the Bible does not, even in one passage, state in language about the meaning of which there cannot be the least doubt, that she, though descending from Adam by ordinary generation, had not the slightest taint of sin, and that she is the only one of that

(1) See Appendix XV.

class of whom this is true?" He said that it was. It is indeed a most remarkable thing.

Before December 8, 1854, the Immaculate Conception of the Virgin Mary was an open question in the Romish Church. Now, cursed is every one who does not believe in it, a proof that she is not what she boasts that she is, "always the same."[1]

(1) See Appendix VI.

Chapter 9.

Question.—(32) "Do Catholics worship images of Christ and His saints?"

QUESTION 32.—" Do Catholics worship images of Christ and His saints?"

ANSWER.—" No, but they cherish and honour them as representatives and memorials."

ROMAN Catholics, as we shall afterwards see, do a great deal more than that to the images described.

"All civilized people cherish and honour mementoes of their dearest friends, such as busts, pictures, and photographs, etc."

"Etc." means "and so forth." His Grace, therefore, speaks here of "busts, pictures, and photographs, and so forth." This is what, I suppose, we must call "the Archbishop's English," as we speak of "the Queen's English." Are not photographs just a kind of pictures?

"To dishonour or spit upon the pictures of royalty, or the flag of a nation, would be considered a grievous insult to the sovereign or country."

Is not "spitting upon," just a form of "dishonouring?" Is not the difference between the two the same as that between paying a person in cash, and paying him in bank bills? "Archbishop's English" again. Not lifting one's hat or bowing one's head or knee to these pictures, or that flag, would not be considered a grievous insult to that sovereign, or country. Protestants neither "dishonour" nor "spit upon" images of Christ and His saints.

"God Himself ordered images to be made."

If Your Grace can prove that, it will settle the question. We must admit that, whatever the Lord commands is right. Let us look at the proofs in support of his statement which the " learned prelate " brings forward.

"And the Lord said to Moses, make a brazen serpent and set it up for a sign, whosoever, being struck, shall look on it, shall live." (Numbers xxi. 8.)

On this I remark, (1) The words here rendered "for a sign," mean in the original Hebrew "on a pole." The brazen serpent was meant to be seen by the whole camp of Israel, therefore, it was to be set high up. (2) It was not a "representative and memorial" of God or any of His saints, but a mean of healing those who had been bitten by fiery serpents. As such, it was to be looked at by them. Simply looking at it was all that was required of them. Those who had not been bitten, were not required to even look at it. (3) God commanded only one to be made. (4) Seven hundred and seventy-five years after, King Hezekiah found the children of Israel burning incense to it, just what Roman Catholics often do to " sacred images." Did he "praise them in this?" No. He broke the serpent in pieces, and called it Nehushtan—a piece of brass. (II. Kings xviii. 4.) Och! Yir Lardship's Rivirince, His Majesty was a bad Cahthlic, so he wuz. Well, the brazen serpent had outlived its usefulness. It had no power of itself to heal the serpent-bitten Israelites who looked at it. It was only a mean which God appointed for healing them. Now, there was no need of it. It was, therefore, merely a piece of brass. To treat it with respect on account of what the Lord had done by it, was most becoming. But it was made an idol. Incense was burned to it, which was an act of worship. Hezekiah, therefore, very properly shattered it into pieces. Our Lord bids us pluck out our right eye, or cut off our right hand, or our right foot, if the one, or the other, lead us into sin.

"He also ordered cherubim to be made and placed around the ark of the covenant."

According to His Grace, they stood around it as a guard stands around the body of a dead king while it is lying in state. Of course, the cherubim were at some distance from the ark. Well, in reply I say, (1) There were only two cherubim. Of course, they could not surround the ark. (2) They stood on the mercy seat, the top of the ark, one at each end. Of course, they could not stand around the ark. (3) They stood in the Most Holy Place, where they were seen by no man, save the high priest, and even by him, only one day in the year—the Great Day of Atonement. (Exodus xxv. 18-22; Hebrews ix. 3, 4, 7.) The high priest was not commanded to do obeisance to them. Fancy only two "sacred images," and these placed in some room in St. Peter's, where they are seen only by the Pope, and that only one day in the year, and he not required to do homage to them. I need say no more on that point.

God commanded the Brazen Serpent and the Cherubim to be made. He nowhere in His word commands "sacred images" to be made.

The rest of His Grace's answer is too long to be quoted in full. He says that crucifixes and images of the Virgin and saints serve as "an open Bible to remind us of the love of Christ and His saints for us, and to urge us to love them and imitate their example."

If the Archbishop's Church would give her people "an open Bible," properly so called, they would have no need of the one of which he here speaks. The latter is a poor makeshift for the former. There is a regiment of saints in the Romish calendar. The "faithful" cannot love them and imitate their example, without knowing about them. Of multitudes of the saints, multitudes of the "faithful" know nothing. The images themselves cannot tell whom they represent. To carry out His Grace's reasoning, every Roman Catholic should have an image of every saint. An image lacking is a leaf lacking in the "open Bible" of which he speaks. What about loving and imitating saints who never had a being? Of some of them I shall hereafter speak. Some of the Romish saints who had a being, lived like the poor heathen fakirs. For example, Labre, who lately was made a saint, was so filthy in his person that if he were now alive, I am sure no cleanly "good Catholic" would like to clasp him to his bosom. The same is true of St. Francis Assisi. Some of the saints were noted for their cruel treatment of those who served the Lord in a more spiritual manner than they did. Should we "love" such saints and "imitate their example"? The Bible "urges" us to love supremely, and to follow fully but one—the Lord Jesus.

"Pictures and images tend to raise the mind to think more earnestly on the original, or person represented."

This sounds very well, but facts prove that pictures and images as "aids to devotion" are not successful. They help to fix the mind on things seen and temporal, and hinder it from rising to those which are unseen and eternal. The Lord knows our weakness. He loves us. "He knoweth our frame, He remembereth that we are dust." (Psalm ciii. 14.) If He knew that "sacred images" would be for our spiritual good, he would "urge" us to use them. But nowhere in His word does He do so. On the contrary, as we shall afterwards see, He forbids it. I have been at what some would call "first-class" funeral services in Roman Catholic churches. I have seen on these occasions, the pictures completely covered with black cloth. Of course, they could not then have any effect on the minds of those present. But surely, if people need "aids to devotion" at any time, they do so at a funeral.

The Archbishop's condemnation of indecent pictures is quite just.

"In Protestant countries a different order is followed; we find statues of Patriots, Generals, and Poets adorn the highways. Which custom tends most to raise our thoughts to heaven?"

These statues are as common in Roman Catholic countries as in Protestant ones. They are not often found on the highways.

In effect, they are about as good "aids to devotion" as "sacred images" are. Yir Grace, you separate Ginirals and Poets from Pathriots. Thin, you must have the oidayah that Ginirals and Poets aren't Pathriots. Aren't ye rathur sevare on the Ginirals and Poets? beggin' Yir Lardship's Rivirince's pardon for makin' so bould as to spake in that way.

The Archbishop refers to a custom of the members of Parliament, both in England and in Canada, of bowing the knee or head, when passing the throne, or the Speaker's chair, even when the one or the other is empty. He expresses himself in a very clumsy manner. He speaks of the House of Lords and Commons as if the Lords and Commons had but one House. Each have a House. Performing the act here mentioned, to a mere piece of furniture, is in its nature altogether different from the reverence paid by, at least, the great mass of people to "sacred images." The act could be omitted without the least disrespect being shown the authority represented by the person whose that seat is.

"It would be a damnable idolatry to adore any but God;——"

On this point, His Grace is as sound as he could possibly be.

"but to pay the reverence of bowing to sacred images is *not* idolatry."

God says that it is, and that settles the question. He says in Exodus xx. 5, "Thou shalt not bow down thyself to them, nor serve them," that is, as Matthew Henry says: "not bow down to them occasionally, that is, by any sign respect or honour them, much less serve them constantly by sacrifice or incense, or any other act of religious worship." Sometimes, idolatry is described as simply bowing down to images. (See, for example, Leviticus xxvi. 1, and Numbers xxv. 2.) The original of the word rendered in these passages "bow down," expresses, not an act of the heart, but one of the body. It is used where we read of Abraham bowing himself to the children of Heth, of Joseph's brethren bowing themselves down to him, and of Naaman bowing himself in the house of the god Rimmon.

We find it used with one expressing kneeling, in the exhortation in Psalm xcv. 6 : "O come, let us worship and bow down ; let us kneel before the Lord our Maker." "Holy and venerable images" were unknown to the early Christians. In the Archbishop's Church, which boasts that she is one, there are three opinions as to the "due honour" to be given to images of the kind described. One is that they are to be used merely to awaken trains of holy thought. Another is that they are to be adored as a mean of adoring those whom they represent. Another is that they are to be adored the same as those whom they represent. Intelligent heathens "long, long ago," used precisely the same argument in favour of the use of images, that His Grace here does. So do intelligent heathens to-day. But the great mass of heathens in all ages have really worshipped them. The same is true of Roman Catholics. The worship of the golden calf at the foot of Sinai was professedly in honour of Jehovah. (Exodus xxxii. 5.) Yet, Paul calls it idolatry. (1 Corinthians x. 7.) The two golden calves which Jeroboam set up, one in Bethel the other in Dan, were meant to be used as means of worshipping Jehovah. (1 Kings xii. 28.) Jeroboam brought in no other form of idolatry. Yet God said to him : "Thou hast gone and made thee other gods, and molten images to provoke me to anger." (1 King xiv. 9.)

The Lord commanded Saul to destroy utterly, not only the Amalekites themselves, but also all their oxen and sheep, camels and asses. (1 Samuel xv. 3.) Though Saul utterly destroyed the Amalekites, he "took of the spoil, sheep and oxen, the chief of the things which should have been utterly destroyed, to sacrifice to the Lord in Gilgal." (20, 21 vs.) He thought that by so doing, he honoured the Lord. But Samuel said to him that instead thereof, he had done evil in His sight (19 v.), and added : "Hath the Lord as great delight in burnt offerings and sacrifices, as in obeying the voice of the Lord ? Behold, to obey is better than sacrifice, and to hearken than the fat of rams. . For rebellion is as the sin of witchcraft, and stubbornness is as iniquity and idolatry. Because thou hast rejected the word of the Lord, He hath also rejected thee from being king." (22, 23 vs.)

Christ commanded a leper whom He had cleansed, to say nothing to any one about it. The latter, however, went away, and began "to publish it much, and to spread abroad the matter." No doubt, he thought he was honouring Christ by doing so. But the wisdom of Christ's command soon appeared. The cleansed leper would have honoured Him infinitely more by holding his peace according to it. (Mark i. 44, 45.)

God, as we have seen, most plainly forbids us to worship Him by images. It is, therefore, a gross insult to Him to worship Him in that way. When the Roman Catholics of Toronto gave Cardinal Taschereau a public banquet in the Rossin House, they had no intoxicating drink at it. This was very proper, because His Eminence is a strong Total Abstainer. Instead of honouring him, they would have grossly insulted him, if they had not conducted the banquet on temperance principles. But we should also do God's will because we know that it is right. It cannot be otherwise.

"We bow every day to our friends in the streets but don't adore them."

Surely Your Grace does not believe that this is the same as bowing to "sacred images." If you do, I do not. We bow to them to honour themselves, not others whom they represent. If we be sufficiently near them to do so, we shake hands with them, ask about the state of their health and that of their wives and families, tell them what kind of weather we have, and so on. If a person to whom we have bowed once or twice, pay no heed to us, we say: "We will let him bow to us first, next time we meet," and act accordingly. Does Yir Grace uver bow to a statty uv St. Payther, and thin take howlt uv his hand and say: "How d'ye do, Yir Howliness? How is Mrs. Payther? An' how is Paythronilla, yir swate daughter? Oi hope oi see you well this illigant marnin." Does the statty say: "Oi thank Yir Grace, we're all well, barrin mesilf. Oi've a moity bad cowld"? Does Yir Grace thin say: "Och! Yir Howliness must bathe your fate in hat wather, and take a good dhrink uv hat skilligalee without e'er a dhrap uv poteen in it, before going to bid to-noite"? If we should bow to images as we do to our friends, then, as the images will not return our salutation, that is a very good reason for taking no notice of them. Saluting "holy and venerable" images, the Church of Rome regards as a religious act. We do not burn lamps, candles or incense before our friends, or kiss their feet. But this is often done by Roman Catholics to images. I have seen lights before images of the Virgin. The toes of the right foot of the statue of St. Peter in St. Peter's, in Rome, and the corresponding ones of the copy of it in Notre Dame Church, Montreal, are worn with kisses. In the church of Ara Cœli in Rome, is the famous miracle-working doll, the Bambino. The monk who showed me it, lighted two candles on the altar before bringing it out. He said to me: "We have to perform a religious ceremony before we show it."

"To respect the sacred Scriptures because the letters in it represent God's word, to kiss pictures of St. Peter, St. Paul, etc., are acts of reverence to God or to His saints. Would it be idolatry in a mother to kiss the picture of her darling child whom she knows to be in heaven?"

Regarding the first part of the first sentence, I say that it is most becoming to treat with respect bibles which we can see and handle, because the letters in them do not merely represent, but really are, God's word. But what, your Grace, about burning Protestant Bibles? This your Church often does. They cannot be truly called false versions, for they are even more faithful than the Vulgate, the one to which she gives the highest place. This, surely, is not treating with respect the sacred Scriptures, "whose letters represent God's word." Torquemada, the famous inquisitor, caused many Hebrew Bibles to be burned at an *auto da fé* at Salamanca. A strange way of showing respect to the sacred Scriptures, "whose letters represent God's word"! These Bibles are not false versions, for they were in the language in which holy men wrote the Old Testament, as they were moved by the Holy Ghost. In the second part, His Grace says that kissing images of the saints is a way of honouring those whom they represent. This is just an illustration of an idea which he has already expressed. When the General Assembly of the Presbyterian Church in Canada, met in Toronto in 1884, His Grace addressed a letter to that body, for the purpose—as an "Oirish jintleman" would say—of letting out the darkness from its mind regarding the doctrines of his church. One of the subjects on which he spoke, was that of the worship of images. He, of course, expressed himself in the same manner that he does here. Now, Yir Lardship's Rivirince, oid be afther spakin' a few words to you as a friend, axin' yir pardon fur that same. Uv coorse, all prastes, from His Howliniss down, are good Cahthlics. Thin they do be anerin' the saints by kissin' their images. Well, do they bi kissin' faymale as well as jintleman images ? If they do, do they kiss them on the mouth ? Och ! but it's cowld comfort intoirely to kiss a marsel of wood, or sthone, or methal, or plasther. Now, Yir Grace, excuse me, Sur, wudn't it be a grate dale betther if the Pope, the cardinals, the archbishops and the rist uv the clargy to the fut uv the laddher, had aitch wan a livin' faymale image uv flesh and blood cahlled "Misthress," and thin his own name ? St. Payther, the first Pope—as you cahll him—had wan uv that same. Now jist luk here : If His Howliness had his Misthress Layo, he cud say to her : "Me darlint, oi'll cahll you St. Mary, and kiss you in aner uv hur." Thin he cud do that, and giv hur a good hug into the bargin. Nixt, he cud say to hur : "Me jewel, oi'll cahll you St. Catherine, and giv you a kiss fur hur sake." Thin he cud giv hur a smack and a hug, and so an. Ahll, uv coorse, in aner uv the saints. He cud kiss hur to show respict to the jintlemen saints as well as the faymale wans. He'd have a good intinshun. There's a lagion uv both kinds uv saints, so he'd be purty well used to kissin hur by the toime he'd git to the last. At the ind uv aitch occashun, he'd smack his lips, and say : Och ! but that bates intoirely the owld way uv anerin' the saints." Thin Misthress Layo cud do the same to him, ahll, uv coorse, in aner uv the saints. So there ud be plinty uv kissin in the Vathican. Let ahll the rist uv the clargy, yis, and the monks and the harmits, too, go and do loikewoise. If St. Payther cud see it, and spake to thim, he'd say: "Barrin the anerin uv the saints, the kissin, me childer, is ahll roite. I used to do a little uv that same mesilf."[1]

This invention of mine is another reason why the Pope, if he knew of it, should send me the decoration of the Order of Gregory the Great, or some other as good.[2]

His Grace speaks about a mother kissing the picture of her dead child. Of course she would kiss it on the mouth. With all due respect for her feelings, I must say that that is a piece of folly. I would sympathize with her, if she showed respect for something which belonged to her child, for example, a book, a toy, or the little shoes. It would be ridiculous in the mother to kiss a fancy picture in honour of her child. The faces in the pictures and images of the saints, are not portraits of the saints. How does the mother know that her child is in heaven? I ask this question in accordance with the teachings of the Archbishop's Church. May not her child be in Limbus infantum, or in Purgatory?

"The Emperor Leo, the image-breaker, asked St. Stephen, Bishop and Martyr, whether he believed that men trampled on Christ by trampling on His image. 'God forbid,' said the martyr."

According to this part of the story, the saint did not believe so. Yea, his language as given by the Archbishop may mean: "God forbid that I should believe such a thing." But it is plain from what follows, that he did believe it. The account of his death has no bearing whatever on the question. His Grace does not bring forward one passage from Scripture in support of his views on it.

(1) "Good Catholic" gentlemen who have read the foregoing "new and improved method" of honouring the saints by means of images, will be very apt to make use of it when, with matrimonial intentions, they visit the ladies.

(2) See page 64 of Review.

Chapter 10.

Questions—(33) Does it not insult Christ to pray to the saints?—(34) How can the Saints hear our prayers?—(35) Does not the Catholic Church suppress the Second Commandment?

"QUESTION 33.—" Does it not insult Christ our only Mediator to pray to the saints?"

HIS GRACE says in reply that "Christ is our only great and Primary Mediator with the Father," and saints are only secondary mediators or intercessors. The Bible says nothing about two kinds of mediators. It tells us that as there is but one God, there is also but one Mediator between God and men, the Man Christ Jesus. (1 Timothy ii. 5.) Christ says: "No man cometh unto the Father, but by Me." (John xiv. 6.) John says: "If any man sin, we have an advocate with the Father, Jesus Christ the righteous." (1 John ii. 1.) Him the Father heareth always (John xi. 42), for His intercession is founded on His sacrifice. He is ever ready to hear the cry of those who call on Him in truth. He says: "Him that cometh to Me, I will in no wise cast out." (John vi. 37.) The penitent thief needed not to go to Him by a saint. (Luke xxiii. 42, 43.) Yet the Virgin Mary and John were at the foot of Christ's cross, and so could have heard him.

"If Catholics pray to the saints for mercy and salvation, expecting them directly from them, then it would be an insult to Christ, but they do not; they only ask the saints to pray to Christ for them, considering the prayers of the glorified saints in heaven to be more powerful than those of sinners on earth."

The English of this quotation is not of the very best quality, but I shall not stop to review it. We have no warrant whatever in the Bible for asking dead saints even to merely pray for us. As we shall afterwards see, reason itself forbids our doing so. We take with us into the other world, our recollections of this one. Saints who have crossed the river, therefore, think on their friends who are yet on this side of it, and, therefore, it is quite likely that they pray for them. Yea, more, it is quite likely that they pray for the conversion of the whole world. But we have no proof that they do, or even that they know what is going on in the world. But, supposing that the saints in glory do pray for us, that is no proof that they are able to hear us when we cry to them. The Church of Rome teaches that the saints in Purgatory pray for men on the earth, but prayers are never addressed to the former. The Romish Church makes little account of the Scripture saints, with very few exceptions, or even of eminent saints of a later date. Of many of her saints, we have, judging from their teachings and what we are told of their lives, great reason to doubt that they are in heaven. Some of her saints never had a being. Some, it is doubtful that they ever had. Roman Catholics pray far oftener to the saints than they do to the Father or the Son. They often ask blessings from the saints directly and personally. I have already referred to prayers to Joseph and Mary. Let us look at one or two others. "Holy angels . . . be present with me, and defend me from the assaults of evil spirits. . . . Cleanse me from all filthiness." "O Peter, blessed shepherd, of thy mercy receive our prayers, and loose, by thy word, the chains of our sins; thou to whom power is given to open heaven to the earth, and to shut it when opened." "O glorious Nicholas, conduct us to the port of salvation where peace and glory reign." "O John, help us to walk in the way of holiness." "O Michael, glorious prince, chief and champion of the heavenly host, . . . vouchsafe to free us all from every evil, who with full confidence have recourse to thee."[1] This is very unlike what His Grace here

---

(1) We have good reason to believe that Michael, the Archangel, is the Lord Jesus. The Church of Rome, however, believes him to be only a created being, though most highly exalted. Her prayers to him, must, therefore, be judged accordingly.

says about praying to the saints. How can the prayers of the glorified saints in heaven be "more powerful than those of sinners on earth"? The sinners here spoken of, are really saints who, as they are on earth, are not yet made perfect in holiness. "God heareth not sinners," that is those strictly so called. His Grace, as we shall see hereafter, teaches that saints on earth have merits. He must, therefore, believe that those in heaven have greater. Roman Catholics often pray to God to hear them for the sake of the merits of the saints, which is really putting the saints in the place of Christ. Their Church says that silent, as well as spoken prayer, should be addressed to them. Sins are confessed to them as well as to God and the priest.

According to the Archbishop's Church, we have all, so to speak, to present to God a vessel full of good works. Some of mankind have done more than their vessel would hold, in other words, they have been better than God's law required them to be. These "overflow" merits are too precious to be cast away. "Gather up the fragments that remain, that nothing be lost." They are, therefore, put into a heap along with the merits of Christ. Beside this heap stands "Mother Church" with a shovel. Here, I would ask: If the merits of Christ be of infinite value, what need is there of adding to them those of creatures, even if the latter could have merits? But to go on. The vessels of the far greater part of mankind are more or less—as an "Oirish jintleman" would say—full of emptiness—some very much so. Their owners must, therefore, bring them to "Mother Church," and make a request of her like that which the foolish virgins made of the wise ones, —"Give us of that heap to fill our vessels." She does so, but not "hoping for nothing again." If what she gives be as good as she represents it, she deserves to be well paid.

The merits of creatures—admitting that there is such a thing—must, necessarily, be of limited value. One would, therefore, naturally suppose that on account of the great numbers who have, for hundreds of years, been helped from that heap, many very much so, the creature merits in it would, long ago, have disappeared. The merits of the new saints who are, from time to time, added to the calendar, are not sufficient to keep up the needed supply. But no—a most remarkable thing!—these merits have not been in the least degree lessened. They are like the widow's meal and oil in the days of Elijah, and the loaves and fishes used by Christ in two of His miracles.

We come now to certain passages of Scripture which the "learned prelate" brings forward in defence of praying to saints. He first says, in general, that Paul "recommended himself to the prayers of his brethren, the Christians." We find him doing so in Romans xv. 30; 2 Corinthians i. 11; Ephesians vi. 18, 19; Colossians iv. 3; 1 Thessalonians v. 25, and 2 Thessalonians iii. 1. The Archbishop refers to Philippians i. 19, where Paul speaks of the benefit which he knows that he shall receive, in part, through the prayer of those whom he addresses. He might have referred also to Philemon 22, where the Apostle speaks in like manner. But we never find him asking the saints in glory to pray for him, or expressing the hope of receiving any blessing through their doing so. He would have acted very differently, we may be sure, had he believed that their prayers were more powerful than those of his brethren on earth.

"St. Stephen, first martyr, prayed for his persecutors, that is mediated for their pardon."

He prayed for them, but did not "mediate for their pardon." He could not do the latter. A mediator is "one who stands between two parties at variance, in order to reconcile them." He must have power to bring this about. Only Christ can be a mediator between God and men. Only He atones for sin, and imparts to His people both the will and the power to return to God. He is an intercessor as well as a mediator. But it is impossible for one to be merely a mediator of intercession, as the Romish Church says the saints are. Stephen did not pray also to the saints to pray for his persecutors. Why did he not, if he believed that their prayers have great power? Of course, his persecutors did not pray to him. The case of Stephen here mentioned, does not prove that the saints in heaven pray for their enemies on earth, and, therefore, of course, also for their friends here. But suppose that it does, that is no warrant for our praying to them.

"This privilege of mediation" (His Grace should rather have said "intercession") "is not lost by death, because it proceeds from love, and love does not die. Faith and hope will pass away with earth; but love enters into the portals of heaven, nay even descends into hell."

Faith and hope, as far as they are connected with earth, will certainly pass away with it. That they will utterly pass away, is doubtful. That love goes down into hell, is the greatest nonsense possible. In hell, there is nothing but wickedness.

To prove that love goes down into hell, the Archbishop refers to Luke xvi. 27, 28, where the rich man is represented as "praying Abraham to send Lazarus to earth to warn his five brethren there, of the punishment awaiting their crimes if they did not repent." Now, it is most likely that it was mere selfishness which moved the rich man to do so. He, no doubt, believed that if they should come where he was, they would add to his sufferings. "The more closely the lost have been related to each other on earth, the more bitterly they will upbraid and torment each other in hell." But supposing that this rich man is to be regarded as moved by love to his brethren on earth, that circumstance is simply the imaginary origin of an imaginary act. This passage is a parable. We must not interpret it in opposition to what we are elsewhere plainly told about hell. What we have to do with, is not the origin of this prayer, but the answer to it. It is the only instance in Scripture of prayer to a glorified saint. The thing asked was refused, which certainly does not encourage one to pray to the saints. It was asked of Abraham directly. The rich man did not ask Abraham to pray to God to hear his prayer. The person who prayed was in hell. His Grace thinks that because glorified saints pray for men on earth, we should pray to them. His Church teaches that the saints in Purgatory pray for men on earth. Then we should pray to *them* also. The Archbishop refers to this parable as a proof that souls in hell pray for men on earth. Then we should pray to them also. We have, therefore, "mediators of intercession" in Heaven, Earth, Purgatory, and Hell!!

Before going further, I would notice two things in the Archbishop's language here. He says that love "even descends into hell." "Descends even" etc., would be more elegant. He next says: "The rich man died and was buried in hell, he loved even there his brothers." The comma after the word "hell," makes His Grace say that the rich man was buried in hell. Truly a strange burial place! But let us lay the blame of this on the printer. It is well known that he often makes sad havoc of an author's language. Let us blot out that comma, put a period immediately after "buried," and then read as follows: "In hell, he loved even there his brothers." This is not nonsense, but the English is—as is often said of a hat—"shocking bad." "Even in hell he loved his brothers," would be much better.

"Christ has said, in heaven the just shall be as angels of God. (Mark xii. 25.) And the angels pray and intercede for us." (Zachariah i. 12.)

Therefore, according to His Grace, the just in heaven "pray and intercede" for us, and, therefore, we should pray to them. There is no need of using here both words "pray" and "intercede." Either is sufficient. But let us now look for a little at the first of the passages to which the "learned prelate" refers. He utterly misinterprets it. He makes it describe the just in heaven as they are at present, which it does not do at all. Reading on from the 18th v., we learn that the Sadducees on one occasion asked our Lord, what they thought was a very puzzling question about "the resurrection" and marriage. (23 v.) They did not refer to the resurrection of the just, but to the resurrection in general. They themselves did not believe in any. (18 v.) In His reply, our Lord speaks only of the saved, in connection with the resurrection. He makes no mention whatever of the lost. It is true that both in the passage which the Archbishop quotes, and in the kindred one in Matthew xxii. 23-30, He uses simply the word "they," when speaking of those who shall arise from the dead. But what I have just said regarding His reply, is proved by the kindred passage in Luke xx. 27-36. The clause in each of the three passages relating to the angels in heaven, does not by itself prove it, as we shall afterwards see. Our Lord here speaks only of the resurrection of the saved, because that was sufficient for His purpose, and a pleasing subject, whereas that of the lost was a painful one. Well, instead of speaking about the saints now in glory, as the Archbishop interprets the passage under consideration, He speaks of a very striking difference between the state of His people in this world and in the next. He says that while they marry and are given in marriage in the former, they shall not do and be so in the latter. Though marriage was instituted in Eden, it was designed only for this life. As His Grace says of faith and hope, it "will pass away with earth." The angels do not marry, neither shall the saints in the future state. As Bishop Ryle says: "Death being no more—there shall be no need of births to supply the place of those who are removed. Enjoying the full presence of God and His Christ—men and women shall no more need the marriage union, in order to help one another." As Matthew Henry says: "Where there are no burials, there is no need of weddings." It is true that in many other respects, the righteous shall, hereafter, be as the angels. But as the subject under consideration, is death and the resurrection, the only instances of equality between them here mentioned, are immortality and not marrying. It is true that in this respect, the lost also shall be as the angels. As Matthew

Henry says: "In hell, . . . the voice of the bridegroom and the voice of the bride shall be heard no more at all." But for the reasons already given, our Lord does not here speak of *them*. For the same reasons, He says nothing regarding the fallen angels, though they also, in being immortal, and not marrying, are as those who have "kept their first estate, and not left their own habitation." I am surprised that His Grace does not bring forward the passage in Mark to which he refers, as a proof that the single state is holier than the married one. Many of his proofs are no stronger.

We come now to the second passage. We have very good reason to believe that the angel spoken of in it, is the Lord Jesus who interceded with the Father on behalf of His Church which was greatly afflicted during the days of the prophet. Read from the 8th v. In many passages in the Old Testament, Christ is spoken of as an angel. If this interpretation be correct, the passage gives no warrant for praying to saints or angels.

"Prayers of the saints are offered up before the throne of God in heaven (Apoc. v. 8): 'Four-and-twenty ancients fell down before the Lamb having every one of them harps, and golden vials full of odours, which are the prayers of the saints.'"

His Grace should have mentioned also the four living creatures. The same is said of them, that is said of the "ancients." Now, in the 8th chapter, 3rd and 4th verses, we read of an angel offering up the prayers of all saints with much incense on the golden altar before the throne. This can be none other than the Lord Jesus our Great High Priest. The much incense is His own merits, only through which, our services, as well as our persons, are accepted by the Father. Peter says that spiritual sacrifices are acceptable to God by Jesus Christ. (1 Peter ii. 5.) One passage of Scripture does not contradict another. In the 9th and 10th verses of the chapter from which the Archbishop quotes, we have the song of praise to the Lamb from the four living creatures and the four-and-twenty "ancients." But they do not, in it, ask Him to accept the prayers of others which they offer. It is most likely that they represent the Church, and that these prayers are their own. It will be noticed that the prayers here spoken of, are simply those of saints, whereas those spoken of in the 8th chapter, are those of all saints. Again, the prayers here spoken of, are called odours or incense. Those spoken of in the 8th chapter, are represented as mingled with much incense. In the Old Testament, prayer is sometimes spoken of under the figure of incense. Prayer is an offering to God of a sweet smelling savour when the merits of His Son are added thereto. Christ's offering of Himself was one of a sweet smell to the Father, and when the merits thereof are added to the prayers of His people, they make them the same. The passage which His Grace quotes is in the highest degree figurative, and, therefore, no doctrine can fairly be founded on it. According to his interpretation of it, it proves too much, for it proves that glorified saints present our prayers to the Father, which is a very great deal more than simply praying to Christ for us.

But I must now pass on to other Questions and Answers. Before doing so, I would just say again that though it could be clearly proved that glorified saints pray for us, that does not prove that we should pray to them.

Q. 34.—"How can the saints, who are so far away in heaven, hear our prayers?"

A.—"Heaven is not far away, it is where God is, and 'God is nigh unto us.'" (Philippians iv. 5.)

God is everywhere. Therefore, according to His Grace, heaven is everywhere, therefore, the saints are everywhere, therefore, they are equal to God. The passage here quoted, read where it stands, seems to refer to the second coming of Christ. It is to the same effect as 1 Peter iv. 7, where it is said: "The end of all things is at hand; be ye therefore sober, and watch unto prayer." Even though heaven should be near us, it does not follow from that, that the saints know what is taking place on the earth.

"God hears and sees us and the angels and saints in heaven can know the mind of God, and through it know what passes on earth as far as God permits."

"Can know the mind of God," that is, as He knows our mind. The highest angel can know it only as God reveals it to him. If angels and saints know the mind of God, they, of course, know all things, therefore they are equal to God. True, His Grace uses the "saving clause" "as far as God permits." But if they know God's mind, He cannot hinder them from knowing anything. It is not very easy to see, on account of the fog, in what direction our "Dear Roman Catholic Friend" is steering. This seems to be it—We pray to the saints to pray to God to hear our prayers. God makes known to them that such prayers are addressed to them. Then they pray to God to hear these prayers. A very round-about way of praying to God! But if our prayers be not pleasing to God, it is not likely that He will tell the saints of them. We are commanded to ask of the Father in the name of Christ. If the Father accept our prayers for the sake of His Son, there is no need of the saints praying for us. "As far as God permits." Supposing that he does not make known to the saints the prayers addressed to them, what then? It seems, then, a matter of uncertainty that God makes known to the saints such prayers. This gives us poor encouragement to pray to them.

"The angels rejoice upon the conversion of a sinner. . . . There shall be joy before the angels of God upon one sinner doing penance" (Luke xv. 10.)

This, however, does not give us the least warrant to pray to them. "Doing penance." Is that going with gravel or unboiled peas in one's shoes, eating bread with ashes in it, becoming a total abstainer from soap and water, wearing the same clothes so long that an odour more powerful than pleasant is produced, or the like?

Q. 35.—"Does not the Catholic Church suppress the Second Commandment, 'Thou shalt not make unto thyself any graven thing or image'?"

Of course, the "learned prelate," as the counsel of his Church, pleads "Not guilty." He says that both Protestants and Roman Catholics believe that there are ten commandments, but differ about the division of them. What follows is too long to be given in full. I shall give what is essential in as few words as possible, and with full justice to his arguments.

He says that what the Protestants call the first and second commandments, are only one. They "concern the worship of God." What the Protestants call the third "forbids to profane the holy name of God." This is, according to His Grace, the second.

There are really *four* commandments concerning the worship of God. The first relates to the *object* of worship—God only. The second relates to the *manner* of worship—not by means of images. The third relates to the *spirit* of worship —reverently. The fourth relates to the *time* of worship—one day in seven, which God claims as specially His. The first and the second are perfectly distinct from each other. We can worship other gods than the true God, and we can professedly worship the true God by images. God forbids us to do both. There is no sin in treating the first and second commandments as only two branches of the same, provided we carefully obey both. The Archbishop's Church has never gone the length of blotting out of the Scriptures what she calls the second part of the first commandment. But she almost invariably blots it out, where she can conveniently. Not the slightest notice is taken of it in Butler's Catechism, which is recommended by the four Romish archbishops of Ireland; nor in Plunkett's Abridgment of Christian Doctrine; nor in Archbishop Reilly's Catechism; nor in a Catechism by Bellarmine.

I may state that in the last, instead of "Remember the Sabbath day to keep it holy," we find "Remember to keep holy *the festivals*." As very few of His Grace's co-religionists know anything of the Scriptures, the action of his Church just referred to, is very suspicious. What good end can she have in view in trying to smuggle the command against images out of sight, under the one against having other gods than God?

His Grace says that Protestants and Roman Catholics agree regarding the division of the other commandments, till they come to what the latter call the ninth and tenth, but which the Protestants say are only one—"the prohibition of coveting the neighbour's house, ox, ass, and wife." His Church, he says, makes two of these commandments, "because the coveting of a wife is a different thing from the coveting of a house, an ox, an ass, for Christ has said, 'the coveting of thy neighbour's wife is equal to adultery.'" (Matthew v. 28.) Coveting one's neighbour's wife is not a different thing from coveting the other things here mentioned. His wife is clearly mentioned as a specimen of the "anything which is our neighbour's," which we are in the close of the commandment forbidden to covet. If coveting one's neighbour's wife be "equal to adultery," what need is there of a command against it? The Romish sixth commandment, the Protestant seventh, distinctly says: "Thou shalt not commit adultery." His Grace does not quote here correctly, even from his own Bible. Our Lord does not say that coveting one's neighbour's wife is equal to adultery, but that "whosoever looketh on a woman"—she may be a maid or a widow—"to lust after her hath committed adultery with her already in his heart." Here, He in effect states, what is a maxim in sound philosophy, that "to will is to act."

His Grace refers to Deuteronomy v. 21, where the ten commandments are repeated. There, our neighbour's wife is the first mentioned of the things which we are forbidden to covet. This is no argument in favour of the Archbishop's views on this question. The corresponding passages in Exodus and Deuteronomy are of equal authority. The fact that the Lord mentions our neighbour's wife second in the one, and first in the other, shows clearly that He speaks in each, only of the sin of covetousness. The "learned prelate" says that the Protestants, by making one commandment of his Church's ninth and tenth, "falsely make the coveting of the wife, the house, the ox, and ass, the same or equal sin." According to him, these are four different sins, that is to say, sins differ according to the object on which they are committed. For example, stealing money, stealing provisions, and stealing clothing, are all different sins. "The same or equal sin." Two or more things may be equal, but they cannot be, numerically, the same. "Equal sin." Two or more things may be equal, but one cannot. Och! Yir Grace, but its mesilf that's shacked to hear an archbishop spakin' so ungrammatically. God here forbids only one sin, though He particularly mentions different forms of it. In this commandment, He, in effect, bids us "keep our hearts with all diligence, for out of them are the issues of life." Christ tells us that obedience to all the commandments is an expression of love—love to God, and love to man. Paul says that love is the fulfilling of the law. In like manner, coveting the different things mentioned in this commandment are just different forms of the same sin. We must bear in mind that the person here addressed, is supposed to covet his neighbour's wife for his own; otherwise, his coveting is forbidden by the commandment, "Thou shalt not commit adultery." The term "wife," as here used, I consider, applies to a woman who is only betrothed, as well as to one who is actually married. In Deut. xxii. 23, 24, "a damsel that is a virgin betrothed unto a husband," is called his wife. Compare what is there said about her and her partner in sin, with what is said in the 22nd verse, about a married woman and her partner in sin. According to this commandment, one seems to be forbidden to covet for his wife, a woman who is even only betrothed to his neighbour.

It could easily be shown that, according to His Grace's reasoning, all the other nine commandments are contained in this one: "Thou shalt not steal."

"The Catholics, therefore, do not suppress the second commandment, but truly say, that it is comprised in the first, namely, 'Thou shalt not,'" etc. (quoting the two as one).

What he has said about our tenth commandment, does not in the least support what His Grace has said about our first and second. His Church utterly fails, both in trying to justify her making two of the former, and only one of the latter. There can be no doubt that the reason why she makes two of our tenth commandment is this: The command against the worship of images is a thorn in her side. She, therefore, very naturally wishes to have it removed. We have seen that she removes it whenever she can conveniently do so. Of course, when it is removed, only nine are left. She must have the full number to show. For this end, she makes two of our tenth. His Grace says, regarding what I have just quoted: "Here it is evident that the worship of the true God is intended and the worship of false gods prohibited, and the making of images for the purpose of adoration." I need not repeat what I have already said on these points. I would say a word merely about the Archbishop's English in this quotation. The last sentence is unfinished. It needs to have the word "prohibited" taken from where it stands, and placed at the end, after "adoration."

His Grace is thoroughly orthodox when he says that our second commandment is not opposed to the Fine Arts.

"The Queen of England has a remarkable devotion to her late husband, and takes great pleasure in exhibiting him to the love and veneration of her English subjects."

"Exhibiting her late husband!" Does she carry his mummy about with her? "Her English subjects." Thin, she doesn't "exhibit her late husband to the love and viniration" of hur Scatch and Wilsh subjects; no, nor aven to hur Oirish wans. Och! its too bad intoirely uv our Quane to do sitch a thing.

"When his statue is unveiled, the people uncover their heads, to express their esteem, and give loud hurrahs. It is not to the marble or bronze the honour is given, but to the Prince and the Queen."

Do they uncover their heads that they may be able to hurrah the louder ? Both hats off and hurrahs are expressions of esteem. Men usually wave their hats when they hurrah. Ladies wave their handkerchiefs. People do not bow to the statue, or kiss its foot. They would act as here described, at the unveiling of a memorial pillar, or the opening of a memorial hall.

His Grace then asks if it be idolatry " to express one's esteem for Christ and His saints by anoc casional bow of the head." He, of course, means a bow to images of them. This case and the one just referred to, are quite different. God— as we have seen—most distinctly forbids bowing to images. We must not say, even in effect, that we are wiser than He.

Chapter 11.

Questions—(36) What is the meaning of the "communion of saints"?—(37) Do Catholics worship relics of saints?—(38) Do we read anything in the Bible about relics?

QUESTION 36.—"What is the meaning of the 'communion of saints,' which we profess in the Apostles' Creed?"

WE do not profess the communion of saints, but we profess to believe in it. The Archbishop says that it is a union like that in any earthly society, by which members of the same body "partake of earnings and and advantages of the body. Christ is the Head of all good Christians, . . . so He gives grace and mercy to His true followers." So far, His Grace is quite sound. Then he goes on to say: "All true Christians in like manner communicate to each other a share of their merits and prayers, so we, being many, are one body in Christ, and every one members one of another." (Romans xii. 5.) It is plain from the rest of his answer, that he here speaks of true Christians on the earth. Well, the best Christian on earth has no merit. Christ says: "When ye shall have done all those things which are commanded you, say, We are unprofitable servants: we have done that which was our duty to do." (Luke xvii. 10.) But "there is not a just man upon earth, that doeth good, and sinneth not." (Ecclesiastes vii. 20.) Though one were to live perfectly, in the strict sense of that word, he would have no merit of which he could give another a share. The angel Gabriel has merit, but even *he* cannot spare any. Only those Christians who have more merits than they need for themselves, are, according to His Grace, true Christians. Only *they* go straight to heaven when they die. But he afterwards tells us that few are so holy on earth, as to do so. Therefore, there are few true Christians on earth. Those who are not true Christians are false ones. But we have no warrant in Scripture for believing that those who die false Christians shall, in the other world, be changed into true ones, and afterwards received to glory. Mention is here made of "merits and prayers." Do not these fancied merits spring, in part, from the prayers? If the prayers have no merit, then "communicating to each other a share of . . . their prayers," is only a clumsy expression for praying for one another.

"Christians in the state of mortal sin, and excommunicated persons, are dead members, and do not communicate in its good works and prayers,"——

We have already seen that every sin is, in itself, mortal. "Every sin deserves God's wrath and curse both in this life, and in that which is to come."[1] Every sin is venial in this sense, that whoever seeks forgiveness of it in God's appointed way shall receive it. The Bible makes no distinction between mortal and venial sins. That distinction is alike absurd and impious. Are not excommunicated persons supposed to be "Christians in a state of mortal sin"? A person cannot be cast out of a society to which he never belonged. How can an excommunicated person be a "dead member"? He has been cut off from the Church. A branch cut off from a tree, cannot be even a dead branch of that tree.

"though they can obtain the grace of repentance through the merits of Christ and the prayers of the Church."

According to this, the prayers of the Church, that is, of the priests, are of as much value as the merits of Christ. The one is not sufficient without the other. Christ and the Church are a company for the obtaining of salvation for sinners, like Brown & Jones, Commission Merchants. Christ, when He was about to be parted from His disciples, commanded them

(1) Shorter Cathechism, Q. 84.

to preach "repentance and remission of sins in His name among all nations." But he did not say one word about the prayers of the Church. If His merits be of infinite value, there is no need of the prayers of the Church in addition to them. If the sinner do not from the heart, ask the grace of repentance through the merits of Christ, the prayers of the Church will not obtain it for him. What we obtain through the merits of Christ, we obtain "without money and without price." But the Church appoints prayers and almsgiving to go together in this way—she will pray; and the sinner will give alms to—her.

Q. 37.—"Do Catholics worship or pray to relics of the saints?"
A.—"No. But they hold them in reverence as belonging to the saints."

As the Roman Catholics justify relic worship on the very same grounds as those on which they justify image worship, the same arguments as those used against the latter, will, of course, apply equally well to the former. These arguments I need not repeat. I would just state that many eminent Romish theologians hold that relics are to receive the same honour as those whose they are. The brazen serpent in the days of Hezekiah was surely worthy of respect, merely as a relic. Yet he caused it to be destroyed, because the children of Israel burned incense to it. Burning lights unceasingly from the beginning of the first day of January to the end of the last day of December, before the bodies or parts of the bodies of the saints,[1] is more than mere reverence of the saints. It is itself a relic—a relic of heathenism.

"Protestants have their relics; in the Tower of London we find relics of Kings, Queens, etc."

Protestants keep these merely as interesting objects. They do not burn lights before them, bow to them, kiss them, or the like. That is, sensible Protestants do not. Those whose

(1) See Appendix XVI.

"attics" are scantily furnished—to use a homely comparison—may do, at least, the bowing to and kissing them. Protestants do not believe that any of the relics referred to, can work miracles, as many of those of the saints are said to have done, and to be still able to do. They do not keep among their relics such rubbish as teeth and parings of toe nails. The saintliness of many of those whose relics they have, was, to say the least, of a very low kind. Of course, they do not hold these in reverence as belonging to saints. But, really the piety of some of the Romish saints was not any better, though, their morals were blameless. Roman Catholics have also relics of kings, queens, etc., or—as His Grace expresses it when speaking about images—"of patriots, generals and poets." These they treat as Protestants do.

But, Your Grace, what about holding in reverence relics of saints which never belonged to them? Take, for example, the brain of Peter which is only a piece of stone, the arm of St. Anthony which is only the dried limb of a stag, the sandals of Peter the fisherman, and Paul the tentmaker, which are of velvet, studded with spangles of gold, the priestly robe in which Peter said his first mass, and his Episcopal cross. Then, there are several entire bodies of each of the Apostles, and still more pieces of the same, several of these the same part. Each is, of course, " the only genuine article. Beware of counterfeits." Further, Your Grace, what about holding in reverence, relics belonging to saints who never had a being? There are several saints in the calendar who are just as imaginary beings as that well-known venerable gentleman, the man in the moon. What an interesting relic his lantern would be!

Your Grace, the following imaginary relics are just as genuine as are many saintly ones which your Church venerates. A pair of earrings, chignon, pair of curling tongs, bustle, pot of rouge, "taypot," sugar bowl and "crame" jug, which all belonged to the Virgin Mary; a "dhudeen" and a "'bacca fob" used by the beloved disciple; a "cruiskeen" in which Pope Peter kept "a dhrap uv rale poteen," uv which he tuk the laste taste now and thin to kape out the cowld whin he was out ahll noite fishin, the shillelah which he sometimes flourished to make those about him kape betther reggilashuns; and a snuff mull, half full of "Irish Blackguard,"[1] used by the Apostle Paul, also the thorn in the flesh (from a blackthorn) which was given him.[2]

In the Tower of London, there are relics of the Spanish Armada, which was destroyed by a tempest in 1588, while it was on its way to visit England. Among these are thumbscrews and other arguments of a like kind, meant to be used for the conversion of the heretics there to the "Catholic" Church. I need not say that Protestants do not "hold them in reverence as belonging to the saints."

"At Washington, many things used by General Washington, such as his clothes, kitchen utensils, etc., are preserved with great care."

Yes, but they are not treated by the people of the United States, as the relics of the saints often are by the Roman Catholics. Fancy Uncle Samuel, who has not been "just terrible smart" for a few days, taking off his old beaver hat, falling on his knees, and kissing, and then touching with his brow, the three-cornered hat, one of the boots, the "tay kittle," or the frying pan of the "Father of his country," hoping by so doing, to get a "powerful sight of good"!

Q. 38.—"Do we read anything in the Bible about relics?"

A.—"Yes, we read that miracles were wrought by their touch. The cloak of the Prophet Elias in the hands of Eliseus divided the waters of the Jordan (4 Kings ii. 14), and the bones of the same prophet raised from the dead a man that was thrown into the saint's sepulchre. (4 Kings xiii. 21.)"[3]

Elias is another name for Elijah, and Eliseus for Elisha. "The same prophet" is, of course, the one of whose cloak His

---

(1) A kind of snuff so called. (2) See Appendix XVII.
(3) 4 Kings in the Roman Catholic Bible, is 2 Kings in the Protestant one. 1 and 2 Samuel in the latter are 1 and 2 Kings in the former.

Grace has just spoken, that is Elijah. Well, according to him, his bones were the means of raising a man from the dead. But we learn from the 11th verse of the chapter from which he here first quotes, that Elijah was taken up to heaven alive. How then could he be buried? Och! och! yir Lardship's Rivirince, shure an' yir spakin in that way makes me sinses as if they wur goin thro a counthry dance. Had the prophet more bodies than one? Some of the Apostles seem to have had bodies *galore*. Did Elijah shed his body as the snake sheds his skin, the lobster his shell, and the deer his antlers? Was it with Elijah's body in the grave, as it was with a skull in a showman's museum, which the proprietor said was Oliver Cromwell's when he was a boy? In the second of the passages here quoted, it is the bones of Elisha which are spoken of. Your Grace, you must plead guilty of gross ignorance, either of the Bible, or of the rules of composition. Take your choice.

What the "learned prelate" here says about the bones of Elijah, reminds me of a remark in an account in the Toronto *Leader*, of the burial of Mr. Joseph, the optician, a member of the Jewish persuasion, and a well-known citizen of Toronto, who died several years ago. It was to this effect: that the ceremonies performed on that occasion were, no doubt, of the same nature as those performed by Joshua at the grave of Moses. Hurrah! Read Deuteronomy xxxiv. 5, 6. Like mistakes were once made by the writer of an article in the Montreal *Witness*, on the Great Day of Atonement. He said that the command for the observance of that Festival is contained in a verse in Leviticus which he professed to quote, without saying where it is. That verse, however, is not found in any part of the Bible. Besides, a whole chapter in Leviticus (xvi.) is devoted to the commands concerning it. The writer referred to, also said that after the High Priest went into the Holy of Holies, he offered sacrifices.

"The handkerchief and apron that touched the body of the great

St. Paul the Apostle, cured the sick and drove away evil spirits." (Acts xix. 12.)

His Grace should have said "handkerchiefs and aprons." They were not relics of Paul, for, at the time spoken of, he was alive. Challoner says: "Relics are the dead bodies or bones of saints, and whatever belonged to them in their mortal life." We have no reason to believe that such things always had the power here described. Paul himself could not always work miracles. In his second Epistle to Timothy, he says: "Trophimus have I left at Miletum sick." (iv. 20.)

"The hem of the garment of Christ cured the poor woman." (Matt. ix. 20.)

So says the Archbishop. But what said Christ to her? "Daughter, be of good comfort; thy faith hath made thee whole." (22 v.) The part of His garment mentioned was not a relic.

"The Bethesda, or washing pool at Jerusalem, when stirred by an angel, cured the first diseased person that was thrown into it."

Of whom was it a relic? The Greek says that it was a pool near the sheep-gate or market. Its waters healed only the first one who stepped into them after an angel had troubled them. "Thrown in"! Hurrah! Your Grace, you make me laugh. I fancy I see a poor sufferer who is most anxious to go into the pool at the right time. Two brawny men have pity on him. They take him up in their arms, swing him backwards and forwards a few times, singing all the while: "Yo, heave ho," then launch him forth.

"So, like an arrow, swift he flies,
Shot by an archer strong."

Down he goes into the pool. Plump. "Splash goes the water." Those near him get a "ducking."

"The arm of the Lord is not shortened, and miracles have not ceased amongst his own true followers and believers."

Of course, those of whom His Grace here speaks, are good children of his Church. It is a noteworthy fact that more "miracles" are wrought among *them*, than among heretics, as the spirits of the dead, in many cases, cease to be seen, in proportion as the spirits of the distillery cease to be swallowed.

"Had we now amongst us any of those sacred relics of the Apostles, we do not doubt that all who believe in Christ and His holy word, would reverence them with great devotion and respect."

They could do so without unduly honouring them. Have we not an abundance of such relics? Do not different places, in some instances, show the same relic? His Grace does not seem to believe that any "sacred relics of the Apostles" are now in existence. I fear that he is somewhat "tainted with heresy."

"The cross upon which our Lord suffered, and which was stained with His blood, retained, as a loadstone does attraction, virtue in a higher degree than did the handkerchief of St. Paul to cure diseases."

We have no scriptural authority for believing that the wood of Christ's cross had the power here ascribed to it. His preaching had not always a converting power. How can it cure diseases in a higher degree than did Paul's handkerchiefs and aprons—not handkerchief and apron—to use the Archbishop's own way of describing these things? Those parts of Christ's cross which were not stained with His blood, are supposed to have as much "virtue" as those which were.

"We have seen with our own eyes miraculous cures effected by the touch of the wood of the real cross of Christ."

We have no proof whatever that the early Christians took charge of the cross on which their Lord suffered. In all likelihood, the Roman soldiers crucified many others on it afterwards. They, of course, would pay no respect to it. The story of the Empress Helena finding it three hundred years after, is a most ridiculous one. As many pieces of the real wood of the cross have been shown as would make a goodly number of crosses of the usual size. Has that wood multiplied as did the loaves and fishes wherewith Christ fed at one time, over five thousand, and at another, over four thousand? I have no doubt that the "miraculous" cures of which His Grace speaks, were due only to natural causes.

"The shadow of St. Peter cured the sick upon which it fell." (Acts v. 15.)

Luke does not say that it did. He says simply that people brought the sick into the streets, in the hope that, at the least, the shadow of Peter passing by, might overshadow some of them, and heal them. Yet, it is altogether likely that what His Grace here says, really took place. How could Peter's shadow be a relic of him? One of his shadows, or even a piece of one, would be a most precious relic for St. Michael's Cathedral.

Before leaving this subject, I would remark that the word "relic" comes from the Latin, and signifies something left behind. The word "relict," which means a widow, has the same origin. A widow may well be called a "relic" of her husband, for she is his "better half." Of course, no good Roman Catholic priest can leave a "relict" behind him when he leaves this world.

Chapter 12.

Questions—(39) Are the religious orders sects in the Church?—(40) Why do monks and nuns make vows?—(41) What do Catholics believe respecting good works?—(42) Have miracles ceased in the Church?—(43) Do Catholics place any faith in holy wells?

QUESTION 39.—"Are the religious orders such as Jesuits, Dominicans, Franciscans, Nuns and Sisters of Charity, sects or divisions in the Church?"

OF course, His Grace, in reply, says "No." He compares them to companies for the carrying on of worldly business, and to the early Christians in the matter of having all things in common. Of course, he says nothing about the long and fierce opposition between the Dominicans and Franciscans on the question of the Immaculate Conception of the Virgin, nor about that between the Jansenists and Jesuits.

"Q. 40.—"Why do monks and nuns make vows?"
A.—" . . . persons binding themselves by vows to the service of God are more acceptable in His sight than others."

We should all vow, in dependence on the grace of God, to serve Him, and be careful to pay our vows. We can glorify Him in the most common acts of life. "Whether therefore ye eat, or drink, or whatsoever ye do, do all to the glory of God." (1 Corinthians x. 31.) We do not need to leave the world to glorify Him. Christ once prayed thus to His Father on behalf of His people: "I pray not that Thou shouldest take them out of the world, but that Thou shouldest keep them from the evil." (John xvii. 15.)

"Those who live holily in religious orders, with the vows of chastity, poverty and obedience, follow Christ more strictly than any others. He was pure, He was chaste and obedient unto death."

By "chastity" is here meant, not only what is the usual and proper meaning of the word, but also single life. According to this, marriage is one form of unchastity or impurity. The absurdity and wickedness of this view of it, I shall point out when I come to discuss what the Archbishop says regarding the celibacy of the clergy. By "obedience" is here meant doing the commands of those in authority over them, by those who have taken these vows, no matter how much they may be contrary to the commands of God. His Grace says: "Those who live holily . . . with these vows." He may well bring in here the word "holily." Some who have taken these vows which are not warranted by the word of God, have been faithful to them. But history tells us that the great mass of those who have taken them, have not. The first, especially, they have most shamefully disregarded, though they abstained from marriage. It is blasphemous to say that as Christ did not marry, those who remain unmarried follow Him in that respect.

"St. Bernard says of those who live in religious orders: 'They live more purely, fall less frequently, rise sooner, walk with greater precaution, are refreshed more frequently with heavenly comforts, repose with greater security, die with greater confidence, are sooner purified, and are more gloriously recompensed.'"

Facts prove that they do not, and are not, as here described.[1] The saint, the "mediator of intercession," just mentioned, was the eloquent abbot of Clairvaux in France. He was not, however, infallible. We must not, therefore, accept what he says, merely on his own authority. But I fear that in his quotation from him, the Archbishop has left out something which, if it were put in, would give a different meaning to the passage from what it has here. I do so for this reason. In his sermon (66) on 1 Timothy iii. 2, 12; iv. 3, he thus speaks: "Take away from the Church *honourable marriage and the undefiled bed*, and see if you will not fill it with fornicators, incestuous persons, effeminate persons, monsters of licentious-

(1) See Appendix XVIII.

ness, and with every kind of lewdness and debauchery." He also mourns over the impurity of the prelates and clergy, who, he says, "in secret committed excesses which it is a shame to mention."

I may remark that this saint, one of those to whom the Romish Church recommends prayers to be offered, was, on several points, directly opposed to her. For example, he was a staunch opponent of the dogma of the Immaculate Conception. He is, therefore, according to what the Church of Rome has now to believe, accursed.

Here is a very remarkable historical fact. Bones of infants have often been dug up in the cellars of convents and abbeys. Discoveries of this kind were made, for example, in England, in the time of Henry VIII. Once, several thousand bodies of infants were taken out of a pond in the neighbourhood of some convents and monasteries. These bones and bodies were not fossils. Of course, they had no connection with the "holy places" mentioned. Then, "how came these children there?" Ah! "say I to myself, say I," in the language of His Grace regarding another question: "It is a mystery above my comprehension."

The following extract from the Westminster Confession of Faith on Vows, may, very properly, be quoted here: "No man may vow to do anything forbidden in the word of God, or what would hinder any duty therein commanded, or which is not in his own power, and for the performance whereof he hath no promise of ability from God. In which respects Popish monastical vows of perpetual single life, professed poverty, and regular obedience, are so far from being degrees of higher perfection, that they are superstitious and sinful snares, in which no Christian may entangle himself." (Chap. xxii. Sec. 7.) Every part of this passage is "founded on, and agreeable to the word of God."

Q. 41.—" What do Catholics believe respecting good works? Do they think fasting, prayer, alms, and mortifications will save them, independent of the merits of Jesus Christ?"

A.—"The Catholics believe no such thing. They believe that good works being the effects of the grace of God operating in their souls, are meritorious when joined with the merits of Christ, for atoning for their sins."

The doctrine here stated, is contrary alike to reason and the Bible. The Church of Rome calls many works good, which are not so in God's sight. What really good works are, I have already described. Well, it is quite true that such works are "the effects of the grace of God operating in our souls." He "works in us both to will and to do of His good pleasure." (Philippians ii. 13.) The grace of God is His undeserved goodness. It is, therefore, utterly unreasonable to say that works, which are the effects thereof, have any merit whatever to atone for our sins. If they had any merit whatever, it would avail only for the time when they would be done. Future well-doing cannot both avail for the present, and satisfy justice for past ill-doing. But again, the Bible most distinctly says that we are not in the very least saved by our own works, but only and wholly through the merits of Christ. In proof of this, I shall quote only one or two passages: "When ye shall have done all those things which are commanded you, say, We are unprofitable servants." (Luke xvii. 10.) "The gift of God is eternal life." (Romans vi. 23.) "Neither is there salvation in any other [than Christ]." (Acts iv. 12.) "Redeemed . . , with the precious blood of Christ." (1 Peter i. 18, 19.) "The blood of Jesus Christ His (God's) Son cleanseth us from all sin." (1 John i. 7.) The Archbishop makes us and Christ partners in atoning for our sins. According to him, the merits of neither are, by themselves, sufficient to do so. It requires the two together. Our merits, if we have any, are, necessarily, of finite value. The merits of Christ are, necessarily, of infinite value. If His merits be imputed to us, we need none of our own. Yea, ours could not, in the very slightest degree, increase His. The following sum in arithmetic will illustrate His Grace's views on the question now under consideration:—

1,000,000,000,000 (Christ's merits.)
0 (Ours.)

2,000,000,000,000 (Our salvation.)

If our merits need to be joined to those of Christ to atone for our sins, His are, of course, not of infinite value. Therefore, He is not God.

His Grace refers to Peter's exhortation to Christians "to labour the more that by good works they may make sure of their calling and election." (2 Peter i. 10.) One passage of Scripture never really contradicts another. Though we are not, even in the least, saved by our own works, we are to labour just as diligently as if we were. Paul uses the fact that God works in us both to will and to do of His good pleasure, as a reason why, instead of doing nothing, we should work out our own salvation with fear and trembling. (Philippians ii. 13.) Another passage which the Archbishop brings forward, is the one in Matt. xxv. 34-46, in which Christ represents Himself as rewarding the righteous and punishing the wicked according to their works. These shall be used simply as proofs of the state of heart of each class. The quotation from the Epistle of James: "Faith without good works is dead," etc., (ii. 17-26,) which His Grace gives, does not, in the least, prove that our good works have any merit. As life in the body shows itself in action, so true faith shows itself in a holy life. The faith which does not show itself therein, is utterly worthless. The sun cannot but shed forth light and heat. To prevent it from doing so, it must be blotted out of being. The living tree cannot but bring forth fruit (using that term in its widest sense). To prevent it from doing so, it must be killed. So he who has true faith in Christ, necessarily loves Him, and, therefore, necessarily, seeks to honour and please Him. If we believe that a fellow-being has showed us great kindness, we cannot but love him, and, therefore, we account it a privilege to be able, in any way, to show our thankfulness to him. So it is with the true Christian. What Cowper says of his own good works is, as true of every one's:—

> My prayers and alms, imperfect and defiled,
> Were but the feeble efforts of a child;
> Howe'er performed, it was their brightest part
> That they proceeded from a grateful heart.

A child has been in the fields on a summer day. It brings home to its mother, as a token of its love to her, a "posy" of the commonest flowers, such as those of the red and the white clover, and buttercups. It could get no others. The "posy" is, in itself, of no value. But the mother, looking at what it expresses, takes it with a loving smile, and pays the giver with an embrace and a kiss. In like manner, the Lord accepts the good works of His people. The doers say of them—to use again the language of Cowper:—

> Cleansed in Thine own all-purifying blood,
> Forgive their evil, and accept their good;
> I cast them at Thy feet—my only plea
> Is what it was, dependence upon Thee.

Good works are not the *root* of salvation, but only the *fruit* thereof. Those who do them are already saved. "He that believeth on the Son *hath* everlasting life." The very moment he believes, his salvation begins. He has it then in security and foretaste. By and by, he shall have it in full enjoyment. Augustine very truly says: "We work not *for* life, but *from* life." Good works are, on the one hand, of no value whatever, and, on the other hand, of great value. A thing may be most useful for one purpose, and most useless for another. A plough would be of no use for reaping with. A reaping machine would be of no use for turning up the soil. So it is with good works. Protestants put them in their right place—Roman Catholics in their wrong one. But, though this subject is a most important one, I must now leave it, and go forward.

Q. 42.—"Have miracles ceased in the Church?"

To prove that they have not, the Archbishop quotes John xiv. 12: "Amen, amen, I say to you, he that believeth in Me, the works that I do he also shall do; and greater than these shall he do." "Remark," adds His Grace, "the word *believers*, not only apostles, but believers." The promise in the first part of the verse quoted, was fulfilled in the natural miracles which the early Christians were enabled to work, as is recorded in the Book of Acts. But we have no reason to believe that power to work them has been continued in the Church to the present day. There is not the need of them now that there was when the Church was being set up. "If miracles were continually in the Church, they would cease to be miracles." Those said to have been wrought in the Romish Church cannot stand examination. The promise in the second part of the verse does not refer to natural miracles. None of the Apostles, or others of the early Christians, wrought any greater miracles of that kind than our Lord did. "What our Lord has in view seems to be the far greater number of conversions, the far wider spread of the Gospel, which would take place under the ministry of the Apostles, than under His own teaching. This was the case, we know from the Acts of the Apostles."

"Miracles not mentioned in the Bible are not objects of Divine faith."

This sentence is as clear as a block of granite ten feet thick. "What is Divine faith?" is a riddle which I am utterly unable to answer.

"Authenticated miracles of the present day are believed upon the testimony of respectable witnesses. It would be folly and temerity to reject them all."

It is not enough that the witnesses are respectable. They may be "good Catholics," not very intelligent, and, therefore, easily deceived. If miracles be proved by respectable witnesses to have taken place, which His Grace considers sufficient proof that they have, why reject any?

Q. 43.—" Do Catholics place any faith in holy wells and fountains ? "

A.—"They hold these in reverence which God has by evident miracles blessed with curative powers."

This is just a roundabout way of saying "Yes." The "evident miracles" wrought by what are commonly termed "holy wells," are only an evident farce. Many "good Catholics" do most unholy things at these "holy wells." His Grace refers to the pool of Bethesda. That was, truly, a miracle-working pool. It was so at irregular times, and it cured only one each time—the first who went into it after the angel had troubled its waters. His Grace, in this instance, does not give the diseased person kind friends to throw him into the pool, as he does in his answer to Q. 39, but makes him go down into it on his own feet. But it is long since a miracle was wrought there.

"The arm of God is not shortened, and He is with His Church to the end of the world; and can attach His graces to whatever objects He pleases."

Quite true. But because God can do a thing, it does not follow that He does it. He has good reasons for working in one instance, and for not working in another. He can help His Church without giving her holy wells.

"He has imparted curative powers to the herbs and minerals of the earth, so can He do with anything else."

Some herbs and minerals cure one kind of disease, others another. We do not, however, call the cures wrought by them miraculous. God has imparted " curative powers " to pure water, both when taken inwardly and applied outwardly. Many are greatly benefitted by the same use of sea water, and of mineral waters, such as those of the Caledonia Springs, and St. Léon in Canada, and of Vichy in France. No one, however, thinks of calling the cures wrought by them miracles, and such springs as I have mentioned, holy wells. I may here remark that many persons found at holy wells, greatly need the bath for their bodies, and the washtub for their clothes.

"But faith and hope are necessary to obtain miraculous cures, so that God is the ultimate source of all graces and mercies."

Many have gone with unlimited faith and hope to holy wells, without receiving any benefit. Some have been cured at them, but their diseases were of the kind which faith and hope are fitted to remove. The mind has often a powerful effect on the body. Every doctor knows that if his patient have faith in him, it is a very great help towards the latter being cured, if a cure be possible. But it would be absurd to call such cures as I have spoken of, miracles. In many instances, cures wrought by holy wells have lasted but a very short time.

"Witness the wonderful cures at the fountain of Our Lady of Lourdes, which no sane man can deny."

Is it raley Yir Grace that oi hear spakin? There are thousands and thousands and thousands uv paypel in Canady that only laugh at thim miracles. Well, you say they're insane, uvry wun uv thim. They're at large, fur there aint enough uv places to kape thim in. Now, what kin you expict but bloody murthur and killin in uvery direcshun? The tho't uv it's enough to scare me from puttin me nose out uv doors. Jist think uv wun whin he gits up some marnin, findin he's been kilt in his slape by some uv thim wandherin lunatics! Water from the fountain referred to, can be had at places far distant from it. Of course, it is as powerful in one place as in another. Well, a great deal of the genuine water of Lourdes comes from where the blue milk is got—"the cow with the iron tail." Fancy a water of Lourdes man, and a milkman, each with a jar in his hand, meeting beside her! There is a fountain of Our Lady of La Salette. The feelings between the caretakers of the two fountains are of the same nature as those between two rival steamboat companies. A caretaker of the latter fountain once said: "It is all up with our Lady of La Salette, Our Lady of Lourdes has cut her out."

A priest in the first province east of Ontario, once brought a cask of miraculous water from Lourdes. For every bottle of it that he took out, he added one of Canadian. ("Encourage home manufactures.") Of course, the contents, by and by, became like the knife which Pat got from his brother Barney, after the former had first put in a new blade, and next put a new handle to the blade. Yet, strange to say! the miraculous power of the water was not, in the least degree, lessened. No doubt, it had, many a time, been in Canada, for there is continually going on, a drawing up into the sky of water from the earth in some parts, and a sending it down in others. If it be true that he who is "once a priest" is "always a priest," why may not water "once miraculous," be "always miraculous"?

"Some Protestants bring water from the river Jordan in which Christ was baptized, and they hold it in reverence."

Quite true, but they do not expect any miracles to be wrought by it.

Chapter 13.

Questions—(44) What do Catholics believe concerning purgatory?—(45) Why do Catholics fast?—(46) Why do not Catholics eat meat on Fridays?—(47) Did not Christ say : "It is not that which goeth into the mouth," etc. ?

QUESTION 44.—"What belief do Catholics hold concerning purgatory?"

ANSWER.—"That it is a place or state of punishment, in which persons who have not fully satisfied the justice of God on account of their sins committed during life suffer for a time before entering into heaven."

THE Scriptures tell us most distinctly that we cannot in the slightest degree, by our sufferings or our doings, or both, satisfy the justice of God for even one of our sins, and that one of the least heinous—what the Romish Church calls a venial sin—but Christ has fully satisfied that justice by the decease which He has accomplished at Jerusalem, and we have simply to trust in His finished work. If Christ's merits be all-sufficient, we have not to suffer to atone for our sins. God is not unrighteous. He does not exact satisfaction, both from the sinner and his Surety. If Christ's merits be not all-sufficient, He is not God.

"Purgatory is the Limbo or third place spoken of by St. Peter (1 Peter iii. 19), where the souls of the just were detained and to whom Christ went to preach again."

Peter here speaks about Christ preaching to "the spirits in prison." Whatever that prison was, it could not be purgatory. These spirits, the Archbishop says, were souls of the just. If they were in purgatory, they were on their way to glory. In the sentence which we have just been considering, it is said that those who are in purgatory, suffer there for a time before entering into heaven. Well, what need was there of Christ preaching to those who, by and by, were to be with Him for ever, for all who leave purgatory go to heaven, not one to hell? What benefit could they receive from His preaching? His Grace says that Christ went to "the spirits in prison" to preach to them again. They must, therefore, have rejected Him, and "not received His words" when they were in the world. They, therefore, died in mortal sin and went straight to hell. If they rejected Christ when He first preached to them, was it unlikely that they would do so when He should preach to them again? How they treated Him when He preached to them in prison, we are not told. Of course, I am only taking the Archbishop on his own ground. His Grace's orthodoxy here is not above suspicion. He teaches what very strongly resembles the doctrine of Future Probation, a doctrine contrary to the teachings of his Church. She says that those who go to hell stay there for ever. On that point, she is thoroughly sound.

"Be at agreement with thy adversary betimes," etc. (Matt. v. 25.)

The kindred passage in Luke xii. 58, 59, should also have been referred to. The Archbishop should have added to his quotation the 26th verse, which tells us that those cast into prison shall not come out thence till they have paid the uttermost farthing. The whole passage, instead of being an argument in favour of purgatory, is plainly against it. We have seen that we cannot pay the first farthing of the debt which we owe God's justice. If then we must stay in prison till we pay the last, we must stay there for ever.

"St. Paul says: 'That the good works of every man will be tried of what sort they are,' etc., and the man himself shall be saved yet so as by fire." (1 Corinthians iii. 13, 15.)

His Grace does not here quote Scripture correctly. Paul says that the fire shall try every man's *work*. If works be known to be good, there is no need of trying them to find out what sort they are. In the last of the verses quoted, Paul speaks of one being saved "as by" fire, not "by" fire—a great difference.

"The second book of Maccabees says that 'it is a holy and wholesome thought to pray for the dead that they may be loosed from their sins.' This book is not allowed by Protestants to be canonical, but even taking it as a history it proves that the Jews offered sacrifices for the dead and were not reproved for these practices by Christ."

The dead spoken of in the book to which the Archbishop here refers, were idolaters who fell in battle. (2 Maccabees xii. 39-45.) They, therefore, died in, what the Church of Rome terms, mortal sin. They, therefore, went straight to hell. Further, this circumstance happened fully 150 years before the birth of Christ. We have no proof that it was usual, at that time, among the Jews to offer sacrifices for the dead. Whether it was or was not, there is not the slightest warrant for such sacrifices in the Old Testament. Again, we have no proof that the Jews offered them in the time of Christ. We have every reason to believe that they did not. Christ would not reprove the Jews for sins which their forefathers committed, if they themselves were free from them. The following absurd reasoning is of the very same nature as the Archbishop's here. A's great-grandfather committed several acts of dishonesty. B did not reprove A for them. Therefore, he approved of the dishonesty of A's great-grandfather.

"Few pass out of this world so very pure as to enter at once into the beatific vision of God;———"

The Scriptures speak of only two places after death—heaven and hell. Paul represents all believers as being present with the Lord immediately after leaving the body. The penitent thief went straight to paradise after death. The beggar, Lazarus, was carried by angels from this world into Abraham's bosom. At death, the spirits of just men are made perfect.

"the very wicked go to hell———"

On this point, the Archbishop is quite orthodox. But it is not only the *very* wicked who go to hell. "He that believeth not the Son shall not see life" (John iii. 36), it matters not how correct his outward life may have been, and how great a profession of religion he may have made. But His Grace's Church sends to hell also, all those who are knowingly and wilfully outside of her. It matters not how strong may be their faith in Christ, how warm their love to Him, how closely they may follow His example, and how much they may labour for His glory. According to the word of God they are the excellent of the earth—the Lord delights in them. According to the Church of Rome they form part of the "very wicked."

"and the very good go to heaven,"——

In one sense, His Grace is quite orthodox here also. By going to heaven, he means going straight to it. Well, all believers go straight to heaven when they die. They are all "very good," for their souls are then made perfect in holiness, as we have already seen. But that is not what the "learned prelate" means here. He speaks of those who are better than God requires them to be—who do more than love the Lord their God with all their heart, and with all their soul, and with all their strength, and with all their mind; and their neighbour as themselves (Luke x. 27)—who, in fact, are more than perfect. They have superabundant merits, the benefits of which are conveyed to the needy by indulgences. From these indulgences the Church receives certain benefits. Thus there is joy all around.

"but tepid Christians go to purgatory."

"Tepid" means lukewarm. That was the state of the Church at Laodicea, and Christ said that He would, therefore, spue her out of His mouth. (Rev. iii. 16.) Well, masses are offered up for the repose of the souls after death, of even popes, archbishops, and bishops. If they be in purgatory, they must, of course, have been only lukewarm Christians when they were on earth.[1]

In grammar, the verb has an imperfect, perfect, and pluperfect tense. But the Church of Rome has no perfect members. Those belonging to her who are not " very wicked," are either imperfect or pluperfect.

" The family of Christ as members of His mystic body, is composed of the saints reigning in heaven, the true Christians obeying His laws on earth, and the souls in Purgatory; all can assist each other by their prayers and merits."

Each one of these three classes, it seems, has merits. Then, no one needs help from another. If I have enough of a thing, I do not need to ask another to give me more of it. The saints in heaven are, of course, perfectly holy and happy. They, therefore, need help neither from each other, nor from the other two classes. If the true Christians on earth can help them, they do not need to pray to them. How can the souls in purgatory—the souls of lukewarm Christians—have merits? If they have, they need neither the prayers of the saints in heaven, nor those of the true Christians on earth. According to the Archbishop, these three classes should pray, each to the others in the same class, and to those in the other two. Who, on earth, ever really heard a prayer to him from heaven, or from purgatory?

We read in Scripture of those who through fear of death are all their lifetime subject to bondage. (Hebrew ii. 15.) It is impossible for those to be anything else, who really believe in purgatory, and, therefore, look forward to suffering hereafter inconceivable torments, for, it may be, a vast number of ages, ere they pass into glory.

Is it known when any one is released from purgatory, his

---

(1) By his will, His Grace directs that two hundred masses shall be said for the repose of His soul. He must, therefore, have looked on himself as a lukewarm Christian. It may be said that this is a mark of his humility. Be that as it may, those who offer up prayers for the object mentioned, do thereby, according to his teaching, say that they fully agree with him.

term of imprisonment there having run out? If so, how is it known? What means of intercourse are there between here and there? If not, it is very disheartening to his friends on earth. He may have to suffer many ages after they have prayed many prayers, and paid many dollars, "his spirit to free from dire purgatorial pain." Those who have had masses said or sung "for the weal of a departed soul," cannot know for a certainty, that their wish has been carried out. The priest may, in his heart, have meant them for another, in which case the latter will receive all the benefit that is to be had from them—the former none.

How shall it be with those "tepid Christians" who go to purgatory just before the end of the world? Shall their sufferings be condensed?

"It is want of due appreciation of the infinite sanctity of God, and the purity of those who shall enter into His glory, to suppose for instance that there is only one step for the criminal from the gallows into heaven."

There was but one step for the penitent thief from the cross into paradise. Several years ago, a man named O'Leary was hanged in Toronto, for a most brutal murder which he committed in Georgina, Ont. On the scaffold, he said that he would share in God's glory before the setting of that day's sun. Of course, he expected to go straight to heaven. His spiritual adviser, Father Rooney, was standing close to him at the time, but he did not tell him that he was mistaken. As O'Leary read his speech, it is most likely that Father Rooney saw it before. Yet prayers were offered up for the repose of the soul of Bishop McDonnell, of Kingston, twenty years after *his* death.

"There is an example of the thief on the cross, one that none may despair, and only one that all may fear.",

For "all may fear," read "none may presume." This has not the slightest bearing on purgatory.

Unless we obtain rest for our souls in this life, we shall not obtain it after death. Christ promises to give it to all who come to Him. (Matthew xi. 28, 29.) The real purgatory is the blood of Jesus. That cleanses from all sin. (1 John i. 7.)

The teaching of the Archbishop's Church regarding those who die, may be stated in the following figurative manner: The first class good go to heaven by a through express train, without stopping at purgatory. The first class bad go in the same manner to hell. The second class good, and the second class bad, which, really, are "one and the same," stop at purgatory, not for refreshments, but for purification. When the time is up, they continue their journey, and go on to heaven. Purgatory is a station on the straight line to heaven. It is not a junction to which the first class wicked go so far on the way to heaven, and there change cars for hell.

Q. 45.—"Why do Catholics fast?"
A.—"To imitate Christ the true model of all Christians. He fasted to show us an example."

Christ fasted forty days and forty nights. In that, we, of course, cannot imitate Him.

"The Apostles fasted and prayed when they were about to perform any great action. In many places of sacred Scriptures we are counselled to fast."

The Apostles did not look on their fasting as meritorious. The Scriptures do not represent voluntary fasting as so. The Church of Rome does.

"Fasting subdues the flesh and brings it under subjection, and takes away the spirit of revolt."

"(Rom. viii. 13). 'For if you live according to the flesh you shall die; but if by the Spirit you mortify the deeds of the flesh, you shall live.'"

That is to say: "If you eat, you shall die eternally; but

if you fast, you shall live eternally." His Grace does not take into account the clause "by the Spirit." In Galatians v. 19-21, the Apostle mentions the deeds of the flesh, but he does not class eating among them. A person may fast, yet do these deeds.

Q. 46.—" Why do not Catholics eat meat on Fridays ?"
A.—"Friday being the day on which He died, it is meet that His followers should mortify themselves by abstaining from the most nutritious food."

One who is in good health, will do himself no harm by refraining for a day from eating the flesh of beasts or birds. On the contrary, it may be a benefit to him to do so. "The foinest pisinthry in the wurld" seldom see "butcher meat." How many rosy cheeked, strapping lads and lasses are brought up on the "halesome parritch, chief o' Scotia's food." There are many who, from principle, are vegetarians. The Church of Rome allows the faithful to eat fish at any time. This is said to be excellent food for the brain. She also allows them to eat eggs. Yet on "lean days," she does not allow them to eat fowls. But all that is in the fowl is in the egg. Time and heat make the difference between them. She allows the faithful in the Province of Quebec, to eat at any time, a certain fowl which feeds on fish.[1] One can spend a day very comfortably without eating "meat." Some would find it a greater trial to refrain for a day, from tobacco, whiskey, and swearing.

"It is a custom dated back to the earliest days of the world, that on the anniversary of the father's death children fasted."

Your Grace has no authority for saying so. Your Church observes the anniversary of Christ's death every week—as an "Oirish jintleman" might express it.

---

(1) I do not know the English name of it. The French Canadians call it the "bernaise." That name I spell according to its sound.

Q. 47.—"Did not Christ say: 'It is not that which goeth into the mouth that defileth a man'?"

A.—"That is true. It was not the apple that defiled the soul of Adam, but his disobedience in eating it."

This is meant to blow into invisible dust, an argument against Roman Catholics not eating "meat" on Fridays. Yet His Grace is here as good a Protestant as one could find "in a day's walk." We will not be exact about the name of the fruit spoken of, for no one knows whether it was an apple, an orange, a peach, or some other kind of fruit.

Chapter 14.

Questions—(48) What is the meaning of rosaries ?—(49) What are scapulars ?—(50) Why do Catholics make the sign of the cross ?—(51) Why have Catholics their children baptized ?—(52) Is baptism absolutely necessary for salvation ?—(53) What becomes of children who die unbaptized ?—(54) Will merely pouring the water suffice for baptism ?—(55) Is immersion necessary for baptism ?—(56) What is the meaning of confirmation ?

QUESTION 48.—" What is the meaning of rosaries or beads ?"
ANSWER.—" They are a mode of reckoning prayers——"

PRAYERS should not be counted out to God, like articles of merchandize.

" but yet on account of their use are blessed and held in veneration as reminders of the mysteries of the love and sufferings of Jesus Christ commemorated by the prayers counted on them."

Very few Roman Catholics take this highly sentimental view of the rosary. The great mass of them use it merely to enable them to know how much to say of this prayer, how much of that, and how much of another—as the Archbishop calls them. The rosary is made up of 166 beads. On one, is said the Creed. On each of fifteen, is said the Lord's Prayer. On each of the remaining one hundred and fifty, is said the Hail Mary. Neither the Creed, nor the Hail Mary, is a prayer. Very little is said in the Creed, and nothing in the Lord's Prayer and the Hail Mary, about "the mysteries of the love and sufferings of Jesus Christ." On the rosary, the Hail Mary is said ten times oftener than the Lord's Prayer, in other words, ten times more honour is given to the Virgin Mary, than to God.

Q. 49.—" What are scapulars ?"

A.—"They are badges worn in honour of Jesus Christ and the Blessed Virgin."

The Archbishop then goes on to compare them to the decorations of knighthood. Multitudes of those belonging to his Church, however, wear them as charms to keep them from danger. Of course, they have been blessed by the priest. His blessing is to the scapular, what Samson's uncut hair was to *him*.

Q. 50.—"Why do Catholics frequently make the sign of the cross?"

A.—"Because with St. Paul they glory in the cross of our Lord Jesus Christ." (Gal. vi. 14.)

With the great mass of Roman Catholics, making the sign of the cross is merely a matter of form. They trust more in two lines crossing each other at right angles, than in "the merits of Jesus Christ who died on the cross."

As an argument in defence of "Catholics" making the sign of the cross, His Grace here quotes the testimony of Tertullian, who lived in the second century, that the Christians in his day did so, in connection with all their actions. Of course, the fact that they did it, is no proof that it was right. Tertullian himself does not defend it, for he immediately adds: "If for these, and other acts of discipline of the same kind, you demand a text of Scripture, you will find none; but tradition will be alleged as the prescriber of them." Had His Grace quoted this passage, it would have been an argument rather against him, than in his favour. Let us—to use an expression of our "Dear Roman Catholic Friend's"—hope that he stopped where he does, not cunningly, but unwittingly, not seeing what would follow if he should go on to the end.

"Some Christians have a prejudice against the symbol of salvation, but without valid reason."

They have as valid a reason as Hezekiah had for destroying the Brazen Serpent. How often the cross or the sign of it, is used for superstitious purposes, for example, preserving one from lightning, storms, diseases, devils, and ghosts!

"A weathercock symbolizes change."

Cocks used to be common ornaments on the tops of steeples of French Roman Catholic churches. As these are turned about by the wind, His Grace thinks that they are not suitable on buildings belonging to a Church which never changes. A cock on the top of the steeple of a Roman Catholic church, is a memorial of a certain event in the life of him whom the Archbishop's Church calls the first Pope, which was not to his honour.

Q. 51.—" Why do Catholics have their children baptized? Did not Christ say to His Apostles, 'Go and teach and then baptize,' but children are incapable of being taught, consequently they are not capable of being baptized?"

"Do have"—except in an entreaty—is bad English. "Capable of being"—as used in the last sentence—should be "qualified" or "entitled to be." Let us now listen to His Grace's answer to the opponents of infant baptism. Surely it will be like the blowing up of a tremendous charge of nitro-glycerine or dynamite under them, after which, these heretics shall be "like the baseless fabric of a vision, leaving not a wrack behind." He says:

"—— children who are not capable of being taught should be baptized for the remission of original sin in which we are all alike born. . . . 'In sin did my mother conceive me.' (Psalm L—in the Protest.Ver. li.—7) . . . 'We are born children of wrath.' (Ephesians ii. 3.) Sin is remitted in baptism. . . . 'Do penance and be baptized,' etc. (Act ii. 38.) . . . 'Rise up and be baptized,' etc. (xxii. 16.)"

The opponents of infant baptism are "nivir a ha'porth" the worse of the Archbishop's reasoning. He had a "good intinshun," but he has utterly failed to carry it out. What he here says, has not the slightest bearing on infant baptism.

I believe that infant baptism is warranted by the word of God, but His Grace has not succeeded, in the very least, in proving it. He is quite sound when he says that all are alike born in original sin. But he is the very opposite, when he says that sin is remitted in baptism. Neither water, nor spittle, nor bread, nor oil, nor fire, can take away sin. Only blood can—"the precious blood of Christ as of a lamb without blemish, and without spot." Ananias and Sapphira were baptized, but their sins were not remitted. Simon Magus was baptized, but his sins were not remitted. If baptism took away sin, Christ would have sent Paul to baptize, instead of preaching the Gospel. (1 Corinthians i. 17.)

Q. 52.—"Is baptism absolutely necessary to enter the kingdom of God?"

A.—"Yes. Christ has said so. 'Unless a person be born again of water and of the Holy Ghost he cannot enter into the kingdom of God." Baptism of desire, at least, is necessary. A person should wish to perform everything enjoined by our Lord.

In the Question, after "necessary," read "to enable one to enter," etc. The passage which the Archbishop quotes, cannot refer to baptism. It contains a part of the words of Christ to Nicodemus, shortly after He had entered on His public ministry, before He had appointed the ordinance of Baptism. Had Christ meant water baptism, He would have said so plainly, for Nicodemus was very ignorant in spiritual things. If His words refer to water baptism, then those of John the Baptist, "He shall baptize you with the Holy Ghost and with fire," must refer to baptism with natural fire. "Water and the Holy Ghost" seem to mean the Holy Ghost purifying the soul, as water does the body. What is essential is the baptism of the Holy Ghost. That and water baptism are not necessarily connected. In my remarks on the Archbishop's Answer to the last question, I have given proofs that they are not. The penitent thief had only the baptism of the Holy Ghost. Many at the present day, have received that baptism, who, owing to mistaken views, or want of opportunity, have not received water baptism. But His Grace says: "Baptism of desire"—which, I suppose, means "desire of baptism"—"at least is necessary." This is in opposition to what he has just said, that baptism itself is absolutely necessary. But the penitent thief had no "baptism of desire," for baptism was not yet appointed. Those true Christians who believe that the observance of the ordinance of baptism is not now binding, have, of course, no "baptism of desire." His Grace is perfectly sound when he says that one should wish to perform everything enjoined by our Lord. But one cannot wish to perform what he does not know or believe that He has enjoined.

Q. 53.—"What becomes of children who die without baptism?"

A.—"Of these there has been no revelation in Scripture, but from the texts above quoted, they are excluded from the beatific vision of God, inasmuch as they have not been engrafted on Christ, and made partakers of redemption through Him. . . . 'Except a man be born again of water,' etc. (John iii. 5.)

Bad English here, Your Grace. For "Of these" read "Concerning these." For "has been" read "is." After "quoted," read "it is plain that." The Archbishop—as we have already seen—believes that tradition is of equal authority with the written word. Surely it is not silent regarding infants dying unbaptized. According to him, they go to hell. It cannot be otherwise with them, if they have no part with Christ. They, therefore, form part of the "very wicked." This is all owing to the want of a little water applied to their bodies in a certain way, and to no fault whatever of theirs. Truly, this is a most horrible doctrine.

"Hence the Catholics are so anxious to have their children baptized as soon as possible after birth."

"*After* birth." Ah! yes; just so. What has Your Grace to say about *ante-natal* baptism? Very few Protestants have ever heard of such a thing, but it is quite common in your

Church, "in extreme cases." It is only carrying out the doctrine of salvation by baptism.

Q. 54.—"Will mere pouring the water on the person to be baptized suffice for baptism ?"

"Mere pouring." In certain instances, baptism is administered by means of a syringe. To these I refer a sentence or two back. But let us hear the "learned prelate's" answer.

A.—" No. The person baptising must say at the same time, 'I baptize you in the name of the Father and of the Son and of the Holy Ghost,' and have the intention of doing what Christ intended. (Matthew xxviii. 19.)"

According to this, though a child should be baptized, if the baptizer had not a right intention, the baptism is worthless, and if the child die in infancy, it will, in fact, be the very same as if it never had been baptized. Consequently, according to His Grace's views which we very lately considered, it will go to hell. Its salvation or its damnation, therefore, depends wholly on the will of the baptizer. A most horrible, as well as most absurd doctrine. His Grace, as we have seen, says that sin is remitted in baptism. But, according to what he here says, the baptizer can, just as it pleases himself, either remove sin from the person whom he baptizes, or cause it to remain on him. If a person have not been rightly baptized, he, of course, cannot lawfully be a priest. One must be a priest before he can be a pope. Well, then, I defy any one to prove that any one has ever been rightly baptized in the Romish Church, that any one has ever lawfully been a priest in it, that any priestly act has ever been valid, and that any one has ever lawfully been a pope. The Romish Church teaches the doctrine which we are now considering—that of intention—in relation to the administration of her other sacraments. It, therefore, makes her like the earth, as described in Genesis i. 2, "waste and void."

Q. 55.—"Is it necessary for the person to be baptized to be put completely under the water?'
A.—"No."

Let us now watch the firing of His Grace's ten thousand ton gun at the Baptists. Stand aside, yiz that duzn't want to be kilt! Fire! Bang!

"Although this is a valid form; the pouring of the water on the person signifies the washing of his soul from sin, and is the outward sign of the inward grace of the sacrament. St. Peter says 'It is not the exterior washing of the body but the internal washing of the conscience that remits sin.' (1 Peter iii. 21.)"

This is not what Peter really says, but what the Archbishop considers is his meaning. He then gives the Apostle's own words, and so ends his Answer. We look to see if there be now the very slightest trace of the poor Baptists. No doubt, His Grace thinks that he has blown them into invisibility. Lo! they are as hale and hearty as ever. Laughingly, they say: "It gives His Grace pleasure to fire at us, and it does not hurt us in the least." I believe that it can be clearly proved from Scripture that it is not at all necessary for the person to be baptized, to be put completely under the water. But I must say that the Archbishop has not here proved that it is not. Poor body! He has not "done well, and as was fitting the question, which was what he desired." He has done "slenderly and meanly," but then "it was that which he could attain unto."

Q. 56.—"What is the meaning of confirmation?"
A.—"Confirmation is the imparting of the Holy Ghost by the imposition of the hands of the Bishop, and by prayers and anointing the forehead with holy chrism."

According to this, on whomsoever the bishop lays his hands, with the accompaniments described, he receives the Holy Ghost. Well, in Scripture, the gift of the Holy Ghost is

Review of "Answer" to Question 56.

represented as followed by one or other of two results not necessarily connected : (1) Enabling the person receiving Him, to work miracles, to "speak with tongues," or to prophesy. (2) Purifying his heart. Now, it need not be asked: Does every one, or even any one, on whom the bishop lays his hands in confirmation, thereby receive power to work miracles, to "speak with tongues," or to prophesy? Or does he become a better person? Alas! is it not the case that multitudes who have been confirmed by the bishop, are, in more senses than one, only confirmed sinners? If sin be remitted in baptism, as His Grace says it is, the Holy Ghost must also be given them. How then can He be given in confirmation?

* "This sacrament was given by the Apostles, and whatever was done by the Apostles is continued yet in the church." (Acts viii. 14-17.)

In no part of the New Testament do we find the slightest mention of Christ having appointed the sacrament of confirmation. Let us look at the passage to which the Archbishop here refers. We are told in it that the Apostles sent two of their number, Peter and John, from Jerusalem to the converts in Samaria, "who when they were come down, prayed for them, that they might receive the Holy Ghost. Then laid they their hands on them, and they received the Holy Ghost." These two Apostles were not bishops such as His Grace speaks of. It is a most remarkable fact that one of them was Peter. Had he been the Chief of the Apostles, as the Church of Rome says he was, he would have sent, not been sent. There was on this occasion prayer, but no "anointing the forehead with holy chrism." There can be no doubt whatever that those who then received the Holy Spirit were enabled to work miracles, for Simon Magus offered Peter and John money if they would give him power to bestow the Holy Ghost on any one on whom he should lay hands. He had no wish to be himself, a better man. He had no wish to be able to make others better. But he thought that he would make great gain if he could sell others the power to work miracles.

St. Paul says: "Who also hath sealed us and given the pledge of the Spirit in our hearts." (2 Cor. i. 22.)

He of whom the Apostle here speaks, is God. He needs not to pray for the gift of the Holy Ghost. He does not "anoint our forehead with holy chrism." The anointing which we receive from Him (v. 21) is accompanied by the entrance of the Spirit into our hearts. This passage, therefore, gives no support whatever to the Romish rite of confirmation, which is only an outward thing.

His Grace next quotes Acts xix. 5, 6, where we read of Paul laying his hands on about twelve disciples in Ephesus, thereby bestowing on them the Holy Ghost, which enabled them to speak with tongues, and prophesy. This does not call for any special remark.

"The graces received from the Holy Ghost in confirmation are seven."

Then follows a quotation from Isaiah xi. 2, 3.

This passage is a prophecy of the coming Messiah, the Lord Jesus. There is no mention in it of bishop, prayers, and "holy chrism." As we have already seen, the gift of the Holy Spirit and confirmation are not necessarily connected. Many there are who have been confirmed, who are still the slaves of sin and Satan.

"We know the effects of the descent of the Holy Ghost upon the Apostles and early Christians by their being filled with the Spirit of God, and were endowed with fortitude to confess Jesus Christ."

When the Holy Ghost came down on those here spoken of, they were filled with the Spirit of God. That is, when the Holy Ghost came down on them, they were filled with the Holy Ghost. They could not, in these circumstances, have been filled with any other. "By their being filled . . . and were endowed." "O horrible, most horrible" English. Of the same quality is the reasoning in this passage. The descent of the Holy Ghost on the day of Pentecost, had no connection with bishops and "holy chrism."

"In the combat with the enemy of our salvation through life, we frail mortals require all the graces and mercy from God, through Christ and through the sacraments established in His Church, to enable us to triumph over the enemies of salvation."

"The enemy of our salvation . . . the enemies of salvation." Yir Grace, is it raley possible that wun who was so long at school as you wur, can't spake more properly than that? A bishop's hands having been laid on his head, having been prayed for, and having had his forehead anointed with "holy chrism," are but poor helps to one in his "combat with the enemy of his salvation."

Chapter 15.

Questions—(57) Why do Catholics confess their sins to the priest?—(58) Can the priest, as man, by his own power forgive sins?—(59) Does not confession encourage the sinner, etc.?—(60) Is confession always necessary?—(61) Are there any exceptions to the law of confession?—*Objection* (3) But do we not read in Scripture, etc. (Luke v. 21)?—*Question* (62) Can a priest forgive the sins of any one he pleases?—(63) Is it blasphemy to say that a man can forgive sins?—(64) Is the Catholic mode of obtaining forgiveness more difficult than the Protestant?—*Objection* (4) But do not we read, "If we confess our sins?" etc.—*Question* (65) Did the first Christians confess?—(66) Was confession continued in the Church?—*Objection* (5) But was it not introduced by the Council of Lateran?—*Question* (67) Is not confession practised in some Protestant Churches?—(68) Do the married clergy of the Greek Church hear confessions?

QUESTION 57.—"Why do Catholics confess their sins to the priest?"

THE Answer to this question takes up nearly three pages of His Grace's book. It is a greatly "tangled skein," and contains many repetitions. The same is true of the answers to several other questions connected with this one, which take up nearly five pages more. I shall, therefore, notice only the principal points in this one. I may state that a great many questions remain to be considered.

A.—"Because they are ordered to do so by the sacred Scriptures. (St. James v. 16.) 'Confess your sins one to another, and pray for one another that you may be saved.'"

If this passage mean that we should confess to a priest, then, after one has confessed to him, they should change places, and the priest confess in his turn. If one must confess to a priest, but the priest be not required to confess to him, then, while he must pray for the priest, the priest is not required to pray for him. In like manner, we are commanded to love one another, to bear one another's burdens, 'to seek one another's good, and to forgive one another. Therefore, according to His Grace's reasoning, we must love the priest, but he is not required to love us; we must bear the priest's burdens, but he is not required to bear ours; we must seek the priest's good, but he is not required to seek ours; we must forgive the priest if he have wronged us, but he is not required to forgive us if we have wronged him.

It is plain that the command under consideration gives no authority whatever for what is commonly termed auricular confession. But how can it be obeyed in any other way? It can in several. One is, when he who has wronged another, acknowledges it to him. We cannot be reconciled to our brother who has somewhat against us, unless we own to him that we have done him wrong. "Where crimes are of a public nature, and have done any public mischief, then they ought to be more publicly confessed, so as may best reach to all who are concerned."[1] Another is, when we "confess our faults to some prudent minister, or praying friend, that he may help us to plead with God for mercy and pardon."[1] None of these cases is the least like the confession which the Archbishop advocates. "We are not to think James puts us on telling everything that we are conscious is amiss in ourselves, or in one another."[1] James does not say as in His Grace's quotation, "that you may be saved," but "that ye may be healed," that is "of your bodily sickness. Also that, if your sickness be the punishment of sin, the latter being forgiven on intercessory prayer, 'ye may be healed' of the former. Also, that ye may be healed spiritually."[2]

"If we are told to confess our sins one to another, for greater reason, we should confess to the priests who have the power from Christ to forgive sins."

Private Christians are as much commanded to forgive one another, as they are to confess their faults one to another. But what about the priests having power from Christ to

(1) Wright in the completion of Matthew Henry's Commentary.
(2) Fausset.

forgive sins? This, most probably, is only "the power of declaring and pronouncing authoritatively whose sins are forgiven, and whose sins are not forgiven," not that of "absolutely pardoning or not pardoning, absolving or not absolving, any one's soul." In the Old Testament, the Prophets were often said to *do* things, when they *declared* them about to be done. There is not in Scripture the slightest trace of anything like the Romish confessional. Admitting that the Apostles could absolutely remit and retain sins, they could do so only with a knowledge of men's hearts which God was pleased to give them. But that knowledge no man has now.

"It is one of the most merciful institutions of Christ."

"It" is, of course, the Confessional. Well, in the language of truth, it is one of the most cruel, debasing and polluting institutions of Satan.

"The confession, with the absolution of sins has been the means of the sanctification of the frail followers of Christ, 'for we all sin in many things.'"

It has been the cause of a most enormous amount of the most abominable sins. It could not be otherwise. Many of the questions put by the priests to their penitents are of the filthiest nature possible. No brothel literature could excel them in filthiness. Priests are allowed to ask as many of that kind in the Confessional, as they please. Some years ago, a person in England published a translation of questions relating to impurity, for the guidance of priests when hearing confession, in books approved by the Church of Rome. He added neither note nor comment. Yet he was punished for publishing immoral literature. Think of ministers of religion, one of them now a saint, planning new filthy questions as one would new patterns for wall-paper, carpets, or Christmas cards! While doing so, they must have wallowed in filthy thoughts, as a hog wallows in the mire.[1]

(1) See Appendix XIX.

"This ministry is most consoling for the repentant sinner, for there is a natural yearning in the heart of man when he sincerely repents, to confess his sins."

Those sins which we have committed against our fellow-beings, we should confess to those whom we have wronged, as well as to God. But we are not required to confess to any but to God, those sins which we have committed against Him only. If a man believe that by confessing his most secret sins to a priest, he will save his soul, he will readily confess them.

"At the hour of death how many Protestants have called for the ministrations of the Catholic priests?"

Not very many. Those who have, were as much Protestants, as Madame Tussaud's wax works are human beings. Would Your Grace call Charles II. a good Protestant, to whom Father Huddlestone was brought when he was dying, and who died, as some say, with the wafer in his throat and a prostitute by his side?

"We do not hear of a Catholic calling for a Protestant minister to assist him in his passage to eternity."

Several who, by profession, were "Catholics" have done so. Some who have died with the rites of their Church, have, before receiving them, said to Protestants that they had no faith in them, and, therefore, did not wish to receive them. They could not, however, keep the priest away. Some "Catholics" have, at the last, refused the services of a priest, though they did not ask for those of a Protestant minister.

"The secret of the confession can never be violated, hence the people have the most unbounded confidence in declaring their sins in confession, and finding a remedy for them. Some bad priests have been dismissed from the Church, but none through the mercy of God have revealed sins heard in confession."

To violate the secret of the confessional is not, in the

nature of things, an impossibility. It is a most infamous thing, that though a priest should know through the confessional of crimes, yea great crimes, being committed, or plotted against persons whom, otherwise, he could make aware thereof, he must be as silent as the grave to the latter, about them. It is not uncommon for priests to entertain each other with stories of what they have heard in the confessional, giving the names of their penitents. Often, persons who have belonged to vile gangs, and suffered death for their crimes, have "died game"—as it is termed—that is, they revealed neither the names, nor the doings of the gang. That was not "through the mercy of God." The fact stated in the last sentence just quoted, therefore, proves nothing in favour of the confessional.

Q. 58.—"Can the priest, as man, by his own power forgive sins ?"
A.—"No. This power is delegated from Christ, and this forgiveness of sins must be ultimately ratified in heaven." "Were a priest to give absolution to an unworthy penitent this absolution would not be ratified in heaven."

As we learn from the Archbishop's language elsewhere, the priest is here supposed to act in good faith. As he does not know men's hearts, it follows that his absolution is merely a declaring that the sins of the person confessing are forgiven, as the condition of forgiveness is supposed to have been complied with. But the Council of Trent says that it is "equivalent to a judicial act, wherein sentence is pronounced by himself as a judge," and that the priest, "as the minister of God, really absolves from sin; a power which God Himself, the author and source of justification, exercises through His ministry." Thus the priest is really put in the place of God. But though the person confessing has done all that the Church requires of him, and the priest has pronounced him absolved, he cannot be sure that his sins are not yet all on him, for absolution depends on the intention of the priest. The Council of Trent says that "no one is absolved truly and before God, when the priest has not a mind to act seriously and absolve truly." This gives the priest a tremendous power over his people.

Q. 59.—"Does not this confession encourage the sinner to commit more crimes?"

A.—"No. Any penitent who goes to confession with this intention has no contrition for his sins, and every Catholic child knows that he cannot receive the forgiveness of the sins confessed witout contrition."

There is such a thing as "contrition made easy." It is a penitential work. Well, the "learned prelate" elsewhere tells us that penitential work is sometimes commuted into alms, and other good works. The confessional is naturally fitted to encourage men to commit sins. It has that effect. How often, in Popish countries, do people go straight from the confessional to commit deeds of impurity, plunder and bloodshed!

"An amendment of life is a necessary adjunct of confession."

It is of true confession, but not of confessional confession.

Q. 60.—"Is the confession of sins always absolutely necessary for the forgiveness of sins?"

A.—"No. God can forgive sins, when and how He pleases."

Scriptural confession, as I have already explained it, is always absolutely necessary for forgiveness. God never forgives those who refuse to confess to Him. "He that covereth his sins shall not prosper." (Proverbs xxviii. 13.)

"If a sinner have perfect contrition, but had not an opportunity of confession . . . his sins will be forgiven him; but if he despises the sacrament of penance, instituted by Christ, or is too proud to submit to it, he will not obtain the pardon of his sins, because he has no true contrition."

Your Grace, what difference is there between "despises" and "is too proud to submit"? There is no proof whatever in Scripture that Christ appointed the sacrament of penance.

As Protestants do not go to the confessional, they, according to His Grace, go to hell, it matters not how sincerely and fully they confess their sins to God, and how holy their lives are.

> Q. 61.—"Are there any exceptions to the law of confession ?"
> A.—"No, whenever it is possible. The Pope, Bishops, Priests, as well as other Catholics are bound by the law of confession. . . . . The clergy make as much preparation for confession as the ordinary people do, and perform their penance exactly."

It is to be feared that many of the clergy make only a sort of short-hand confession. Take, for example, Pope Gregory XVI. in our own day. He, of course, confessed. Yet, as he was so often "under the influence," etc., he was called by the Italians "Il Bevone" *(The Drunkard)*. Though the "Holy Father" had, doubtless, no spiritual children, properly so called, he had some children which, in more senses than one, were natural ones. In days further back, there were "Holy Fathers" even viler. Antonelli, who was Secretary of State under Pius IX., was a cardinal, though not a priest. He was a noted libertine. In the case of those just mentioned, we have a clear proof that "an amendment of life is" not always "a necessary adjunct of confession."

> OBJECTION 3.—"But, do we not read in Scripture, 'Who can forgive sins but God alone' ?" (Luke v. 21.)
> A.—"Yes, but who said it ? The Scribes and Pharisees."

That is quite true. But they had Scriptural authority for believing that only God can forgive sins. There is not one passage in the Old Testament in which an opposite doctrine is taught. As the Scribes and Pharisees looked on Christ as merely a man, they reasoned quite correctly when they charged Him with blasphemy because He said to the man sick of the palsy : "Man, thy sins are forgiven thee."

"Then our Lord Jesus . . . cured the paralytic to prove that the Son of Man, that is, Christ, as man, had the power to forgive sins." (Matt. ix. 6, Luke v. 24.)

He cured him to prove that He had power to forgive sins, and that He, therefore, was not a mere man, as the Scribes and Pharisees supposed, but God manifest in the flesh.

"Q. 62.—"Can a priest forgive the sins of any one he pleases ?"
A.—" No. . . . If the priest knowingly pronounces absolution on an insincere penitent, he as well as the hypocritical penitent commits the grievous sin of sacrilege."

That is very good. But when a priest hears the confession of one with whom he has committed sin, it is not likely that he will lay on him, or her, a *very* heavy penance. As we have already seen, contrition can be commuted into alms or some other good work, so the sin of sacrilege can very easily be avoided.

Q. 63.—"Is it not blaspheming to say that a man can forgive sin ?"

The answer to this question is substantially the very same as that to Q. 59.

Q. 64.—" Then, the Catholic mode of obtaining forgiveness of sin is much more difficult than the Protestant mode, which is confessin to God alone."
A.—" Yes. But confessing to God alone is only a disguised way of confessing to one-self, who too easily pardons."

Confessing with all earnestness to God in secret, is anything but the confession here described. Ungodly men would rather confess to a priest, if they believed that they could thereby obtain forgiveness, than confess to God in the way which I have just described.

"God knows the sin already."

According to this reasoning, we should not pray to God for the supply of any of our wants, "for our Father knoweth what things we have need of before we ask Him."

"Catholics confess to God also, but in the hearing of the priest, who acts in God's name."

He has no authority from God to do so. A better contrivance than the confessional there could not be for making the people in the hands of the priest, like clay in those of the potter.

OBJ. 4.—"But do not we read: 'If we confess our sins He is faithful and just to forgive us our sins, and to cleanse us from all iniquity'?" (1 James i. 9.)

A.—"We do. But we do not read: 'If we confess our sins to God alone, He is faithful and just to forgive us,' but simply if we confess."

Quite true, Your Grace. But we do not read: "If we confess our sins to God in the hearing of the priest," etc., but simply, "If we confess." Well, then, as nothing is said here or anywhere else in the Bible about the confessional, it is better to confess to God in the Protestant way, as I have already described it. "1 James i. 9" should be "1 John i. 9."

Q. 65.—"Did the first Christians confess their sins?"
A.—"Yes. 'Many who believed came confessing, and showing their deeds, magic, and reading bad books.'" (Acts xix.)

Your Grace, are not magic and reading bad books two kinds of "deeds"? You do not quote Scripture correctly here. You jumble two verses together. In the 18th verse of the chapter referred to, we thus read: "And many that believed came, and confessed, and showed their deeds." In whatever way they had wronged their fellow-men, it was right that they should confess it to them, as well as to God. In the 19th verse, we thus read: "Many of them also which used curious arts brought their books together, and burned them before all men." There is no mention here of any one reading "bad" books, that is, infidel or immoral ones, the meaning which any one not acquainted with the verse just quoted, would put on the "learned prelate's" words. It would be in the highest degree absurd to suppose that on this occasion, things like sentry boxes were set up in some square, into which Paul and his companions went, and then people came and told them their most secret sins in word and deed, yea, also their sinful thoughts.

Q. 66.—"Was confession continued to be practised in the Church?"

Bad English here, Your Grace. Say: "Was confession continued in?" etc., or: "Did confession continue in," or "continue to be practised in?" etc.

A.—"Yes. If it were not of divine institution the practice is so repugnant to the pride of human nature that no Pope nor Bishop would have introduced it."

What the Archbishop here says about confession, does not necessarily prove that it was continued in the Church. To introduce a thing, is very different from continuing it. The confessional is of devilish, not of divine institution. There are different devilish practices which are repugnant to the pride and other feelings of the human heart, but it is wonderful to what men will submit, in the hope of thereby meriting heaven.

OBJ. 5.—"But was it not introduced by the Council of Lateran?"
A.—"No. But the Council of Lateran made confession obligatory at least once a year."

Of course, that Council introduced confession, by making it obligatory.

Q. 67.—"Is not confession practised in some Protestant Churches?"
A.—"There is a kind of confession or telling experiences in the Methodist Church."

The confessional countenanced by the Methodist class-meeting! Hurrah! Fancy those present at a meeting of that kind, kneeling down beside things like sentry boxes, in which ministers are sitting and listening to them, and the ministers "putting the screws" on them by asking, even the women, the most infamous questions conceivable! Well, that is "rich." The Methodist Class-meeting and the Romish Confessional are as wide apart as A and Z are. His Grace's reasoning here is an illustration of the plain saying, "A poor excuse is better than none," and of the figurative one, "Any port in a storm."

Q. 68.—"Do the married clergy of the Catholic Greek Church hear confessions?"

A.—"The people have a great repugnance to confess to a married priest."

Then, there must be something very bad in the confessional. Your Grace, in your Answer to Q. 15, you say that those outside of your Church, calling themselves Christians, "never assume or receive the title of Catholics." Yet, here, you call the Greek Church the "Greek Catholic," as you call your own the "Roman Catholic." You would not have called the Greek Church "Catholic" if she had not "assumed" that title.

The next paragraph takes up a half page, but it has no connection with the question. In it, the Archbishop praises Confession as "one of the most merciful of God's institutions, where justice and mercy meet." If these two attributes meet in it, he might as well have called it "just" as "merciful." He says that he has received many into his Church, the most of whom became "Catholics" from a desire to confess their sins, and obtain forgiveness of them before going to the judgment-seat in the next world. They must have been as ignorant of God's way of peace as wild Zulus. Reference is made to the Absolution in the Visitation for the Sick in the Liturgy of the Church of England. That is no argument in favour of the confessional. Bishop Ryle says of it: "In my judgment, it was intended to bear only a declarative sense. But I can never refrain from saying that the absolution in the Visitation Service is liable to be misunderstood, and its wording is to be regretted."

"Even where there is an uncertainty of obtaining pardon, yet in cases of doubt, and in the last moments of life, a prudent person would have recourse to confession."

There is not the slightest uncertainty about a person obtaining mercy, who seeks it in God's appointed way. "Whosoever shall call upon the name of the Lord shall be saved." (Romans x. 13.) God must change before such promises as that one can fail.

Chapter 16.

Questions.—(69) What is the meaning of Indulgences? *Objection.*—(6) Protestants say that when the sin is forgiven there is no temporal punishment due. *Q.*—(70) By what authority does the Church grant Indulgences?—(71) What is the Mass?—(72) If Christ was once offered on the cross, why offered every day in the Mass? *Obj.*—(7) Is it not contrary to common sense to say that bread would be the body of Christ? *Obj.*—(8) How could Christ hold His body in His own hands?

QUESTION 69.—" What is the meaning of Indulgences?"

ANSWER.—" An Indulgence does not mean forgiveness of sins, nor permission to commit sin, nor not to pay one's honest debts, but it means the remission of canonical penance or other temporary punishments due to sin when the guilt of it has already been forgiven by the sacrament of penance."

YOUR GRACE, is not refusing to pay one's honest debts a form of sin? The "temporary" punishments of which you here speak, are, I suppose, what you elsewhere call "temporal" punishment. But let us hear how these "canonical penances," and so forth, are remitted.

"A magistrate often commutes imprisonment into a fine; so, in the Catholic Church, fasting and other penitential work are sometimes commuted into alms and other good works."

A fine is a form of punishment. It would be most ridiculous to call it a gift. In like manner, alms and "other good works," of which prayer, no doubt, is one, when they are substitutes for "penitential work," are only forms of punishment. Now, alms should be given gladly. The giver should account it a privilege to give. He cannot do so, when he gives as a punishment. God loves a cheerful giver, but he is not a cheerful giver who gives as a punishment. Our Father in heaven delights to bless. We should, therefore, draw nigh to

Him with joy. It is, therefore, dishonouring prayer to treat it as a punishment. How absurd it would be to think of punishing a child by sending it into the presence of its father, who, that child knows, delights to receive it! In Answer to Q. 70, His Grace says :—

"There must be a just and proper cause for granting these indulgences."

In the eyes of the Archbishop's Church no cause of the kind just described, is so "just and proper" as dollars given her.

"The penitent must perform many acts of reparation."

Dollars put into her treasury will stand for these. "The more, the merrier" she will be.

"The sin must be always forgiven by a hearty and true repentance before an indulgence can be gained."

This "penitential work" can be "commuted into alms," that is, gifts to the Church, and—I need not mention any other good works.

I may here say a word on the kindred subject of Dispensations. These enable a person to do, with the approbation of the Church, what, otherwise, would be in her eyes a most heinous sin. Several years ago, when I was pastor of the Presbyterian church in Métis, Que., I married a French-Canadian couple who came to me with a license. The story is an interesting one, but I must tell it in as few words as possible. They said that they were third cousins, and, therefore, could not be married according to the rites of their own Church without a dispensation, which they were too poor to get. They added that the priest had said to them that they could be married by a Protestant minister without a dispensation, and that the marriage would be quite legal. I consulted two Congregational ministers who were near me at the time. They said that they saw no reason why I should not marry the couple. I accordingly did so. It proved, however, to be a case of marriage between a man and his deceased wife's sister's daughter—uncle and niece by affinity. Well, on All Saints' Day (Nov. 1), a few weeks after, they, and all who should countenance them, were excommunicated in the cathedral of Rimouski. There was a large congregation present. The special ceremonies were well fitted to have the following effect on all " good Catholics " present:—

> "To harrow up their soul, congeal their blood,
> Make their two eyes, like stars, start from their spheres;
> Their knotted and combined locks to part,
> And each particular hair to stand on end,
> Like quills upon the fretful porcupine."

After a few more suns had risen and set, the erring ones appeared on bended knees, before the Vicar-General, in the porch of the Cathedral. The Bishop was at the time at Rome, helping to make the Pope infallible. They confessed their heinous sins in having been married within the prohibited degrees without a dispensation, and by a heretical minister. I have not heard if they promised not to do so again. Well, they were taken back into the Church, but separated. An account of the affair appeared in the Rimouski paper, in which I was called, to express it mildly, a non-gentleman. I "stepped into the ring," ready for the fray. The Vicar-General, "the man at the wheel" of the paper, no doubt, thought that he could crush a heretic as easily as he could a cricket, or a bed b-g. Finding that he was mistaken, and fearing that his readers would get too much light, he at length, extinguished my articles by putting the waste basket over them. In course of time, the Bishop returned. The Church-made widower had by this time, raked together twenty dollars. With this he went to His Lordship, who gave him a dispensation in exchange for them. Then the couple went across the St. Lawrence to an Indian settlement, where they were married by a priest. Now, their Church smiles lovingly on them. As the late deeply lamented Wm. Shakespeare, Esq., very justly remarks: "All's well that ends well." I wrote to the Bishop some time after, "making a few remarks" on the question of Dispensations. He replied, saying, among other things, that the Church can, for good and sufficient reasons, grant them. In my reply I said that dollars were good and sufficient reasons. I added a few syllogisms against what he had done. He did not reply —for a very good reason.

I know a case of a Roman Catholic in Canada, who, in plain English, bought a dispensation, whereby he was enabled to marry his brother's widow. This, of course, made her, in one sense, a *dear* wife to him.

The late Duke of Aosta, brother of the King of Italy, was married to the Princess Letitia Buonaparte, his niece by blood, his sister's daughter. Without a dispensation for it, the marriage would have been a most sinful one in the eyes of their Church. But 100,000 lire ($20,000), which "His Holiness" received from the Duke, cleansed it from all sin.

I challenge any one to confute the following propositions: If an action be bad, the Church of Rome ought not, for any reason, to permit it. If it be good, she ought not, in the least, to hinder it.

OBJECTION 6.—"Protestants say that when the sin is forgiven there is no temporal punishment due."

A.—"They do not hold this in practice."

Neither do they in theory.

"Notwithstanding that Christ died on the cross for all mankind, yet even the just suffered temporal losses, sickness, death and the like, as punishment for their sins, though forgiven. St. Paul says, 'that he made up in his flesh that which was wanting in the sufferings of Christ.'" (Colossians i. 24.)

How could Paul's suffering punishment for his sins make up what was wanting in the sufferings of Christ? Your Grace, give us the beginning of this verse: "I, Paul, rejoice in my sufferings for you." Give us also the close: "For His body's sake, which is the Church." Paul does not here say that these sufferings were punishments for his sins. To the Corinthians, he says: "Whether we be afflicted, it is for your consolation and salvation." (2 Corinthians i. 6.) To Timothy, he says: "I endure all things for the elect's sakes." (2 Tim. ii. 10.) These sufferings were not punishments for his sins.

Q. 70.—"By what authority does the Church grant Indulgences?"
A.—"By the authority of Christ Himself."

I need not say that His Grace then holds up to view the well-known keys. A blow on the head with them is supposed to "settle" heretics.

"The Church exercised this power when St. Paul granted an Indulgence to the incestuous Corinthian (2 Cor. ii.), forgiving, as he says, 'in the person of Christ,' the penitent, on account of his extraordinary grief."

We are not told how much of his "extraordinary grief," on account of which he obtained an indulgence, came out of that Corinthian's pocket. ("Penitential work is sometimes commuted into alms.") Your Grace, you have not given this passage much attention. Paul directed the Church at Corinth to excommunicate that member, which seems to have been done at once. As soon as the erring one gave satisfactory proof of his repentance, the Apostle counselled his being restored to his former place, lest if he should still be severely dealt with, he might be swallowed up with over-much sorrow. He would not himself restore him, but if his former fellow-members should do so, he would readily support it. He gave this counsel merely from a regard to their best interests. He set Christ before him. The expression rendered "in the person of Christ," more properly means "in the presence of Christ." Considering that Christ is beholding us, is a most powerful reason why we should be "very pitiful, and of tender mercy." The act of Paul, to which the Archbishop here refers, has, therefore, not the very slightest resemblance to granting an Indulgence.

Q. 71.—" What is the Mass ? "

A.—" It is the same offering Jesus Christ made of Himself to His eternal Father, when, after His Last Supper, He took bread and blessed and broke it," etc. "The body that was given and the blood that was shed for the remission of sins were the real body and blood of Christ that were miraculously there and then offered to His eternal Father. This is the unbloody sacrifice called the Mass; a true, real, propitiatory sacrifice, anticipating the bloody sacrifice which He offered of Himself on the cross."

Christ's Last Supper was His taking bread, blessing and breaking it, etc. He broke the bread. It is forbidden to break the wafer. Let us suppose that Judas did not partake of the Last Supper. Well, according to the Church of Rome, each of the eleven disciples ate a complete Christ. There were, therefore, present on that occasion, twelve complete bodies of Christ. Yet they were all one and the same body. Greater nonsense than this there could not be. There cannot be an expiatory bloodless sacrifice. "Without shedding of blood is no remission." His Grace says that the Last Supper was an "unbloody sacrifice." But he also says that in it, "the real body and blood of Christ were miraculously offered to His eternal Father." Utter nonsense again. If the Last Supper were a "true, real, propitiatory sacrifice," there was not the slightest need of Christ offering Himself on the cross. One sacrifice of infinite value was sufficient. I defy any one to disprove this. If Christ's death on the cross, which Roman Catholics admit was a "true, real, propitiatory sacrifice," was absolutely necessary—and they admit this also—then there was no need of its being "anticipated," as His Grace says was done in the Last Supper. It is blasphemous to speak of "anticipating" that sacrifice. Further, if Christ's death on the cross was a "true, real, propitiatory sacrifice," the Last Supper was not, and, therefore, the Mass is not. If the Mass be the same as the Last Supper, and His Grace says it is, then in it, Christ's death on the cross is anticipated. But it is a gross contradiction in language—to use a homely phrase, a "bull"—to speak of "anticipating" an event which took place eighteen hundred and sixty years ago. It is no more absurd to say: "Christ shall come to our world eighteen hundred and ninety-two years ago." The doctrine of the Mass is a mass—of impious nonsense.

"Christ at His Last Supper exercised His priestly office of Melchisedech, who used bread and wine in sacrifice, and Christ being a priest of that order," etc.

The Archbishop has already said that Christ did this *after* His Last Supper. I suppose he there means to say *at*. "His priestly office of Melchisedech." The Archbishop's English here is, of course, quite correct, though I can make neither "head nor tail" of it. There is not the least mention of Melchizedek using bread and wine in sacrifice on the occasion spoken of in Genesis xiv. 18. He could not use bread and wine as a sacrifice. If he offered a sacrifice separate from them, his act has no bearing on the question of the Mass. If the bread and wine were changed into flesh and blood, though retaining the "accidents" of these substances, into whose flesh and blood were they changed? If not into Christ's, into whose? In that case, what Melchizedek did has no connection with the Mass. If the bread and wine were changed into the body and blood of Christ, then Melchizedek "anticipated" the death of Christ on the cross over nineteen hundred years before He came into the world. There was, therefore, no need of Christ "re-anticipating" it. How, was it offered? Was it by Abraham and his followers eating and drinking it? Did Melchizedek withhold the cup from them? Did each one receive as much as another? Did the bread and wine which Melchizedek offered them, still remain unused, and were the several portions given them, each and all together, the very same bread and wine? Here we find ourselves in another

"Slough of Despond." Melchizedek, it is plain, brought bread and wine to refresh Abram, afterwards called Abraham, and his followers. In many passages of Scripture, bread and wine are spoken of as ordinary victuals.

"He who changed water into wine, multiplied loaves and fishes, raised the dead to life, and created the world out of nothing, can change bread into His body and wine into His blood."

That He can do a thing, does not prove that He will. He cannot make a thing be in two or more places at the same moment. The wine into which the water was changed, had all the qualities of wine. It had not, in appearance, all those of water. It refreshed the body. The wafer is supposed to refresh the soul. The loaves and fishes were multiplied to feed the hungry. The Mass is not a meal. The loaves and fishes, when they were multiplied, were not altogether different from what they appeared to be. What was added to them was not, strictly speaking, the very same as they. What His Grace says about the Mass is as intelligible as, "There was not been good so I extremely having was my."

Protestants do, however, believe in a real presence of Christ in the Lord's Supper. "Worthy receivers, outwardly partaking of the visible elements in this sacrament, do then also inwardly by faith, really and indeed, yet not carnally and corporally, but spiritually, receive and feed upon Christ crucified, and all benefits of His death: the body and blood of Christ being then not corporally or carnally in, with or under the bread and wine; yet, as really, but spiritually, present to the faith of believers in that ordinance as the elements themselves are to their outward senses."[1]

I could easily prove that, according to the Archbishop's Church, the Mass is a commemoration, a representation, a continuation, and a renewal of the death of the Lord Jesus on the cross. How it can be all these, is, of course, according to her, "a mystery above our comprehension."

(1) West. Confession of Faith, Chap. XXIX., Sect. 7.

Q. 72.— "Christ was once offered on the cross: why offered every day in the Mass?"

A.—"Jesus Christ was once offered in a bloody manner, but now that offering is renewed in an unbloody manner, that we may have a continual sacrifice to offer to God, and perennial means of grace for ourselves."

The idea of a bloody offering being renewed in a bloodless manner, is in the highest degree absurd. One might just as well speak of a person putting on a new scarlet coat, but this time, it is blue. Your Grace, you have already said (A. to Q. 71) that the Mass is the same offering which Christ made of Himself to His eternal Father in the Last Supper, which was a "true, real, propitiatory sacrifice, anticipating the bloody sacrifice which He offered of Himself on the cross." Now you say that it is a renewal in a different manner of the latter. These two offerings were quite distinct. How, then, can the Mass be both the offering which "anticipated," and that, too, after the offering which it "anticipated," and a renewal of the offering which was "anticipated"? The thing is utterly impossible. Again, if the sacrifice of Christ on Calvary be renewed in the Mass, then it was not of infinite value. That, I challenge any one to disprove. Why were sacrifices offered continually under the Old Testament? Just because they were not of infinite value.

His Grace next quotes the prophecy about "sacrifice" and a "clean offering," in Malachi i. 11. He may well say of it, as an argument in favour of the Mass, as a woman said of her husband: "He is worth little, but he is a great deal better than none." The passage referred to is a prophecy in figurative language of the spread of the true religion over all the earth. No doubt, Christ referred to it when He said to the woman of Samaria: "The hour cometh, when ye shall neither in this mountain, nor yet at Jerusalem, worship the Father." "The hour cometh, and now is, when the true worshippers shall worship the Father in spirit and in truth." According to the Archbishop's way of interpreting Christ's words, "This is my body," "This is my blood," the passage in Malachi teaches that God should be worshipped only between sunrise and sunset, and, consequently, forbids worshipping Him between the latter and the former, as, for example, in the Midnight Mass.

The original word translated "sacrifice," in the passage in Malachi here quoted, is *mooktar*, which signifies "incense." The one translated "offering" is *mincha*, the name given to the "meat (in the Rev. Ver. 'meal') offering," which was *never* what His Grace calls "a true, real, propitiatory sacrifice." Such sacrifices were *always* bloody. It was the blood which made atonement for the soul. To a Jew, the idea of an unbloody propitiatory sacrifice would have been as ridiculous as that of a lay priest would be to a Romanist. It is true, that in four instances in the Old Testament, the term *mincha* is applied to a sacrifice properly so called. But this describes it as an *offering* to the Lord, for the term properly means "a gift, present, or offering." To describe a sacrifice as *propitiatory*, the term *zebach*, from a word meaning "to slay," is used. Peter calls all Christians priests, and says that they have to offer spiritual sacrifices. Paul uses like languge. Malachi, in the passage quoted, refers to Gospel times. He, therefore, uses the word *mincha*, instead of *zebach*. In many passages, the word *mincha* means simply "a present." For example, Joseph's brethren took him a present (*mincha*). (Genesis xliii. 11, 15, 25, 26.) This, of course, was not a "propitiatory sacrifice. The same is true of Psalm lxxii. 10, where it is said, "The kings of Tarshish and of the isles shall bring presents (*mincha*)."

I shall here set before the reader two arguments against the doctrines of Transubstantiation and the Mass, which I have never seen or heard used by any one else, but which, I think, are of great force.

According to the *first*, the wafer is changed into the soul and divinity of Christ, as well as into His body and blood. Of course, this is the case only when the consecrating priest has a proper intention. Well, then, every one who swallows a wafer, becomes a partaker of Christ's divinity. As God, He is from eternity, is everywhere present, knows all things, and can do all things. He is the same in substance as, and equal in power and glory to, Father, Son, and Holy Ghost. There are, therefore, besides them, as many persons in the Godhead as there are persons who have swallowed the wafer and have it in their bodies. As long as there is a particle of it, no larger than a pin's point, in one's body, he has in him the divinity of Christ, for, according to Rome, a part is equal to the whole. He who has the wafer in his stomach, has Christ in him literally. Therefore, "in Him dwelleth all the fulness of the Godhead bodily." When he drinks, swears, steals, or commits uncleanness, it is God who does so. When he appears before God in judgment, he is God judged by God.

According to this doctrine, also, Christ cannot be truly man, for it teaches that His body can be in millions of places at the very same moment, which man's body cannot. But it was absolutely necessary for our salvation that Christ should have a true body, for it was as necessary that He should be one with us.

According to the *second*, Christ is constantly sacrificed in the Mass. Of course, then the offering of Himself on Calvary was not of infinite value, else it would not have needed to be repeated. Therefore, Christ is not God. The first doctrine is a practical denial of His *humanity*—the second, of His *divinity*. What remains of Him? Nothing. The two doctrines are, therefore, a practical denial of His being.

What I have now stated as following from these doctrines, is most absurd—yea, in some instances, fearfully blasphemous. But I challenge any one to prove that it does not fairly do so.

OBJ. 7.—"Is it not contrary to common sense to say that bread could be the body of Christ?"

A.—"Yes. . . . . Catholics do not adore bread."

If a hungry person were to eat a goodly number of wafers,

he would lose his appetite for the time being. He could not do this on mere "accidents."

OBJ. 8.—" How could Christ hold his body in his own hands ? "
A.—" How could He multiply loaves and fishes, and grain in the earth, but by His almighty power ? "

Quite true, Your Grace, but these things are utterly different from what is supposed to take place in Transubstantiation. The loaves and fishes were not changed—say into grapes—under the "accidents" of loaves and fishes. Each grape was not equal in quantity to the original loaves and fishes, and all that was added to them. It was not the case that the loaves and fishes were not increased in quantity by being multiplied.

"This wonderful action of Christ at His Last Supper far transcends the comprehension of man."

This "wonderful action" was never performed. Downright nonsense "far transcends the comprehension of man."

"But the love of God for His creatures, being infinite, induced Him to do what finite love cannot comprehend."

Bad English and bad metaphysics here, Your Grace. Say "love to His creatures," and "finite intelligence." Love does not belong to the intellect.

"A God who would become man and die on a cross for His creatures would descend to incomprehensible depths to gain their love."

That is, by letting them make Him "descend to the incomprehensible depths" of their stomach, and still lower. (Matt. xv. 17.) This is just what the Archbishop's statement really comes to : "If through certainly, the kettle drum's wings extended paramount, then it follows that all according, certainly, in nature was been. Do you see ? " " How clear you have made it ! "

Chapter 17.

Questions.—(73) Why are the Mass, etc , performed in Latin?—(74) Why does the priest use such strange vestments?—(75) Why so many colours in the vestments?—(76) Why are candles used on the altar during Mass?—(77) Why is incense used in the Church?—(78) Why does the Church use so many ceremonies?—(79) Did Christ use ceremonies?

QUESTION 73.—" Why are the Mass and Liturgies of the Church performed in Latin ?"

ANSWER.—" Many nations retain in their worship the original language in which the Gospel was preached to them by their first apostles or apostolic missionaries."

HIS GRACE then mentions several. That, however, does not prove that they are in the right in having their worship in a language which the people do not understand. It is contrary to the word of God. (1 Corinthians xiv.) Here I would remark, once for all, that Protestants do not condemn the use of Latin in the worship of the Church of Rome, because it is Latin, but because it is an unknown tongue to almost every one of the worshippers. They would condemn the use of any other language of the same kind. They would say nothing against the worship being in Latin, if the worshippers understood it.

"The Jews perform their services in the old Hebrew."

The Reformed Jews do it in the native language of the worshippers. They use precisely the same arguments against services in Hebrew, as those which we use against the Latin ones of the Romish Church.

" Almost every village . . . in Europe have their peculiar dialect or *patois*. It would be most inconvenient and almost impossible to adapt the Liturgy to suit all these people; besides, it would lessen very much the dignity of worship."

For "have their" say "has its," and for "and almost" say "yea, almost." There is a great variety of dialects among those who speak English, yet all who speak it understand, for example, the Liturgy of the Church of England. The like is true of other languages. The instruction of the worshippers is of infinitely greater importance than "dignity," that is to say, pomp. The worship of God can be performed with true dignity, while, at the same time, language is used in it which the most unlearned can understand.

"The people have their prayer books in their own language, in which are translated the prayers used at Mass, ... and can follow the priest when he celebrates."

Suppose a person has not a prayer book of the kind described, cannot read, the light is not good, or his eyes are dim, and he has not his spectacles with him. What benefit can he receive from the services? But suppose he has a prayer book, can read, and has good light and good sight, if he do not understand Latin he cannot follow the priest. He will sometimes be, perhaps, far before him, at others, far behind him.

"Priests always preach in the language of the people,"—

Why do they not pray in the same?

"and recite other prayers before Mass and at different times."

That is, in their native language. Well, why should not the rest of the prayers be also in it? I challenge any one to give a good reason why people should sometimes pray in a language which they understand, and, at others, in one which they do not.

His Grace refers to the use of Latin in the Vatican Council. According to him, all the members thereof understood that language. It is quite likely that some were pretty "rusty" in it. However, the Vatican Council was a very different thing from an ordinary congregation of worshippers. He also refers to Latin being the language of literature in Europe during the Middle Ages, from which fact he argues that it was proper to have the Liturgy of the Church in it during *them*. The great mass of the people in those days were grossly ignorant. Worship should be conducted in the language understood by the greatest number of those who engage in it. The great question with which we have to do as regards that, is, "What is proper for our own day?"

"The Latin language is not an unknown language by any means; all highly educated gentlemen and many ladies in Europe and America know this language."

Very many highly educated persons do not know Latin. Very few ladies do. Many who can read it, understand it very imperfectly when they hear it spoken, especially if it be pronounced differently from what they have been accustomed to, and also when they hear it sung. The great majority of people are not highly educated; very many are highly uneducated. As I have already said, the good of the greatest number is to be sought.

"A Catholic .... finds in China the same language, vestments of the priests, and ceremonies, as he will find in his own country or in Rome."

What good will that do him, if he do not understand the language? He may as well listen to the beating of a gong.

Q. 74.—Why does the priest use such strange vestments when he he is celebrating?"

The "learned prelate" refers to the holy garments of the priests under the Old Testament, which were designed "to add dignity to the priest, and to the worship of God, and to inspire the people with reverence." He argues that, for the same reasons, the priest, "when performing divine services, should wear sacred ornaments." But the ceremonial part of the Old Testament has been abolished.

"Great monarchs, and we might add, respectable people, have their servants dressed in livery."

According to His Grace, great monarchs are not respectable people. Well, Queen Victoria is a great monarch. Therefore, she is not a respectable person. Och, och! Yir Lardship's Rivirince, wood ye be afther spakin' uv the Quane in that way, afther she allowed ye to be presinted to hur in yir cananicals, the first toime sitch a thing wuz done since the Riformashun? Och! sure, an' it's too bàd intoirely!

"The vestments which the priest uses at Mass are most appropriate, inasmuch as the Mass is the commemoration of the sufferings and death of Jesus Christ."

In his Answer to Q. 71, His Grace says that the Mass is the same offering which Christ made of Himself to His eternal Father, a "true, real, propitiatory sacrifice, anticipating the bloody sacrifice of Himself on the cross." In his Answer to Q. 72, he says that the Mass renews that bloody sacrifice. In his Answer to the one before us, he says that the Mass commemorates it. Now, I challenge any one to show how the Mass can do these three things—*anticipate, renew, and commemorate* the death of Christ.

Q. 75.—" Why do priests wear a variety of colour in their vestments?"

A.—" It is to mark the festivals."

There is nothing argumentative in what follows. At the close, he says :—

"A bell is rung occasionally, during certain solemn portions of the Mass, to remind the people to excite a greater fervour and devotion."[1]

The whole of the Mass should be solemn. As the worshippers, with few exceptions, know nothing of Latin, the ringing of a bell, at certain times, tells them what progress they are making in their journey through the service, and

(1) See Appendix XX.

into what postures to put themselves. "To remind the people to excite," etc. In homely language, to tell them to stir up the fire within them. The language used is a specimen of "The Archbishop's English."

Q 76.—" Why are candles used on the altar during Mass?"

We can see the need of them at the Midnight Mass, which is only on Christmas Eve. But why they should be used in broad daylight, I must say, is to me a very dark question, though the candles are lighted. Let us see what light His Grace sheds on it.

A.—" Light signifies joy, hope and sacrifice." .... "The candles on the altar signify the light of faith and hope."

How light can signify hope, and, especially, how it can signify sacrifice, Yir Grace, is intoirely beyant me cumprihinshin. In the first sentence, it is said that light signifies hope. In the second, it is said that the candles on the altar signify the light of hope, as well as of faith. How to reconcile the two, I cannot see. With Goethe, I say: "More light!"

"Lamps were lit by order of God Himself, and kept burning in the Temple." (2 Parl. [Chron.] iv. 20.)

"Lighted" is better English than "lit." These lamps were kept in the Holy Place in the Tabernacle, a room which had no light but from them, and into which only the priests were allowed to enter. Some think that a part was kept burning continually. Be that as it may, those which were not, were lighted in the evening, and put out next morning. There was, certainly, a great difference between them, and the lights on a Roman Catholic altar. The former were in harmony with the Mosaic dispensation, the latter are not with the Gospel one.

"It was the custom in the East to light torches or candles to honour great personages on their visits."

This was always done at night. See, for example, Matt. xxv. 1, 6.

"The torchlight processions of modern times are also in this spirit."

They always take place after sundown. There was a grand torchlight procession one night during the festivities in honour of your silver wedding as a bishop. But if we saw people marching about between sunrise and sunset with lighted torches, we would think that they should be marched into that large, white brick building with a dome on it, on Queen Street, near Parkdale, and put under the care of my old friend, Dr. Clark.

"The candles on the altar . . remind us of the darkness . . at the death of Christ. They remind us, again, of the sacrifice of the Mass offered up in the Catacombs under the earth. Lights are very beautiful ornaments."

I fear, Your Grace, the Mikes and the Pats, the Biddies and the Norahs who go to Mass, know nothing of these fine-spun arguments. Lights are very paltry ornaments when the sun is shining.

Q. 77.—"Why is incense used in the Church?"
A.—"Incense was offered to God from the very beginning of worship."

That was a part of the pomp of the Old Testament service which has given place to the plainness of the New Testament one.

"St. John saw incense offered in heaven."

When he was in the Spirit in Patmos, he did not see things as they really are, but figures of better things. Christ is not as He appeared to him. (Revelation i. 13-16.) Heaven is not like the New Jerusalem which he saw. (xxi. 10-27.)

"The burning of incense . . . was used in the Catholic Church in the earliest ages. It was taken from the vision of St. John."

There are many things in the vision of the beloved disciple which she has not copied. Chapter xvii. looks remarkably like a copy by "anticipation" of the "Catholic" Church.

"David asked . . . 'Let my prayer be directed as incense in Thy sight," etc. (Psalm cxl.—Protest. Ver. cxli.—2.)

Only "*as* incense." That is no authority for the use of incense in worship. Why not have also sacrifices of beasts, for the Psalmist immediately adds: "Let the lifting up of my hands be as the evening sacrifice"?

Q. 78.—"Why does the Church make use of so many ceremonies?"

For the sake of variety, I shall answer this question before noticing what His Grace says on the subject. The fact is that the worship of His Grace's Church is almost wholly a copy of that of the ancient heathens. The Church sought to win the heathens by adopting their forms, only giving them Christian names. Of course, the "learned prelate" gives another reason. He says:

"No polite society is without its ceremonies; witness such as are performed at the court of every monarch, at tribunals and in private houses."

Some of the ceremonies performed at the courts of some monarchs appear to us highly absurd, yea, some appear as impious. But take even those courts where the forms are the simplest. No argument in favour of ceremonies in the Church, would have any force with a thorough republican. In republics there are few ceremonies in halls of legislation and courts of justice. Many of the ceremonies in private houses are really of no use.

"Ceremonies are manifestations of respect which should be used in divine services."

A ceremony may be very simple, yet be far more solemn than a great amount of "pomp and pride and circumstance."

Beauty is sometimes buried under a mass or ornament. The worship of God is "when unadorned, adorned the most." "Majestic in its own simplicity." A gorgeous ceremonial has a powerful tendency to draw men's minds away from the spiritual nature of true religion. But I do not advocate in place thereof, what is often called a "bald" service. "Let all things be done decently and in order." Both extremes are to be avoided. In this matter, as in all others, we need "the wisdom that is profitable to direct."

Q. 79.—"Did Christ use ceremonies?"
A.—"Yes."

His Grace then mentions those which He used when He gave sight to a blind man (John ix. 6, 7), and hearing and speech to a deaf and dumb one (Mark vii. 33), and when He bestowed the Holy Ghost on His disciples on the evening of the day on which He arose from the dead. (John xx. 22, 23.) But these were not used by Him in the worship of God. We have not to imitate Him in them.

Chapter 18.

Questions.—(80) Why do Catholics genuflect when they enter their churches?—(81) Why use holy water?—(82) Why do Catholics communicate under one kind? *Objection.*—(9) But did not Christ say: "Except you eat the flesh of the Son of Man, and drink His blood," etc.? *Q.*—(83) What do Catholics mean by the sacred ministry, or the priesthood?—(84) Why do not priests marry?—(85) Can men and women live chastely without being married?—(86) Why are the priests called Fathers?

QUESTION 80.—"Why do Catholics genuflect when they enter their churches?"

ANSWER.—"To adore our Lord Jesus Christ. In the tabernacle of their churches is generally preserved the most Blessed Sacrament, ... in which all Catholics believe that He is really present."

"BOW the knee" is just as elegant as "genuflect," though not so "highflown." We have already seen that Christ is not present in the consecrated Host. But even if Transubstantiation be a reality, no Roman Catholic can be sure that He is in it, because the wafer cannot be consecrated unless the priest has, at the time, a right intention.

Where the Host is allowed to be carried in public procession, Roman Catholics often order Protestants to do it homage when it is passing by them, or they are passing by it. Even according to the teachings of their own Church, they have no right to do so. Admitting the doctrine of Transubstantiation to be true, that of Intention has to be considered. According to it, though the priest should go through all the necessary forms of consecration, yet, if he have not while doing so, a proper intention, the Host remains unconsecrated. It is, therefore, in reality, only a flour-and-water lozenge. Of course, then, no one has a right to order me to do homage to the Host, until he can clearly prove to me that the consecrator had a right intention. After he has done that, we can take up the doctrine of Transubstantiation. The first will, however, be more than enough for him.

Q. 81.—" Why does the priest bless water and sprinkle it on the people before Mass on Sundays ?"

A.—" Water can be blessed and sanctified as well as any other creature that God has made."

So can dust.

"The word of God and prayers are used over the water for its consecration, hence it is sprinkled over the people."

It does not necessarily follow that a thing is right because the word of God and prayers were used at it.

"In the old law, Moses sprinkled the altar and the people with the blood of victims."

Why use water now, instead of the blood of victims ?

"Holy water reminds people of the blood of Jesus Christ by which they are sanctified; and also of baptism, when they became children of God."

This is the case, at the most, with very few of them. If all baptized persons are children of God, then no baptized person can go to hell.

Q. 82.—" Why do Catholics only receive communion under one kind, that is, under the form of bread ?"

A.—" Because under that form, Christ has declared that He is whole and entire; body and blood, soul and divinity. 'I am the living bread that came down from heaven,' etc." (John vi. 51, 52, 59.)

The words of Christ here quoted, were spoken long before the Lord's Supper was instituted. They cannot, therefore, refer to it.

" The Apostles themselves practised this form of communion,

'And they were persevering in the .... breaking of bread,' etc." (Acts ii. 42.)

"Bread." Plain bread, not the "body and blood, etc., of Christ." "Breaking." The wafer is not allowed to be broken. This could not have been "the sacrifice of the Mass."

"Communion of one kind was invariably given to the martyrs"

It was not. Even if it had been, it was contrary to the word of God.

"It was also given under one kind to children and to the sick."

Children have no right to either one, or both kinds. Private communion is contrary to the word of God.

"The cup is not essential."

It is as much so as the bread, according to every account which we have of the institution of the Lord's Supper. If both be not essential, neither is. I challenge any one to disprove this.

"The priests always receive under both kinds, for when Jesus Christ instituted this adorable sacrament, He told His Apostles to receive the cup: 'Drink ye all of this,' but that command was not given to the faithful in general."

"The priests." That is, the officiating ones. When priests partake of the Mass as private communicants, the cup is withheld from them also. Christ gave the bread to the very same persons as, neither more nor fewer than, those to whom He gave the cup, that is, at least, eleven of the Apostles. If, then, the command, "Drink ye all of this," was not given to the faithful in general, neither was the one, "Take, eat, this is My body." If the latter was given to them, so also was the former. Och! Yir Grace, but it's mesilf that's sarry fur you. Shure now ye're in a toight place. You may twist yirsilf as much as you plaze, an' throy to git out uv that same, but you can't do it at ahll, at ahll. Yir Grace doesn't same to be much acquainted wid yir boible.

OBJECTION 9.—"But did not Christ say: 'Except you eat the flesh of the Son of Man and drink His blood you cannot have life in you?' Therefore, you must partake of the cup."

An intelligent Protestant would not use an argument like this. He would first refer to the different accounts of the institution of the Lord's Supper which we have. Then he might use as an illustration the words of Christ just quoted. As I have already said, they do not refer to the Lord's Supper. But let us hear how His Grace answers this objection.

"Communicants partake of the true body and blood of Christ under each species. It is a miraculous partaking of the body and blood of Christ. It is a mystery above our comprehension."

To those who admire this kind of reasoning, this is just the kind which they will admire. The following are also "mysteries above our comprehension": A man's pulling himself out of a pit by the hair of his head, carrying his head in his mouth, kicking himself, playing hide-and-go-seek with himself, and carrying a sword in each hand and a pistol in the other.

"If Christ says, 'This is My body and this is My blood,' it is not for us to contradict Him and say that it is not His body and blood."

He says to "the faithful in general," "Drink ye all of this." It is, therefore, not for us to contradict Him and say that only some may. What say you in reply to that, Your Grace? Christ calls Himself, for example, a Vine, a Door, and a Rock. "It is not for us to contradict Him," etc.

Q. 83.—"What do Catholics mean by the sacred ministry or the priesthood?"

The answer to this question takes up two pages of the Archbishop's work. I have already noticed in one place and another of this Review, everything of importance in it. I would, before going to the next question, say a word on each of the two following statements.

"Christ came to save and to transmit the means of salvation to the people of every country, and of every age; to the Americans as well as to those to whom the Apostles preached in person."

If His Grace here mean the people of the United States of America, he is like the person who said that there was mercy for the very worst, yes, even for the Irish. If he mean the people of this continent in general, his phraseology is very clumsy.

"Christ gives grace through His sacraments administered by the bishops and priests of the Church."

His Grace admits that one may receive all the sacraments of His Church, yet be lost for ever. But five of these are not Christ's, though, of course, His Grace does not admit that.

Q. 84.—"Why do not priests marry?"
A.—"Because the Holy Scriptures counsel celibacy."

The Archbishop's language means that they do so in every instance. They do so only in certain ones. They forbid it in none.

"Priests want to be free to take greater care of the spiritual interests of their people, and to attend to the sick and the dying, often of contagious diseases."

Attending to the sick and dying is one form of taking care of the spiritual interests of others. The priests under the Old Testament married. The very same arguments could have been used against their doing so.

The Archbishop next refers to 1 Corinthians vii. But it is as clear as can be, that the Apostle there gives counsel to the Corinthian converts, suitable to the circumstances in which they were at the time placed. They were suffering persecution. He speaks of "the present distress," and of their having "trouble in the flesh." (26, 28 vs.) He does not forbid them to marry. (28 v.) He says merely that it is inexpedient for them to do so. He makes the same distinction here

REVIEW OF "ANSWER" TO QUESTION 85.   183

between what is unlawful and what is inexpedient, that he does regarding food, in 1 Corinthians x. 23. Roman Catholic priests are forbidden to marry, though the Maronite clergy, who are in communion with the Church of Rome, are not. His Grace says that priests in his Church being forbidden to marry, is "only a point of discipline." That it is so, and not one of faith, is, after all, really a matter of not the very slightest consequence. Any priest who should be known to be married, would, for that reason, be deposed. He would not be deposed for impurity, unless the greatness of the scandal should make it unavoidable. The counsel in 1 Corinthians vii. is addressed to "the faithful in general." So, then, if it prove that priests should not marry, it also proves that the people should not. Your Grace, an argument which proves too much, is worth nothing.

Q. 85.—"Is it possible for men and women to live chastely without being married?"

A.—"Yes. . . . We find an immense number of this class in the army and navy, and in all walks of life, living chastely."

The Archbishop's reference to the army and navy is a most unfortunate one for himself. It is well known that there is a very great deal of immorality in garrison towns, and at naval stations. Look at that most infamous piece of legislation for the sake of the British army in India, the "Contagious Diseases Act," which legalizes unchastity.[1]

"Priests from their youth choose this state of celibacy, and none are promoted to holy orders except those who have the gift of chastity from God. . . . Those to whom it appears to be given are chosen to become priests."

"Those who have the gift." These words express certainty. "Those to whom it appears to be given." These express only probability. Both clauses describe the same persons. The

---

(1) Since writing the above, I have seen it stated by Miss Frances Willard that the Act mentioned has been repealed. Whether it has, or not, I cannot say.

history of the Archbishop's Church abounds in proofs that priests, monks, and nuns have not all the gift referred to. Some of the most notorious for unchastity have been "Holy Fathers."[1]

"Priests, by reason of their office, attend and anoint the sick in contagious diseases, etc."

The "learned prelate" has already used this as an argument for priests not marrying. It does not prove that they live chastely.

"The world would be very low indeed if the love of God did not reign in many souls superior to the love of marriage or creatures."

According to this, the single state is holier than the married. There may be very good reasons why some should not marry, but it is in the highest degree dishonouring to God to say that one should not, because by marrying, he will expose his soul to greater danger than by remaining single. God appointed marriage while man was in a state of innocence. It is one of the only two relics of Paradise which we have. The Virgin Mary, who, the Romish Church says, was conceived without sin, entered into the married life. There is no earthly state which is free from inconveniences. Marriage has its share of them. But it has also its advantages, and the rose is not to be rejected on account of its thorns. May it not then, Your Grace, except in particular instances, add to the usefulness of a minister of the Gospel, instead of lessening it?[2] Peter, whom the Church of Rome calls the first Pope, was married. So was Philip, the evangelist. A bishop is forbidden, not to have a wife at all, but to have more than one at a time. But I shall have to refer to this again.

"In the early Church, men who were married were chosen by Christ Himself as Apostles, but we know that they abandoned their wives and left them as widows, and the Deacons were ordained to look after them."

(1) See Appendix XXI.   (2) See Appendix XXII.

We have not the slightest proof that the Apostles acted as here stated. When Paul wrote his first Epistle to the Corinthians, Peter was living with his wife. (ix. 5.) The deacons were appointed to look after the poor "in general." They did not belong to the ministry as they do in the Archbishop's Church. But let us hear what the learned prelate says in support of his statement just quoted.

"And in those days, the number of the disciples increasing, there arose a murmuring of the Greeks against the Hebrews for that their widows were neglected in the daily ministration." (Acts vi. 1.)

The Greeks here spoken of were Greek-speaking Jews, as distinguished from those who spoke the Hebrew of that time. The widows were plainly widows, strictly so called, not "grass" widows. Well, then, these widows were widows of Greek-speaking Jews. Your Grace, you say that they were the so-called widows of the Apostles. Therefore, according to you, the Apostles were not Hebrew-speaking Jews. Hurrah! One is always learning. These widows were widows in the strict sense of the word, as I have already said. According to you, the Apostles —who must have been dead—were concerned about their support. Did a poor man ever say to you: "Wood ye be so koind, Yir Grace, as give me a little charity, fur me widdy is down wid the fayver, and me fatherless childer have nothing to ate"? You are not "mighty in the Scriptures," but as a reasoner, I gaze on you as "Misther Maloney" says he did on the "Christhial Exhibishun":—

> "Wid conscious proide ——,
> Until me soite is dazzled quoite,
> And cannot see fur starin'."

The expression "their widows," in the passage in Acts, which His Grace here quotes, is used just as when we speak of cities, national societies, or churches providing for their poor, their widows, or their orphans.

His Grace's account of the reason why deacons were first

appointed in the Christian Church, is, certainly, a very droll one. It is to the following effect: The twelve apostles, counting as one, Matthias who was appointed successor to Judas, who were all married men, left their wives as "grass widows." By right, they should have provided for their wants. But they preferred laying this burden on the infant church. Accordingly, they called the multitude of the disciples to them, and addressed them after this manner: "Brethren, it is not becoming that we should trouble ourselves with attending to the wants of our grass widows. Wherefore, look ye out among you seven men of honest report, full of the Holy Ghost and wisdom, whom we may appoint over this business." If Judas left a widow, and she belonged to the church, she certainly deserved help. There were, therefore, in all, thirteen widows—twelve "grass" ones, and one properly so called. Seven deacons were appointed to attend to their wants, and only theirs. Seven into thirteen will go once, and six over. Therefore, each deacon had to attend to the wants of one widow and six-sevenths of another. Hurrah! I wonder if any of the deacons ever came into collision with another, while they were attending to the wants of the six fractional widows. Seven deacons to six widows were too many. "Too many cooks spoil the broth." Of course, if the twelve were not all married—though, according to His Grace, all were—the labours of the deacons would be so much the lighter.

Q. 86.—"Why are the priests called Fathers!"

A.—"Because they were so named in the Apostolic times. . . . . 'Men, brethren, and fathers, hear ye the account which I now give unto you.'" (Acts xxii. 1.)

The words here quoted, are the beginning of Paul's address to the multitude from the stairs of the castle at Jerusalem. Is it not more likely that those in it whom he called "Fathers," were simply aged persons than priests?

Chapter 19.

Questions.—(87) What do the Catholics believe of Christian marriage?—(88) Why does not the Church permit divorce? *Objection.*—(10) But did not Christ permit divorces in certain cases? *Q.*—(89) Why does not the Catholic Church approve of marriages between Protestants and Catholics?—(90) Why are priests sent for to anoint the sick? *Obj.*—(11) Was not this anointing only to cure the body, and to be discontinued? *Q.*—(91) Does belief in one's own predestination ensure salvation?—(92) Has God destined some people for heaven—others for hell?—(93) Will all be saved on account of the death of Christ?—(94) What will become of those who never heard of Christ?—(95) What do you think of those who say, "There is no God"?

QUESTION 87. — "What do the Catholics believe of Christian marriage?"

ANSWER.—"That it is a sacrament instituted by Christ to give grace to the man and wife to lead pure lives in the married state. 'This is a great sacrament,' etc " (Eph. v. 32.)

THE Scriptures never represent marriage as a sacrament. The word translated "sacrament," in the passage in Ephesians here quoted, means "mystery." Paul so terms the union between Christ and His people, which He represents under the figure of husband and wife. If people can lead pure lives in the married state, it cannot be hurtful to their souls. But many married persons do not lead pure lives. Therefore, marriage does not give them grace to do so. If marriage be a sacrament, why should the priests be denied it?

"It elevates love to a supernatural one."

In his Answer to Q. 85, the Archbishop says, " . . . if the love of God did not reign in many souls superior to the love of marriage." That is, "if the love of God did not reign superior to supernatura llove." What distinction can Your

Grace make between them? Is it not cruelty to the priests to forbid them to use the means whereby their "natural" love can be "elevated to a supernatural"?

"It is an indissoluble contract, to end only by the death of one of the parties."

It is not like a commercial partnership for a specified time, or during mutual consent. It is this view of it which is expressed in those passages of Scripture which say that only death can dissolve it.

Q. 88.—"Why does not the Church permit divorce?"

A.—"Because Christ has forbidden it, saying, 'Whom God has joined together let no man put asunder.'"

A contract has, necessarily, conditions. If husband and wife are faithful to these, no one has a right to separate them on such grounds as difference of colour, religious creed, rank, or temper.

Objection 10.—"But did not Christ permit a man to put away his wife for adultery?"

A.—"Yes; but He does not say that he can marry another; on the contrary, He says that 'he who marrieth the woman so put away commits adultery,' which He would not do if the woman was released from her husband."

When one of the parties in a contract breaks, or does not fulfil, the conditions thereof, the contract is thereby made void. The woman of whom Christ here speaks, has, by her unfaithfulness as a wife, made void the marriage contract. It would be unjust to doom the husband to a single life for her sin, but it would be quite just to do so to her. Under the Gospel, the wife should, in this matter, have the same rights as the husband.

The Archbishop next refers to Paul's statement that "a man or woman is bound to his wife or her husband as long as either lives." By "either," he, of course, means "the other."

I need not repeat what I have already said on this point. But, in 1 Corinthians vii. 15, the Apostle uses language regarding wilful desertion, the natural meaning of which is, that it is a lawful ground of divorce. What has been said regarding adultery, is equally true of it. Wilful desertion may be termed want of conformity to the marriage contract—adultery, transgression thereof.

But the Archbishop's Church has more than once permitted divorce. The Council of Verberius, in 752, "authorized divorce, even on suspicions roused against the wife." Pope Celestin allowed it on accusation of heresy. Innocent IV. sanctioned a divorce in favour of King Alfonso of Portugal. Pius VII. allowed Napoleon to divorce Josephine.

Gregory II. and one of the Bonifaces allowed bigamy, which was much worse than allowing divorce, admitting, for the sake of argument, that that is wrong.

Q. 89.—" Why does not the Catholic Church approve of marriages between Protestants and Catholics ? "

A.—"Because they introduce a subject of great discord between man and wife. .... When the wife goes in one direction and the husband in another, they are generally divided."

"Generally." Of course, not always. Therefore, husband and wife can sometimes go in opposite directions, without being divided. Only one who can understand Transubstantiation, can understand how this can be.

"There is also a subject of constant dispute about the education of their children."

This implies that the constant disputation is a separate thing from their going in opposite directions. To me, it seems that the first is one form of the second, as Irishmen are a part of mankind. As regards constant disputation, yet being only generally divided, I have just to look grave, shake my head, and exclaim, " A mystery above my comprehension ! "

"As the Catholic Church aims at peace and good will, it discourages those of different religious creeds to unite in matrimony."

"Aims," etc. By having universal sway. "Different religious creeds." Of course, Protestants and Roman Catholics. Well, I fully agree with it here; but, of course, we look at the matter from different standpoints.

I would, in closing this part of my review of the Archbishop's work, remark that, as we have just seen, the Church of Rome classes marriage among her sacraments. As we have also already seen, she teaches that the validity of a sacrament depends on the intention of the priest who celebrates it. Therefore, if the priest, when he professes to marry a couple, has not a proper intention, they are not married, and, consequently, receive no grace from their marriage. It is, therefore, utterly impossible to tell who have been really married.

Q. 90.—"Why do Catholics invariably call for the priest to anoint them when dying?"

In reply, the Archbishop quotes James v. 14, 15. In commenting on this passage, it is remarkable that he takes not the slightest notice of the prayer of faith, and the restoration of the sick man to health therein spoken of. He says:—

"We see here the advantages of this sacrament. The relieving of the sick person, and if he has been in sins, they are forgiven. Many sick persons are deprived of the use of speech when dying, and cannot confess their sins, but if they have real sorrow for them in their hearts, God forgives them—through the merits of His Son Jesus Christ infused into the soul through this sacrament. If ever the poor sinner requires strength from above, it is when the gates of eternity are opening upon him, and here a merciful God steps in to reconcile the sinner on earth before the time of reconciliation has passed."

It is utter nonsense to speak of the merits of Christ being infused into the soul. We obtain all the blessings of salvation through them. We are justified for the righteousness of Christ imputed to us. We are sanctified by the Holy Ghost bestowed on us through Him. His Grace evidently confounds the former with the latter. There is no Scriptural warrant for classing extreme unction as a sacrament. To say the least, the idea of the soul being benefitted by a certain kind of oil being put on certain parts of the body, is most ridiculous. "Strength from above," is, in its nature, a very different thing from reconciliation to God, which, I suppose, is the "reconciliation" of which His Grace here speaks. We are reconciled to God by the death of His Son, not by holy oil. The Romanist is supposed to be reconciled to Him before he receives extreme unction. If he be, he needs no holy oil. If he be not, holy oil will do him no good. If he be prepared for death by extreme unction, what need has he of going to purgatory? The Archbishop is quite orthodox when he says that, at death, the time of reconciliation passes away.

If the bishop who blessed the holy oil—which can be blessed only on a Maundy Thursday—had not a proper intention at the time, the oil was not blessed, consequently, the anointing with it is to no effect. Further, if the priest who administers the rite, do so without a proper intention, the person anointed receives no "strength from above." Think of a man's salvation depending on the will of a priest!

"The Church from the very beginning administered this sacrament."

It is quite true that she administered this rite—not sacrament—in the beginning, but that does not prove that she is still to do so.

"The Catholic Church alone retains all the merciful institutions of Christ; no other Church even pretends to it."

No doubt, His Grace means that all, not merely some, of the institutions of Christ are merciful. Those of His which she has retained, she has wofully disfigured. To these she has added many.

"OBJ. 11.—" Was not this anointing only to cure the body, and a ceremony that was to be discontinued?"

A.—"We do not read so in the Bible—for St. James says, 'if the sick person be in sin it will be forgiven him,' which does not refer to the cure of the body."

It is most singular that, though he quotes the passage in full, His Grace does not see, as it were staring him in the face, these words: "And the prayer of faith shall save the sick man, and the Lord shall raise him up." Here we are told as plainly as possible, that this anointing was to be used as a mean of restoring to health, the person anointed. The Church of Rome uses extreme unction for the health of the soul, not for that of the body. She never administers it to any but those whose recovery is hopeless. Her extreme unction is, therefore, wholly different from the anointing of which James speaks.

"What was ordained for the first Christians ought to be good for the present."

But it might not be the will of God that this ceremony should be continued through all time coming. Whether it was His will that it should or not, can very easily be known. Let the Church of Rome use anointing as here described, along with the prayer of faith, as a mean of healing the sick, and if, in that case, the sick man is invariably restored to health, it is a clear proof that the administration of the rite should be continued. That will be better than volumes of argument.

Q. 91.—"Is it anywhere mentioned in Sacred Scriptures that earnest belief in one's own predestination for the kingdom of heaven ensures salvation?"

A.—"Such a doctrine is nowhere to be found, but the contrary can be seen in many places in the Bible."

If any believe that the Bible teaches the doctrine here stated, it is only lunatics who do. His Grace has heard of the doctrines of predestination and assurance, and, not understanding them properly, he here jumbles them together "in wild confusion dire." His reply to the piebald doctrine which he has made, is all labour lost. He might as well try to refute the notion that the earth is flat, by proving that Toronto is the capital of Ontario. The doctrine, which it is clear that he opposes, is this, "Can a person have assurance of his salvation?" which is very different from the one which he states. The most ignorant fishwife could not express it in a more bamboozled form than the "learned prelate" here does. But let us now look at his attempts to prove that assurance of one's salvation is an impossibility.

He quotes one passage from the Old Testament: "No man knoweth whether he is worthy of love or hatred." (Ecclesiastes ix. 1.) This is a difficult passage, but looking at what immediately goes before it, and what immediately follows, it seems to mean that "in this world, the providence of God makes no open and marked distinction between the righteous and the wicked." The Vulgate here does not quite correctly translate the original. As I shall afterwards show, the Bible, in the plainest language possible, teaches that one can be sure that he is saved. One part of God's word never really contradicts another. His Grace next quotes in full the following passages from the New Testament, which I shall merely indicate: "Working out salvation with fear and trembling." (Philippians ii. 12.) "The just man scarcely saved." (1 Peter iv. 18.) "Making sure our calling and election." (2 Peter i. 10.) "Taking heed least we fall." (1 Corinthians x. 12.) I cannot go fully into a discussion of the question here brought up. I would just say in reply, that God's keeping His people from perishing does not in the least free them from the obligation to labour by keeping His commandments. While they trust wholly in Him to keep them from falling, and to present them faultless before the presence of His glory with exceeding joy, they must work the very same as if they could save themselves. That God works in them, instead of being a reason why they should do nothing, is a reason why they should work out their own salvation with fear and trembling. (Philippians ii. 12.)

Let us now look at some passages which prove that assurance of one's salvation is a possibility. Christ says that whosoever believes in Him shall not perish but have everlasting life. (John iii. 15, 16.) If, then, we believe in Him—that is, trust wholly in Him—we cannot perish. To say that we can, is to make Him a liar. John the Baptist says: "He that believeth on the Son hath everlasting life." (36 v.) If, then, we believe on Christ, heaven has already begun with us. Christ says that His people shall never perish. (x. 28, 29.) Paul says that where God has begun a good work, He will finish it. (Philippians i. 6.) God says: "I will never leave thee, nor forsake thee. (Hebrews xiii. 5.) This promise refers to the soul, as well as to the body. Peter says that God's people are kept by His power through faith unto salvation, that is, their glorification. (1 Peter i. 5.) These are promises which are the foundation of assurance. Let us now look at one or two expressions thereof. "Neither death, nor life, etc., shall be able to separate us from the love of God which is in Christ Jesus our Lord." (Romans viii. 38, 39.) "We know that . . . we have a building of God," etc. (2 Corinthians v. 1.) "Our conversation is in heaven; from whence also we look for the Saviour," etc. (Philippians iii. 20, 21.) "I know whom I have believed," etc., "The Lord shall deliver me from every evil work," etc. (2 Timothy i. 12; iv. 18.) "These things have I written unto you . . . . that ye may know that ye have eternal life." (1 John iv. 13.)

"We must entertain strong hopes of salvation through the merits of Jesus Christ, and keep His commandments."

Here, the Archbishop is thoroughly evangelical. If we look for salvation wholly to the merits of Christ, we are fully warranted to entertain the strongest hopes possible—in other words, assurance. No one who entertains such hopes, shall hereafter find himself a castaway. He who rests on Christ will keep His commandments. Faith "establishes the law." (Romans iii. 31.)

Notwithstanding what I have said on the passage just quoted, I must add that His Grace has very confused ideas regarding the merits of Christ. Here, he plainly speaks of them being simply accounted to us, and of us obtaining salvation only in that way. In his Answer to Q. 90, he speaks of them being infused into the soul. If they were, they would become ours, not legally, but actually, which is utterly impossible. In his Answer to Q. 41, he speaks of our good works being meritorious, when joined with the merits of Christ, for atoning for our sins. He thus represents the merits of Christ as not of sufficient value without ours.

"A certainty of salvation, which no man can have, might lead to carelessness and its consequences."

To use the "learned prelate's" own words, "the contrary can be seen in many places in the Bible." We have already seen that one *can* have a certainty of his salvation. Let us now look at what it says about the effects thereof. "Be ye steadfast, unmovable," etc. (1 Corinthians xv. 58.) "This one thing I do," etc. (Philippians iii. 13, 14.) "When Christ, who is our life, shall appear," etc. (Colossians iii. 4, 5.) "Rejoice evermore." (1 Thessalonians v. 16.) One could not, if he had not an assurance of salvation. "Denying ungodliness," etc. (Titus ii. 12-14.) "Beloved, now are we the sons of God," etc. (1 John iii. 2, 3.) Where there is assurance of salvation on a proper foundation, there will, of necessity, be holy activity.

The paragraph which we have just been considering, is directly opposed to the one immediately before it. If a certainty of salvation be apt to be followed by the bad results of which the Archbishop speaks in the latter of the order of these, instead of "entertaining strong hopes of salvation," as he says in the former, we "must" do, we "must entertain" strong doubts thereof—the stronger the better.

Q. 92.—"Has God destined some people for heaven—others for hell?"

A.—" No."

The Archbishop then proceeds to give his reasons for saying so. These we shall presently consider. The doctrine which he clearly has in view, is the Calvinistic one of election, though, as is almost invariably the case with its opponents, he does not state it fairly. It is distinctly taught by Augustine, one whom the Archbishop's Church counts among its saints, the mediators of intercession. I do not use this fact as an argument to prove that the doctrine is true. I use it merely to show how vain is the boast of the Church of Rome that she is one in doctrine. I have not space here to discuss fully a doctrine so mysterious as this one is. My object in this work is not so much to fully defend doctrines which I believe, as to reply to His Grace's arguments against them. I shall, therefore, here notice only what the "learned prelate" says against election.

"It would be the greatest blasphemy to suppose that a God so infinitely just and merciful could act thus."

This is a reply to the whole question, which is twofold, and, therefore, to the first part, as well as to the second. Let one read the first part of the question, and then the passage in the answer just quoted, and he will be amused at the result.

"The most cruel earthly tyrants can torture their enemies, but they cannot create them for torture."

They would do the latter, if they could. If they could create any for torture, they would, of course, create innocent beings. The "learned prelate's" language under consideration, is very foggy—"mysterious above my comprehension." This seems to be his meaning—that because "the most cruel earthly tyrants *cannot* create their enemies for torture, God *would* not create innocent beings for it." Most inconclusive reasoning! That creatures *cannot* do a certain thing, does not prove that God *would* not. I firmly believe that God would not bring any one into being, just to damn him, but the Archbishop's argument here does not prove that He would not.

In His decree regarding the wicked, "God appears as a judge, fixing, beforehand, the punishment of the guilty; and His decree is only a purpose of acting towards them according to the natural course of justice. Their own sin is the procuring cause of their final ruin, and, therefore, God does them no wrong." Your Grace, though you reject the doctrine of God's eternal decrees, you surely will not reject that of His eternal foreknowledge of all things. Now, Christ said of Judas: "Good were it for that man if he had not been born." Yet, God gave Judas being, though He knew from all eternity what he would do, and what his end would be. I challenge you to get yourself out of this difficulty.

"God gives to all His creatures means to gain heaven : if they do not use them, it is their own fault, not the fault of God."

The Archbishop here seems to represent God as a father who gives every one of his sons enough to set him up in business, and then leaves him to "sink or swim." If any fail, it is not the father's fault. Now, it is quite true that man sins freely, but it is no less true that, without the grace of God, he cannot keep His commandments, and do those things which are pleasing in His sight. Christ says: "No man can come to Me, except the Father which hath sent Me draw him. (John vi. 44.) Man's inability of himself to turn to God, is strikingly represented by the figures of a new birth, a creation, and a resurrection. Paul says: "I have planted, Apollos watered, but God gave the increase." (1 Corinthians iii. 6.) If the sinner can change his own heart, it is as needless to pray to God to change it, as it would be for a farmer to pray to Him to plough and sow his fields. At the same time, man's free agency in sinning, is as clearly taught in Scripture. Christ says: "Ye will not come to Me that ye might have life." (John v. 40.) We cannot harmonize God's work in man, and man's free agency—man's inability, and his accountability. We must accept these doctrines simply on the authority of God's word, in which they are stated with equal clearness. Here, again, we find His Grace at variance with St. Augustine, though he solemnly promised to expound Scripture according to "the unanimous consent of the Fathers." Yea, he is at variance with himself. In his Answer to Q. 36, he says that Christ gives grace and mercy to His true followers. In his Answer to Q. 41, he says that good works are the effects of the grace of God operating in men's souls. In his Answer to Q. 56, he says that in the combat with the enemies of our salvation, we frail mortals require all the graces and mercy from God, through Christ and the sacraments of His Church. In his Answer to Q. 90, he says that the poor sinner requires strength from above through extreme unction. In his Answer to Q. 94—one which we have yet to consider—he says that few of the heathen will be able to live according to the light which they have, "unaided by the grace of our Lord Jesus Christ."

"God predestined for heaven those whom He foreknows will freely keep His commandments."

Bad English, here, Your Grace. Say: "who He foreknew would." Your theology in this quotation is like the landlady's coffee, of which her boarder said, "very good—what there is of it." God knew from all eternity who would keep His commandments. Those who keep them, do so freely. I take your words just as they stand. But you plainly mean that God chose to save those of whom you speak, on the ground of what He foresaw in them. In other words, He chose them because He foresaw that they would choose Him. Now, Paul says that God "hath chosen us in Christ before the foundation of the world, that we should be holy and without blame before Him in love." (Ephesians i. iv.) Here, our holiness is said to be the *consequence* of our election, not the *cause* of it. Only by the grace of God, His people are what they are. (1 Corinthians xv. 10.) As an intelligent Being, He, of course, did not bestow His grace on them without purposing beforehand to do so. That purpose must have been in His mind from all eternity, otherwise He would be a changeable Being. Yet God's decree and man's freedom are in perfect harmony, though we cannot understand it.

"It would be unworthy of God to force any man to love and obey Him."

God cannot. Such obedience would be His own. The feelings and actions of one being never can be those of another. The doctrine that God is almighty, does not mean that He can act contrary to His perfections, or do what is a contradiction. He cannot lie. He cannot repent as man can. He cannot make a being that is self-existent and everywhere present, that knows all things and can do all things. He cannot make a square circle, or a foursided triangle.

Q. 93.—"As Christ died and paid the ransom for all mankind, will not all be saved, no matter what they do ?"

A.—"No. Christ ransomed all, and called them from bondage; but all, though ransomed, do not accept the call."

If all be "called from bondage," all must be saved. "Who hath called you out of darkness into His marvellous light." (1 Peter ii. 9.)

"'Many are called, but few are chosen,' because they do not keep God's law. 'If you will enter into life,' says Christ, 'keep the commandments.'" (Matt. xix. 17.)

The words in the last of these passages were addressed to one who hoped to merit heaven by his own works. Christ gave him to understand that in order to do so, he must always and perfectly keep the commandments; yea, that he must have done so in the past part of his life. But the Bible teaches most distinctly that we are saved "by grace through faith, . . not of works." (Ephesians ii. 8, 9.) Though Christ has "put away sin by the sacrifice of Himself (Hebrews ix. 26), we must believe in Him. Where there is true faith in Him, there will necessarily be a holy life. Yet good works, properly so called, are not the *root* of salvation. They are only the *fruit* thereof. As Augustine says: "We work not *for* life, but *from* life." [1]

I would not have brought out in this work so much Calvinism—as it is commonly termed—had not the last three questions stated by the Archbishop, and his Answers thereto, obliged me to do so.

Q. 94.—"What will become of those who never heard of Christ, or redemption through Him?"

A.—"God is a good father, and will not punish those who had not the advantage of knowing His holy will."

This needs explanation. If by "His holy will," the Archbishop means the Gospel, what he says is quite true. God will not punish any for not having improved privileges which they have not enjoyed. But we read of people sinning without law, that is the word of God, and of the law written in the hearts of the heathen. (Romans ii. 12, 15.) God shall judge men according to the light which they have possessed.

"If these persons keep the laws of God written on their own consciences by nature herself, and do the best they know, God will be merciful to them."

The difference between "keeping the laws of God," etc., and "doing the best they know," is just the same as that between one year and twelve months. What do you mean, Your Grace, by "God will be merciful to them"? Do you mean that they will go to heaven? Well, they will, if they keep His laws as I have described in my remarks on your Answer to the last Question. But the light of nature is "insufficient to give fallen man that knowledge of God, and of His will, which is necessary unto salvation." "The Scriptures assure us that there is no salvation for sinful men in any other name but that of Jesus Christ—that there is no salvation through Him but by faith, and that there can be no faith

---

(1) See Page 122.

nor knowledge of Christ but by revelation." (Romans x. 14-17.) "God does nothing in vain; and were the light of nature sufficient to guide men to eternal happiness, it cannot be supposed that a divine revelation would have been given."[1] But it is equally true that God will deal less severely with those who have been less highly favoured than He will with those who have been more highly favoured. (Matthew xi. 20-24; Luke xii. 47, 48.)

"But how few will do this, unaided by the grace of our Lord Jesus Christ; hence the necessity of sending to these people missionaries to preach to them the true doctrines of Christ, and to administer to them Baptism, and the other Sacraments instituted by our Divine Redeemer, for especial help to salvation."

That is, they cannot "keep the laws of God written on their consciences, etc., and do the best they know," "unaided by the grace of our Lord Jesus Christ." Therefore, in order to enable them to do so, the Gospel must be preached to them. In other words, a brighter light must be given them to enable them to make use of a feebler one. In addition to the Gospel —which they are not likely to get from the "learned prelate's" Church—they must have Baptism, Confirmation, the Mass, Orders, Penance, Marriage, and Extreme Unction. Och! but Yir Grace is a profound theologian.

Q. 95.—"What do you think of those who say 'There is no God'?"
A.—"There are some people who wish to proclaim that there is no God."

They do not *wish* to proclaim it. They actually proclaim it. The question just asked, says so.

"These fools believe in themselves, and always think they are some great people."

Quite correct, Your Grace. Lay on, and do not spare these atheistical fellows.

---

(1) Shaw on the Confession of Faith. Chap. I. Sect. 1.

"Now, who are those who believe in God?"

That seems a very easy question, but let us hear the Archbishop's Answer to it.

"They are the wise, the religious, and best instructed, and most numerous the world ever saw."

A choice specimen of "the Archbishop's English." Hurrah! Yir Lardship's Rivirince, there's many a schoolboy that cud roite betther English than that. Its mesilf that's graved to be compilled to say that same.

"Those who deny the existence of God are to be severely punished for their sins, if God exist,—

Here, the "learned prelate" is thoroughly orthodox.

"and hence they wish to deny his existence altogther."

We have already seen that they do not merely *wish* to deny it, but that they actually do so. The Archbishop, no doubt, means that they try to prove that a personal God is nothing but a fable. He expresses himself in a very clumsy manner.

"They acknowledge that they exist themselves, and that they did not create themselves, and that the first man and woman certainly must have been created. They could not make themselves."

To what is here said about themselves, infidels will assent. But to what is said about the first man and the first woman, they will not. Many believe that the latter came by degrees from monkeys, and these from still lower beings, till, at last, we come to a "fortuitous concourse of atoms." There is, however, a great variety of opinion among infidels. In fact, their creed seems to be just this: "Anything, anything but the Old Book."

"The Darwinian theory, the most absurd that ever was invented, has no foundation whatsoever to rest on, except on the ravings of a disorganized brain."

Allow me, Your Grace, to correct your English once more. Say: "except the ravings," etc. These are the foundation of which you speak.

"In the geology of the world all the discoveries prove the Darwinian theory to be an hallucination."

Your Grace, we have nothing to do with the geology of the sun, moon, or any of the stars. It would, therefore, be better to say: "all the discoveries in geology prove" etc.

"Fossils have been found in the strata and drift of every age of the world, but no incipient man in his state of transition from a monkey, has been discovered, nor any animals in their transient condition from atom to animal."

Your Grace, you would not succeed as a Professor of Geology. There are strata in which no fossils are found. I wrote to an eminent geologist, asking information on this very question. I give some extracts from his answer, but as they would take up too much space here, I shall put them into the Appendices.[1] I would just say, before going on, that they prove your statement, that "fossils have been found in the strata and drift of every age of the world," to be incorrect. You distinguish between men and animals. Man is the species of which animal is the genus. You know a little Latin. You, therefore, know that "animal" means simply "a living being." All men, then, are animals, though all animals are not men.

Here we find ourselves at the end of His Grace's "little book."

Gentle Reader, I am sure that as we have been going together through it, your experience has been like that of "Misther Maloney," at the "Christhial Exibishun" already referred to, which he thus describes:—

> "Fresh wondhers grows
> Before me nose,
> In this subloime Musayùm."

(1) See Appendix XXIII.

Very often, we have found His Grace's ideas comical, his composition clumsy, his scholarship contracted, and his reasoning confused.

With him, the question concerning Purgatory is settled. His state is now fixed for ever. Yet a little while, at the very longest, and thou and I, Reader, also, shall go hence, and be no more. There is nothing more certain than that we shall do so—nothing more uncertain than when we shall. But if we be in Christ, the moment we are absent from the body, we shall be present with the Lord.

> "Done is the work that saves!
> Once and for ever done!
> Finished the righteousness
> That clothes the unrighteous one."

We have simply to trust wholly in that work—that righteousness. Reader, if thou have not already done so, do it at once. What a solemn thought it is that every thought that we think, every word that we utter, and every act that we do, tells on the eternity before us. This life is like the vessel which the potter is shaping. He can do with it as he pleases. But he cannot, after it has been hardened in the furnace. Death does, in a moment, to our life, what the furnace does, by degrees, to the potter's vessel. Reader, that thou mayest be saved, is my heart's desire and prayer to God for thee.[1]

(1) See Appendix XXIV.

Note on Review of "Answer" to Question 33,
(PAGE 98.)

"*The rich man died and was buried in hell,*" etc. After my criticism on this statement of the Archbishop's was printed, I compared the latter with the corresponding passage in the Vulgate. I find that His Grace is supported by his own Bible, and, therefore, the printer has not blundered in this case, The Vulgate distinctly says that the rich man was buried in hell — that is, the place which we now commonly call by that name. Its words are these: "*Mortuus est autem et dives, et sepultus est in inferno.*" (Luke xvi. 22.) A most ridiculous translation. The Greek is: "*Apethanē de kai ho plousios, kai etaphē. Kai en tō hadē eparas tous ophthalmous autou,*" etc. (22, 23.) Both the Authorized and the Revised Versions make his burial, and his being in "hell," two perfectly distinct things — which is the correct rendering. The Revised Version has, instead of "hell," "Hades," that is, here, simply "the place of the dead where the conscious soul of the wicked awaits judgment in anguish, afar off from the resting place of the blessed." In the Authorized Version, "hell" very often means simply the separate state between the moment of death and the resurrection. Sometimes it is applied to the abode of the righteous, sometimes to that of the wicked. It is used even in those passages which speak of Christ's "continuing under the power of death for a time." See Psalm xvi. 10; Acts ii. 31. But where the rich man in the parable was, when he prayed to Abraham, was really hell (as we now commonly understand the term) begun, for his state for woe was fixed for ever. See Luke xvi. 25, 26.

"In the period that elapses betwen death and the resurrection it must be obvious that neither the happiness of the righteous nor the misery of the wicked is complete. The time of separation of soul and body is necessarily a time of anticipation of their ultimate reunion. This anticipation is the object of hope and joy to the one, and of dread and misery to the other."—*Dr. Wardlaw.* " Many expressions of Scripture, in the natural and obvious sense, imply that an intermediate and separate state of the soul is actually to succeed death."— *R. Watson.* " According to the teaching of the early Church, the soul after death was consigned to a place of happiness or misery in Hades, and there remained till the day of judgment. . . . Tertullian alleges the example of the rich man and Lazarus as proving that the soul is now in a state of happiness or misery, awaiting its union with the body and the final award of judgment."—*Blunt's Doctrinal and Historical Theology.*

Man is a twofold being. The righteous and the wicked dead cannot, therefore, be, the one as happy and the other as miserable, as they shall be when their souls and their bodies shall be reunited. But, in the meantime, their happiness and their misery are full, according to their respective capacities.

The salvation of the righteous is completed in their glorification. See Romans viii. 30. Hence, as we often put a part for the whole, the glorification of believers is sometimes called in Scripture their salvation, because it is the last, the crowning part thereof. See Romans xiii. 11; Hebrews ix. 28; 1 Peter i. 5. In like manner, the damnation of the wicked shall not be completed till the last day.

APPENDICES.

APPENDIX I.—(*Page 1.*)

THE Archbishop's Church most distinctly teaches that heretics are to be put to death, when that can be done with safety. She may well be termed, "drunken with the blood of the saints, and with the blood of the martyrs of Jesus." (Revelations xvii. 6.) The following are a few—only a very few—proofs thereof. In less than thirty years, during the thirteenth century, half a million of "holy warriors," under Simon de Montfort, put upwards of 1,000,000 of Albigenses to death. It is said that 100,000 Albigenses fell in one day. In the fourteenth century, during thirteen years, in only one of the Waldensian valleys, that of Loyse, above 3,000 persons were destroyed. It is said that within thirty years after the establishment of the Inquisition, 900,000 Christians were put to death. The Duke of Alva boasted of having caused the execution of 18,000 Protestants in the Netherlands in six weeks. Grotius reckons the number of Belgic martyrs at 100,000. Bossuet reckons the slain only in Paris, at the St. Bartholomew Massacre in 1572, at 6,000; Davila at 10,000, and throughout France at 40,000; and Sully, the latter at 70,000. I have copies of the medal struck in honour of that event, by order of Gregory XIII., who was Pope when it took place. I bought them at the Pope's Mint in Rome. On one side is Gregory's likeness, on the other, an angel holding up a cross in his left hand, and with a sword in his right, destroying heretics. Above, is the inscription in Latin: "Slaughter of the Huguenots, 1572." I saw in the Sala Regia in the Vatican, the picture painted in honour of the same event, by Vasari, at the command of the same Pope. In the foreground, a man is lying on his back on the earth. Bending over him, is another who clutches his throat with his left hand. In his right, he holds a dagger which he is about to plunge into his body. In the middle ground, a body is being thrown from an upper window into the street. This was done to Admiral Coligny's. In the background, armed men are forcing their way into a house. All the other pictures in the hall have explanatory inscriptions beneath them. This used to have one—
"Pontifex Colignii necem probat" (The Pontiff approves of the death of

Coligny)—but it has been painted out, most probably, because it would not please Protestant visitors. In this hall, Cardinals Taschereau, Gibbons, and six others, received their scarlet hats from the Pope.

I saw in the Spanish chapel in Florence, a picture of black and white spotted dogs tearing wolves in pieces. The dogs are the Dominicans, whose dress is partly black and partly white. The wolves, of course, are heretics.

I saw over the tomb of Loyola, in Rome, a piece of sculpture representing Truth destroying Heresy. Of course, we know what is meant in this case, by the one and the other.

During the five years of "Bloody Mary's" reign in England, 300 persons suffered death for religion.

APPENDIX II.—(Page 5.)

THE following is another instance of the kind of liberty of which I speak :—

"VIVE LA LIBERTE.

"When the farce of electing General Bonaparte consul for life was being enacted, Colonel Lannes issued to his regiment the following characteristic order of the day : 'Soldiers ! We are about to take a *plebiscite* for the appointment of General Bonaparte as consul for life. Opinions are free, and I have no intention to influence any man's vote. I only wish to make it known that the first man who refuses to vote with the ayes shall be immediately shot as a traitor. *Vive la Liberte!*'"

APPENDIX III.—(Page 30.)

A M. HENRI LASSERE found—as he believed—great benefit for his sore eyes from the water of Lourdes. Moved by gratitude for it, he wrote a book entitled, "Notre Dame de Lourdes," which was the mean of bringing many to the place. At length, he found a copy of the four Gospels, which he read with great interest. With a desire to benefit his countrymen, he translated, as well as he could, into elegant French the story contained in them, arranging it as a common history. For a Roman

Catholic, the translation was a very fair one. In the preface, he expressed his regret that "the Gospel—the most illustrious book in the world—is become an unknown book." It was published with the consent of the Archbishop of Paris, and the approval and benediction of the Pope ! Edition followed edition, till the twenty-fifth appeared. Probably one hundred thousand copies were sold, at four francs (80cts.) each. As the work was under the sanction of the Pope, the copies bought were treated with all due respect. Twelve months and fifteen days after "OUR MOST HOLY LORD, POPE LEO XIII." gave it his approval and blessing, "the Sacred Congregation" discovered that an error had been committed. Straightway, a decree was issued from the Apostolic Palace of the Vatican, condemning M. Lasserre's translation, and putting it in the *Index Expurgatorius*. "An infallible blessing was removed to make room for an equally infallible curse." But, no doubt, it has been the mean of doing much good which cannot be undone. We have in this circumstance:—(1) A proof of what the present Pope thinks of permitting the people in general to read the word of God ; (2) A curious instance of Papal Infallibility. The Pope may well say of his infallibility, as *Punch* represents a British officer saying to another about going to India: "It's a hawid baw" (horrid bore).

APPENDIX IV.—(Page 29.)

I TAKE the following from the *Montreal Witness*:—

A TRIBUTE TO THE BIBLE.

The *London Christian* says that a Roman Catholic contemporary, in an article upon Sunday schools, pays the following tribute to the Bible:—

"It is certain that the Bible, even looked at as a human production, is the very best book in the world. No other is equal to it in vivid description, in varied interest, in force of expression, in power of appeal to the heart and conscience. When read intelligently so as to bring out its meaning, it never fails to make an impression on young people.

"The writer, too, goes on to quote the opinion of the Roman Catholic Bishop of Birmingham, that Bible histories 'seem to us to destroy half the beauty of the Scripture narrative, by not giving them in the Scripture language. We see no reason, so far as they may do so with propriety, why Roman Catholic children should not have the same advantage as Protestants have in a familiarity with the sacred text—a familiarity which, with Protestants, undoubtedly does more for their intellectual culture than all mere literary study put together."

To this we can only add : Neither do we. We earnestly hope thta the effect which the writer of the article attributes to the reading of the Bible, " with care and reverence, and with prayer for the grace and blessing of God," as he properly puts it, may not be confined any longer to the children in our Protestant schools.

Father Northgraves, of Ingersoll, Ont., in his " Mistakes of Modern Infidels (p. 16), says :—

"We may well conceive that as the elimination of the liberty we possess from the human soul would deprive man of an important mean of merit, that it is better that for the sake of those who will make a good use of it, God should give us that liberty, even though He knows that many will abuse it, and that He in His justice will punish such abuse."

The Father's Church should act on this principle, and say : " As not allowing people full liberty to read God's book, and judge for themselves, deprives them of a liberty which God has given them, and of an important mean of grace, it is better for the sake of those who will make a good use of it, that I should give them that liberty even though some will abuse it, leaving it with God to punish in His justice the latter class." I am an unbeliever in the kind of merit of which the Father speaks in the passage just quoted.

APPENDIX V.—(Page 38.)

ST. CALLISTUS I. was a Sabellian. St. Liberius and St. Felix II., rival Popes, were both Arians ; Vigilius and St. Martin, Eutychians ;[2] Eleutherius, a Montanist ; 'Marcellinus, an idolater ; Zosimus, a Pelagian ; Honorius, a Monothelite ; John XXII., a Materialist. John X. was made Pope by his concubine. Her daughter was the concubine of Ser-

(1) He was, also, a scoundrel. At one time he had charge of a bank, but he used undue liberties with the sums entrusted to him. When the depositors applied for their money, he had " nothing but ciphers to show for it." He then discovered that he was not very well, and believing that a change of air would do him good, "governed himself accordingly." Absconding with other people's money is, therefore, of very ancient date (third century), but I cannot see that it is, therefore, lawful. St. Callistus should be the patron saint of embezzlers.

(2) Yet Vigilius also acknowledged the Council of Chalcedon which excommunicated Eutyches. He likewise made four different confessions of faith. This was very accommodating. He was, of course, very *vigilant* for his own interests.

gius III. The latter made their son Pope. John XII., who was made Pope when he was only eighteen, was guilty of blasphemy, perjury, profanation, impiety, simony, sacrilege, adultery, incest, sodomy, and murder. He drank a health to the Devil, invoked Jupiter and Venus, lived in public adultery with the Norman matrons, and committed incest with his father's concubine. He was killed in the act of adultery, most probably, by the injured husband. Boniface VII. murdered his predecessor and his successor. He was "a thief, a miscreant, and a murderer." Gregory VII. was guilty of simony, sacrilege, magic, sorcery, treason, adultery, impiety, and murder. Boniface VIII. was guilty of the same sins, with sodomy added thereto. He said that men have the same souls that beasts have, that the Gospel is a mixture of truths and lies, that the doctrine of the Trinity is false, a virgin conceiving is impossible, the incarnation of the Son of God as ridiculous as transubstantiation, and that he believed in the Virgin no more than in a she-ass, and in her Son no more than in the foal of a she-ass. John XXIII. denied all the truths of the Gospel. He was guilty of "all mortal sins and an infinity of abominations." He violated three hundred nuns. Sixtus IV. was guilty of murder and debauchery. He established bawdy-houses in Rome, on which he laid a tax which brought him 200,000 ducats a year. Fancy the same person "Our Lord God the Pope," and head of the Roman bawdy-houses! He plotted the murder of Lorenzo and Giulio di Medici during high mass. Alexander VI., by his grossly vile life, made himself the execration of all Europe. "Rome, under his administration and by his example, became the sink of filthiness, the headquarters of atrocity, and the hotbed of prostitution, murder and robbery." Leo X. was devoid alike of religion and decency. Gregory XVI. was called by the Italians "Il Bevone" (The Drunkard). He had, at least, two children—natural ones in more senses than one. "Kirwan" (Dr. Murray) saw them in Rome—fine looking young women. More could be said, of a like kind, regarding the Popes, but let the foregoing suffice.

APPENDIX VI.—(Page 35.)

IN the cathedral of Santa Maria del Fiore, in Florence, there is an old tablet on which is an inscription in Latin, in which the Virgin Mary is called the Mother of God (Deipara), but not the slightest reference to her Immaculate Conception is made.

The Franciscans and the Dominicans were most bitterly opposed to each other on this very question. The former maintained that the Virgin

Mary was conceived without the taint of original sin. The latter denied it. Both parties, to prove that they were in the right, sometimes used means which were not " over proper."

Keenan's "Controversial Catechism" received the approval and license of the late Archbishop Hughes. The editions published in Britain in 1846 and 1853, bear the formal approbations of the four Roman Catholic Bishops in Scotland. In it is the following :—"Q. Must not Catholics believe the Pope himself to be infallible ?" "A. *This is a Protestant invention; it is no article of the Catholic Faith;* no decision of his can bind, on pain of heresy, unless it be received and enforced by the teaching body, that is, by the Bishops of the Church." Since the Vatican Council, this has been removed from the work, but pains have been taken to make it seem the *very same edition*—nay, the very same thousand of that edition—and no hint of any change is given.

Bishop Langevin, of Rimouski, once recommended me to read Milner's "End of Religious Controversy." Well, here is a passage from that work: "The Church does not decide the controversy concerning the conception of the Blessed Virgin, and several other disputed points, because she sees nothing absolutely clear and certain concerning them, either in the written or the unwritten word ; and therefore leaves her children to form their own opinions concerning them. She does not dictate an exposition of the whole Bible, because she has no tradition concerning a great proportion of it." (*Letter XII.*, p. 169.)

Any one who now speaks thus of the conception of the Virgin Mary, is, according to the Church of Rome, damned. Yea, the same is true of any one who has ever done so (alas ! for poor Milner), for, according to her, it has ever been an article of faith in the Church that the Virgin Mary was conceived without sin.

Bishop Langevin is one of those who, so to speak, made the Virgin Mary immaculate in her conception. A marble tablet in St. Peter's, Rome, near the so-called chair of that Apostle, records the fact just stated.

The Rev. D. A. Gallitizen—one of the shining lights, in controversy, of the Romish Church—says, in " A Defence of Catholic Principles " (p. 147) : " I shall not lose any time in defending the infallibility of the Pope, *which never was an article of Catholic communion ;* our creed or profession of faith, printed in all countries and in all languages, and to be seen by anybody who chooses to read with open eyes, *contains no such article.*"

APPENDIX VII.—(Page 35.)

THEY have been persecuted by the Romish Church, some say thirty-three times, others thirty-six. One of the severest persecutions which they suffered, was in 1686. Their Church-mark—to use a commercial phrase—is a lighted candle on a dark background, under an arch of seven stars, and the motto *Lux lucet in tenebris* (The light shineth in darkness). [1] Another device which they often use, is a lily among thorns, and the motto, *Emergo* (I come out).

APPENDIX VIII.—(Page 38.)

THE following is a list of the dates at, or about which, certain doctrines and practices appeared, or were officially proclaimed, in the Archbishop's Church. It shows clearly how vain is her boast that she is "always the same." "Those who live in glass houses should not throw stones":—

	A.D.
Prayers for the dead, making the sign of the cross, and the observance of Good Friday, Easter, and Whitsunday, about	200
Exorcism, fasting, burning of incense, and the doctrine of Baptismal regeneration	250
Gorgeous robes, mitres, croziers, tapers, the worship of images, relics, saints and angels, and the observance of Lent, Christmas, and Ascension Day	375
Worship of the Virgin Mary	450
Processions before Easter	535
Worship in Latin	600
The Pope made universal Bishop	606
Adoration of the Cross	631
All Saints' Day	830
The Rosary, and Consecration of Bells	965
All Souls' Day, and Canonization of Saints	998
The celibacy of the priests made obligatory	1074
The doctrine of the Infallibility of the Church	1076
The use of the Scapulary	1090
The canon of the Mass	1110
Festival of the Immaculate Conception	1138
The doctrine that there are seven Sacraments	1160
Sale of Indulgences	1190

(1) See end of Preface.

viii.   APPENDIX IX.

Dogma of Transubstantiation decreed, and Auricular Confession
    made obligatory 1215
Elevation of the Host 1220
Festival of Corpus Christi 1264
Year of Jubilee appointed to be kept every hundredth year . . . 1299
The " Hail, Mary," appointed to be used in prayer 1325
Procession of the Host 1336
Year of Jubilee changed to every fiftieth year 1350
The cup officially withheld from the laity 1415
Dogma of Purgatory decreed 1430
Year of Jubilee changed to every twenty-fifth year 1468
Doctrines of human merits and of satisfactions, the Vulgate officially
    declared to be superior to the Scriptures in the original lan-
    guages, the Apocrypha to be a part of the word of God, and
    tradition to be of divine authority 1546
Dogma of the Immaculate Conception 1854
Dogma of the Pope's Infallibility 1870

APPENDIX IX.—(*Page 38.*)

SEVERAL years ago, I read a statement in the newspapers to the following effect: Among the papers left behind him, by a minister of the Church of England, who had lately died, there was found a dispensation from the Pope permitting him to marry. Other papers proved that the "Holy Father" had granted the same privilege to several of his brother ministers. Of course, by their marrying, they would the more hoodwink Protestants, and be the more able to advance the interests of the Church of Rome, which, in her eyes, would be, as His Grace expresses it, "to the greater honour and glory of God." That what I have just related did happen, is not impossible. "For ways that are dark," the "heathen Chinee" cannot surpass "Mother Church." There is a common saying : "All's fair in love or war." She says : "All's fair for the greater honour and glory of God," that is, extending her power.

    The late Sir Allan Macnab, of Hamilton, Ont., was, at first, a Protestant in name. Towards the end of his life, he became a Romanist. He showed the Bishop that if he were to avow publicly his change of religious profession, he would be elected to a seat in his own house, instead of one for Hamilton in Parliament. The Bishop, therefore, allowed him to act as if he were a good member of the Church of England. Scarcely any of his friends knew about Sir Allan's hypocrisy, till they came to his funeral, which was conducted according to the rites of the Romish Church.

APPENDIX X.—(*Page 43.*)

In the Holy Synod of the Greek Church, composed of the Metropolitan, archbishops, and bishops, rests all spiritual power as to worship, discipline, etc. Only as regards temporal affairs is the Emperor of Russia chief. " He only claims the right as emperor to receive appeals from the ecclesiastical courts, and to give law to priests as well as to the rest of his subjects. He is head of the Church in much the same sense as the kings of England and the German princes are, none of whom ever presumes to administer the sacraments, or to perform any appropriate functions of a clergyman or priest."—*Murdock's Mosheim.*

APPENDIX XI.—(*Page 46.*)

"CANDIDLY compare Connaught and Ulster, in Ireland. In the one, Popery almost exclusively prevails; in the other, Protestantism is in the ascendency. What a difference between them! Compare Ireland and Scotland—and although the land of St. Patrick is far richer than that of St. Andrew, yet how heaven-wide the difference between them! Compare Spain with England, Italy with Prussia, Rome with Edinburgh, Belfast with Cork—how wide the difference! Come across the Atlantic and continue the comparison on our own Western continent. Compare Mexico to New England, Brazil[1] to these United States, the city of Mexico to that of Boston, or New York, or Cincinnati! How great the contrast! Come yet nearer home. Compare the worshippers at St. Peter's in Barclay Street with those at St. Paul's in Broadway; compare the attendance on your own ministry at St. Patrick's with those who worship God at the Brick Church, or at La Fayette Place, or at University Place. How wide the difference intellectually, socially, morally! And why is it that Papal countries and communities thus suffer, and so sadly suffer, when contrasted with other communities where there is an unshackled conscience and an open Bible? There must be some general law or cause in operation to produce results so uniform. What is that law or cause? Sir, it is the influence of that system of religion which you are seeking with so much zeal and ability to extend. The traveller in Europe need not be told when he crosses the lines that separate Papal from Protestant States; the obvious marks of higher civilization declare the transition with almost as

(1) Since this was written, Brazil has begun to show that she will not be domineered over by the Romish Church.

much plainness as would a broad river or a chain of mountains. Popery, with infallible certainty, degrades man. Do you ask how? In this wise:

"It takes from him the Bible, the revealed will of God, with all its clear light, with all its high motives to excite the soul to high and holy action ; and without which neither civilization nor religion can be long maintained."—*Kirwan's Letters to Bishop [afterwards Archbishop] Hughes· First Series, Letter V.*

The liberty which Italy now enjoys, she owes, not to Protestants, but to professing Romanists. It grieved them to see their beloved country, in consequence of Papal rule, so far below Protestant ones. They were willing to yield the Pope all due obedience in spiritual things, but not in temporal. They, therefore, arose in their might, and "broke his bands asunder, and cast away his cords from them," as regards the latter. May the time soon come when they shall do the same as regards the former!

APPENDIX XII.—(*Page 54.*)

A STILL better authority—the London Religious Tract Society—gives the following numbers: Roman Catholics, 190 millions; Protestants, 174 millions ; those belonging to the Greek Church, 80 millions.

The Rev. James Johnston, F.S.S., has been comparing the increase of population during the last hundred years with the respective increases of Protestants, Roman Catholics, and followers of the Greek Church, and the result is very striking. Protestants in Europe have increased from 37,700,000 to 134,000,000, or nearly fourfold ; Roman Catholics from 80,190,000 to 163,000,000, or twofold , and the Greek Church from 40,000,000 to 83,000,000, also twofold. Of course, it is impossible, in a case like this, to obtain perfect exactness.

It has been stated, on good authority, that had all the natural increase of the Roman Catholic population in the United States, from 1800 till now, remained with that Church, they would to-day number over 22,000,000, instead of only 9,000,000 or 10,000,000.

APPENDIX XIII.—(*Page 67.*)

" WE will first take the two passages in the Gospel of St. Matthew. For the purposes of this argument, the words addressed to St. Peter need not be distinguished from the words addressed to the disciples, as they are in each case identically the same.

APPENDIX XIII.

" I. The phrase 'binding' and 'loosing' meant, in the language of the Jewish schools, declaring what is right and what is wrong. If any Master, or Rabbi, or Judge declared a thing to be right or true, he was said to have loosed it; if he declared a thing to be wrong or false, he was said to have bound it. That this is the original meaning of the words has been set at rest beyond possibility of question since the decisive quotations given by the most learned Hebrew scholars of the seventeenth century." "They—the despised scholars of a despised Master—were to declare what was changeable and what was unchangeable, what was eternal, what was transitory, what was worthy of approval, and what was worthy of condemnation." "Eighteen hundred years have passed, and their judgments in all essential points have never been reversed." " . . . if, as is commonly supposed, the words (John xx. 23), by some peculiar turn of the Fourth Gospel, are identical in meaning with these in St. Matthew. In that case, all that we have said of the address to Peter and the address to the disciples in the First Gospel applies equally to this address in the Fourth."

" II. Such, then, was the promise, as spoken in the first instance. In the literal sense of the words, this fulfilment of them can hardly occur again." (*Stanley's Christian Institutions,* chap. vii., pp. 144, 145, 147.)

"'The keys of the kingdom of heaven' simply means the power of admitting proper persons to the Church, and excluding improper persons from it. Keys, you know, were the ancient emblems of authority." "To bind and to loose here (Matt. xvi. 19) are equivalent to bidding and forbidding, to granting and refusing, to declaring lawful or unlawful. The Apostles were endued with the Holy Ghost, that they might infallibly declare the will of God to mankind, and determine what was, or was not, binding on the conscience—to show what persons ought, or ought not, to be admitted to the Church—and to decide on the characters of those whose sins were, or were not, forgiven. And whatsoever in these, or similar things, they bound or loosed on earth, would be bound or loosed in heaven. This is also the meaning of John xx. 22, 23, already quoted. This, Sir, I believe to be the common sense, the fair and just interpretation, of a passage on which your Church has built up a priestly power, that has overshadowed the earth and enslaved nations. Where now, Sir, is your supremacy of Peter—your power of the keys—your power of absolution? Gone, like the morning cloud before the sun." (*Kirwan's Letters to Bishop* [*afterwards Archbishop*] *Hughes.* Second Series, Letter III.)

APPENDIX XIV.—(*Page 78.*)

St. Buonaventura's Psalter has the Psalms and the *Te Deum* both altered so as to apply to the Virgin Mary. More than once it has been approved by the Vatican authorities. It is published in Rome, in Italian, and sold for two pence. The following is a translation of the *Te Deum* as it appears there. It may well be called the *Te Deam* ("Thee, O Goddess"):—

" We cause our praises to ascend to Thee, O Mother of God; we extol Thee, O Mary the Virgin.
All the earth worships Thee, the Spouse of the Eternal Father.
To Thee, all Angels and Archangels, to Thee all Thrones and Principalities humbly bow themselves down.
To Thee, all the Powers and the highest Intelligences in the heavens, and all Dominions yield obedience.
To Thee, all Choirs, to Thee, Cherubim and Seraphim joyously minister.
To Thee, all angelic creatures continually sing with the voice of praise.
Holy, Holy, Holy Mary, Mother of God, Virgin and also Mother.
The heavens and the earth are full of the glorious majesty of the fruit of thy womb.
The glorious choir of the Apostles unitedly praise Thee, the Mother of its Creator.
The pure assembly of the blessed Martyrs in concert extol Thee, the Mother of Christ.
The glorious army of the Confessors calls Thee the holy temple of the Trinity.
The lovely choir of the holy Virgins joyously praise Thee, the example of humility and of Virgin purity.
The whole heavenly choir honours Thee as Queen.
The Church throughout all the world acknowledges Thee, and calls on Thee.
Mother of the Divine Majesty.
The venerable, the true Spouse of the King of heaven, holy, loving and pious.
Thou art the Mistress of the Angels, Thou art the gate of Paradise.
Thou art the ladder to the kingdom and the glory of heaven.
Thou art the marriage bed, Thou art the ark of piety and of grace.
Thou art the source and spring of mercy; Thou art the Spouse and Mother of the King of eternal ages.
Thou art the temple and sanctuary of the Holy Spirit, and the noble dining hall of the most holy Trinity.

Thou art the mediatrix between men and God, kind to us mortals and the light of heaven.

Thou art boldness to those fighting, an advocate to sinners; Thou art a compassionate refuge to the wretched.

Thou art the dispenser of heavenly gifts, the destroyer of devils and of the proud.

Thou art the Mistress of the world, the Queen of Heaven, and, after God, our only hope.

Thou art salvation to every one who seeks Thee, a haven to the shipwrecked, comfort to the wretched, and a refuge to those in peril.

Thou art the Mother of all the Blessed, after God, their full joy, the joy of all the inhabitants of heaven.

Thou art the promoter of the righteous, the receiver of the strayed, Thou art the Promise of old to the Patriarchs.

Thou wert the light of truth to the Prophets; Thou wert the praise of the Apostles and their wisdom; Thou wert the teacher of the Evangelists.

Thou wert boldness to the Martyrs, an example to the Confessors, the boast, the glory and joy of the Virgins.

To free man from the exile of death, Thou didst receive the Son of God into thy womb.

When Thou hadst vanquished our old Foe, the kingdom of heaven was opened again to the faithful.

Thou, with thy Son, art seated at the right hand of the Father.

O, Virgin Mary, Thou intercedest for us with Him who we believe shall one day be our Judge.

We, therefore, pray Thee that Thou wouldst come to the help of thy servants; to us redeemed with the precious blood of thy Son.

O, pious Virgin Mary, hear us! cause us to be rewarded with eternal joy with thy Saints.

Save thy people, O Lady, that we may be made partakers of the inheritance of thy Son.

Be our guide, our support and defence for ever.

Every day, O Mary, our Lady, we salute Thee.

And we desire to sing thy praises with heart and voice for ever.

Vouchsafe, O sweetest Mary, now and ever, to preserve us from sin.

O Pious One, have mercy on us; have mercy on us!

Show mercy to thy children: for in Thee, O Virgin Mary, we have put all our trust.

In Thee, sweetest Mary, we all hope: defend us for ever.

To Thee be the praises, to Thee the kingdom, to Thee the power and the glory for ever and ever. Amen.

APPENDIX XIV.

Compare the foregoing with the original, of which the following is a metrical version :—

TE DEUM LAUDAMUS.

"We praise Thee, O God: we acknowledge Thee to be the Lord," etc.
—(*Old Latin Hymn.*)

To Thee, O God, we joyous raise
Our voices in a song of praise.
As Him who over all has sway,
To Thee we hearty homage pay.
With rev'rence, all the earth to Thee,
Eternal Father, bows the knee.
All angels and all pow'rs on high,
Aloud to Thee in concert cry.
Ever to Thee ascends the hymn
Of cherubim and seraphim,
O holy, holy, holy, Lord,
The God of Hosts; the rays which poured
Abroad are by Thy majesty,
With brightness fill immensity.
Thee praise, those whom Christ gave command
To preach His cross in ev'ry land.
Thee praise, those who before made known
The coming of th' Anointed One.
Thee praise, those who held fast the faith,
And their lives lov'd not to the death.
The holy Church, in ev'ry place,
Unites with heart to seek Thy face,
The Father of a majesty
Extending through infinity ;
Him whom we for our Saviour own,
Thy glorious, true, and only Son ;
Also the Spirit who imparts
The balm of joy to bleeding hearts.
O Christ, to Thee we praises sing,
Thee who of glory art the King.
Thou, when to save man Thou did'st come,
Abhorredst not the Virgin's womb.
When o'er death's bitter agony,
Thou had'st obtained the victory,
A place in heav'n Thou did'st provide
For all who in Thy blood confide.

APPENDIX XV.

Thou sitt'st at God's right hand on high,
Clothed with the Father's majesty.
Thou shalt return, and righteously
Shall quick and dead be judged by Thee.
Help, therefore, on Thine own bestow,
Saved by Thy blood from endless woe.
A place appoint them, Lord, we pray,
Among Thy saints in endless day.
Thy people send deliverance,
And bless Thine own inheritance.
Rule o'er them by Thy mighty pow'r,
And lift them up for evermore.
We magnify Thee day by day,
And worship Thy great name for aye.
Help us, O Lord, that, this day, we
May from all sin ourselves keep free.
To us, O Lord, Thy mercy show,
Who merit naught but endless woe.
Lord, cause to shine on us Thy face,
As in Thee all our trust we place.
Lord, I have trusted in Thy name,
Then let me ne'er be put to shame.   T. F.

The Litany of the Blessed Virgin is the Litany altered so as to apply to her. I have room for only the following specimen thereof: "In all time of our tribulation, in all time of our wealth, in the hour of death, and in the day of judgment, from all torments of the damned deliver us, O Virgin Mary."

In the *Pouvoir de Marie* (published in France) for April, 1890, is the following: "We see at last, that according to the purposes of the divine Goodness, the Blessed Virgin *having to give her consent* that the Son of God should become our Saviour, and having given it with perfectly free will, she also has willed and procured our salvation."

APPENDIX XV.—(*Page 81.*)

IN the Piazza di Spagna, not far from the buildings of the Society of the Propaganda, in one direction, and the Depository of the Bible Society, in another, is a magnificent pillar in honour of the Immaculate Conception. The statue of Moses at the base has an open Bible on which is the original of Genesis iii. 15. Mr. Ben Oliel, the missionary to the Jews in

Rome, his brethren, his kinsmen according to the flesh, remarked to me that though the Church of Rome has mistranslated that passage in the Vulgate, so as to make it apply to the Virgin, she has not dared to alter the original in that inscription, thereby publicly condemning herself.

In the square of St. Dominic, in Bologna, there is a monument in honour of the Virgin. It is of brick, which is to be veneered with white marble. A part has been veneered evidently a good while ago. The exposed brickwork is becoming very mossy. The whole has a neglected look.

APPENDIX XVI.—(Page 110.)

THIS is the case, for example, in the Church of St. Eustache in Paris, where St. Geneviève is buried, in St. Peter's Cathedral, and St. Paul's Church in Rome, where are said to be parts of the bodies of these saints, and in the Gesu in the same city, where Loyola is buried. When I saw the tomb of St. Geneviève, in 1885, a priest in a surplice was standing beside it, reading prayers. In St. Peter's, eighty-six gold lamps are kept perpetually burning.[1]

APPENDIX XVII.—(Page 112.)

ST. VERONICA is said to have handed our Lord her handkerchief when He was on His way to Calvary. He wiped His face with it, and returned it to her with His likeness on it. According to other accounts, it was she who wiped His face with it. The result was the same. This handkerchief is one of the relics in St. Peter's. The *vera icon*, or *true likeness* of Christ, said to be on it, has been mistaken for the name of a woman, and she has been made a saint. St. Longinus (in Greek, *longche*) was merely a spear. St. Amphibolus was merely a cloak. St. Almachius was merely the word *Almanac* at the head of the Romish calendar. St. Syridoni was merely the name of Syria. St. Nilammonis was merely the names Nile and Ammon. Rome honours St. Julian, the martyr, and five thousand who suffered with him. His fellow martyrs were only five. The contracted Latin word for soldiers was mistaken for a thousand. Rome honours also Florentinus and Felix, officers who were martyred with eighty-three soldiers. This took place eighty-three miles from Rome. The contracted Latin word for miles has been mistaken for soldiers. These blunders are in the Reformed Martyrology published by Gregory XIII., whose name is

---

(1) Hare, in his "Walks in Rome," gives this number. Other writers give different numbers, some as many as a hundred. But, as Hare is usually very correct in his details, it is quite likely that he is so here too.

connected with the St. Bartholomew Massacre. In a Bull, he commands it, and no other, to be used ; forbids it to be changed in any way, and threatens with the indignation of Almighty God and of the Apostles Peter and Paul, any who do not obey his decree concerning it. St. Prothais, St. Petronilla, a St. Marguerite, the eleven thousand virgins whose remains are said to be in Cologne, and St. Philomena, are all only imaginary saints. One has poor encouragement to pray to them, but prayers to them avail just as much as those which are addresssed to dead real saints. In the Romish Breviary, St. Raphael is prayed to. He is an imaginary saint, an angel, the proof of whose being we have only in that nonsensical book Tobit, which forms part of the Apocrypha. One may as well pray to a lady's ruffle, or a child's rattle, as to St. Raphael. He who prays to him is like a barrel-organist performing before an empty house. Last year, eight Syrian immigrants—six men and two women —arrived at Castle Garden, New York. While they were delayed there, they went into a restaurant. On one of the walls they saw a likeness of Ingersoll, the Arch-Blasphemer of America, which they took to be that of some saint. Accordingly, they kissed it, fell on their knees before it, and "spake in their heart ; only their lips moved, but their voice was not heard." A poor woman once went into a Roman Catholic church in Montreal, where she saw a picture of the Archangel Michael bruising Satan under his feet. She supposed the latter to be a saint suffering for righteousness sake, and, accordingly, as a "good Catholic," paid him due honour. It is just as useful to pray to St. Ingersoll and St. Diabolus, as to, at least, the imaginary saints in the Romish Calendar.

I shall now mention a few relics. The so-called real blood of Christ is preserved in a hundred convents, chapels and churches—in some of these in large quantities. Rome has the linen in which He was wrapped, and the first shirt which His mother made for Him. Fifteen places have the three nails by which Jesus was fastened to the cross, though the Empress Helena used them to make a bit for her horse and to adorn the helmet of Constantine. The real lance which pierced His side is in six churches. The thorns with which He was crowned would hedge in an acre of land. Tours and Carcassone have each the sword and buckler of the archangel Michael. There are three heads of John the Baptist, one of which is divided into various duplicate and even triplicate pieces. Six cities have each the forefinger of his right hand, with which he pointed to Christ when he said : "Behold the Lamb of God !" In the church over the catacomb of St. Sebastian, on the Appian Way, near Rome, is shown a stone on which are marks said to be the print of Christ's feet. In Silesia a letter is shown said to be a revelation made by Christ to St. Elizabeth, St. Bridget and St. Melchtida, in which He tells them that He has shed 72,200 tears for them, 97,350 drops of blood, received 6,696 blows, and so on. When I was in Rome I visited the place where Peter is said to have been crucified. The monk who was my guide, gave me some of the earth, which I keep as a curiosity. He drew it up out of a small hole by a pole with a scoop at the end. New earth must be put in from time to time, else as so much is given away every year, even though in small quantities, water, oil, salt or gas, to say nothing of rock, would, in the course of ages, be reached. I see no reason to doubt that the great Apostle of the circumcision was crucified there, if he was crucified in Rome at all. My great difficulty is about his ever having been in Rome. In one of the walls of a cell in the Mamertine Prison is a dimple said to have been made by Peter's head. Negroes are said to be hard-headed — not in the sense in which Scotchmen are said to be—but I would not encourage anyone to risk striking a stone wall with his head. A William goat or Darby's ram, spoken of in the beautiful ancient negro melody, "Ole Dan Tuckah," would have come off only second best in a butting contest with the first Pope. In the same cell is a spring said to have been produced miraculously to enable Peter to baptize the gaoler. There is just one slight difficulty connected with the story of its miraculous origin. We have clear proof that the spring was there long before Peter's time. The basement of the church of Santa Maria in Via Lata, in the Corso, Rome, is said to be the remains of his own hired house, in which Paul dwelt two whole years during his first imprisonment in that city. There is a spring there, too, which is said to have been produced miraculously, to enable him to baptise the centurion who had charge of him. Be that as it may, the water thereof is very good. Where he is said to have been beheaded are three springs, the origin of which, according to story is as follows:—His head, after leaving the body, leaped three times from the ground before it rested. At each spot where it did so a spring gushed forth. If one cannot believe the story, he is at liberty to do the opposite.

Near the Cathedral of Florence stands a stone pillar on which is a bronze tree and an inscription. According to the latter, it stands on the spot where a dead elm tree came to life, and bore buds and blossoms when the remains of St. Zenobius were removed from their former resting place to the Cathedral. This is something like the account of what Aaron's rod did on a certain occasion. I must say, however, that I see much greater reason for believing the latter than the former.

The bodies of Peter and Paul are at Rome, and parts in three other places. There are three bodies of Matthew. There are two entire bodies of Bartholomew, besides a large part of the body in two places. There are also three heads and a large number of parts of the head, jaws, arms and legs of the same apostle. In one of the churches in Genoa I saw a part of the chain with which John the Baptist was bound in prison. It had a modern appearance. In St. Mark's, Venice, I was shown a slab of dark-veined marble on which he is said to have been beheaded. According to the guide, the red streaks in it were his blood. I said to two visitors beside me : "Can you swallow that? It is too big to go down my throat." They laughed and said : "We have the same difficulty that you have."

APPENDIX XVIII.—(Page 118.)

THE Rev. Joseph Blanco White, at one time chaplain to Ferdinand VII. of Spain, says:—

"The picture of female convents requires a more delicate pencil : yet, I cannot find tints sufficiently dark and gloomy to pourtray the miseries which I have witnessed in their inmates. Crime, indeed, makes its way into those recesses, in spite of the spiked walls and prison grates which protect the inhabitants. This I know with all the certainty which the self-accusation of the guilty can give. It is, besides, a notorious fact that the nunneries of Estremadura and Portugal are frequently infected with vice of the grossest kind. But I will not dwell on this revolting part of the picture. The greater part of the nuns whom I have known were beings of a much higher description ; females whose purity owed nothing to the strong gates and high walls of the cloister, but who still had a human heart, and felt in many instances, and during a great portion of their lives, the weight of the vows which had deprived them of liberty."

APPENDIX XIX.—(Page 148.)

BLANCO WHITE says: "I have known the best among them (the Spanish clergy) ; I have heard their confessions ; I have heard the confessions of young persons of both sexes, who fell under the influence of their suggestions and example ; and I do declare that nothing can be more dangerous to youthful virtue than their company."

Melchior Canus says that Confession of the kind under consideration, teaches people not to shun evil, but to commit it.

The Rev. Mr. Seguin, for several years a Romish priest, who is now an open-communion Baptist minister in Chicago, U.S., has published a pamphlet containing translations of those parts of Dens' and Bishop Kendrick's works designed to assist confessors in questioning penitents regarding sins forbidden by our seventh commandment. Of course, I cannot give any specimens of it. It is most remarkable that good bishops, yea, saints (St. Liguori) for example, could deliberately frame such questions on these subjec's as they have done. It is plain that they were, to them, "sweet morsels." What is said of Babylon in the Book of Revelation, is true of each one of their minds—"the habitation of devils, and the hold of every foul spirit, and a cage of every unclean and hateful bird."

APPENDIX XX.—(Page 173.)

POPE GREGORY IX. (thirteenth century), first ordered a bell to be rung, as a signal for the worshippers to betake themselves to the adoration of the Host.

APPENDIX XXI.—(Page 184.)

BLANCO WHITE says of seven of the friends of his youth and manhood's prime : "Not one was tainted by the breath of gross vice till the Church had doomed them to a life of celibacy, and turned the best affections of their hearts into crime." " One whose talents raised him to the highest dignities of the church of Spain, was for many years a model of Christian purity. When, by the powerful influence of his mind and the warmth of his devotion, this man had drawn many into the clerical and the religious life (my youngest sister among the latter), he sank at once into the grossest and most daring profligacy. I heard him boast that, the night before the solemn procession of *Corpus Christi*, where he appeared nearly at the head of his chapter, one of *two* children had been born, which his two concubines brought to light within a few days of each other."

When I was in Rome, in 1885, I heard a person, in a good position to know, say that those there belonging to the upper classes, if there are daughters in their families, dislike to have priests visit them.

The Council of Constance was very zealous against heresy and heretics. It caused the Bible, and two faithful servants of Christ, namely John Huss, and Jerome, of Prague, to be burned, and declared that no faith should be kept with heretics. But the "Holy Fathers" dealt very gently with harlotry and harlots. Between a thousand and fifteen hundred of the "fallen sisterhood" followed them to Constance. During the Council, the former had "days of feasting and gladness," and made money in abundance. The eagles were gathered together, where the carcase was.

During the fourth session of the Council of Trent, at which only forty-eight bishops and five cardinals were present, and after a discussion varied by abusive language and pugilistic exercises, the Apocrypha, save three books, was, by a majority of *five*, declared to be inspired of God. As long as the Council was sitting, Trent was a favourite resort of swarms of strumpets from "a' the airts the wind can blaw," who, of course, took a deep interest in the discussions, though they did not understand one word of Latin, the language in which these were carried on. The society of these "faire ladyes" cheered the good Fathers in their arduous labours.

APPENDIX XXII.—(Page 184.)

BLANCO WHITE says: "How many souls would be saved from crime but for the vain display of pretended superior virtue which Rome demands of her clergy!" "The cares of a married life, it is said, interfere with the duties of the clergy. Do not the cares of a vicious life, the anxieties of stolen love, the contrivances of adulterous intercourse; the pains, the jealousies, the remorse attached to a conduct in perfect contradiction with a public and solemn profession of superior virtue—do not these cares, these bitter feelings, interfere with the duties of the priesthood? I have seen the most promising men of my university obtain country vicarages, with characters unimpeached and hearts overflowing with usefulness. A virtuous wife would have confirmed and strengthened their purposes; but they were to live a life of angels in celibacy. They were, however, men, and their duties connected them with beings of no higher description. Young women knelt before them in all the intimacy and openness of confession. A solitary home made them go abroad in search of social converse. Love, long-resisted, seized them at length, like madness. Two I knew who died insane; hundreds might be found who avoided that fate by a life of settled, systematic vice."

When Gregory VII., in 1074, decreed that "no priests should henceforth marry, and that such as now had either wives or concubines should relinquish either them or their sacred office," it caused a great commotion among the clergy. Many said: "We will rather lose our priesthood than part with our wives. Let him who despises men see whence he can procure angels for the churches."

Last year, a Maronite priest visited Toronto. During his stay, he celebrated mass in St. Michael's Cathedral. If he was a "single pink," that was not the reason why he was allowed to do so, for all the Maronite priests, though they are in full communion with the Romish Church, are allowed to marry. But the Second Council of Lateran, in 1189, "pronounced the marriage of priests void, on the ground of its inherent unholiness, and prohibited everyone from hearing Mass celebrated by a married priest."[1] Everyone present at the mass in St. Michael's abovementioned, was, therefore, according to this Council, accursed. A beautiful instance of the perfect harmony which exists in the Archbishop's Church! Why does she allow the Maronite priests to marry, but most sternly forbid her own to do so?"

I may here state that the priest who celebrated the mass, did so in Syriac, which, like Latin, is now a dead language. The Maronite clergy are allowed to celebrate mass in it, instead of in Latin. I do not suppose that one present at the Syriac mass in St. Michael's, understood one word of what was said. Perhaps the celebrant himself was not much better. But Syriac is just as good as Latin to those who understand neither.

APPENDIX XXIII.—(Page 203.)

"THE lowest known rocks, which are of a crystalline character, and which present a thickness of many thousand feet, are apparently destitute of organic forms. A few years ago, a supposed fossil was found in some of these crystalline strata, as was named the 'Eozoon'; but although some geologists still maintain its organic nature, the weight of evidence is against this, and the supposed fossil is now almost universally regarded as a mere mineral structure. These lowest strata, therefore, are regarded as azoic formations. They form the Laurentian and Huronian series, and are now generally classed together as rocks of the Archoean Age. There is, however, just the possibility that these beds may have been so altered by metamorphism as to have had their fossils entirely obliterated, but that is altogether unproved and quite problematical.

"The strata of all succeeding formations contain casts and impressions of organic bodies—crinoids, trilobites, brachiopods, etc., etc.; although locally, here and there, some of these strata (owing to the conditions prevailing at the spots where the sediments of which they are formed were laid down) may not exhibit fossils, or may contain very few.

(1) Protestantism and Romanism, Vol. II., p. 373.

"The term 'drift,' to which also you refer, is now applied solely to the 'Drift or Glacial' deposits—accumulations of clay, gravel, boulders, etc., which cover large areas, concealing the underlying beds, throughout the northern portions of the Earth, generally. In the true or lower Drift and Boulder formation, there are no fossils ; but there are plenty in the rocks which immediately preceded the deposition of the Drift beds, and there are many also in the Post-Glacial clays and sands which succeed the Drift deposits proper. In a word, there are no known fossils in the strata which indicate the first periods of the Earth's history ; but (with local exceptions) all the succeeding strata, apart from the lower Drift, are full of them."

APPENDIX XXIV.—(Page 204.)

The following, which has already appeared in print, may not be an unsuitable appendix to what I have said on Question 44, regarding Purgatory, and in the closing paragraph :—

"THE FIRST DAY OF THE FIRST MONTH."

AN ADDRESS FOR THE NEW YEAR'S SEASON.

January 1, 1887.

The moment a candle is lighted, it begins to waste away, till, at last, there is no more of it. Then the light which it gave, is quenched in darkness.

It is the same with time. From the moment an hour, a day, a week, a month or a year begins, it moves on without stopping till it comes to an end. Last night, at midnight, another of the greatest divisions of human life—the year 1886—bade us farewell for ever. For the past twelve months, we have been accustomed to read, to utter and to write that number as the name of the then present year. Now we can do so no longer. That year is now wholly a thing of the past. Never shall it be anything else. All the dead of mankind shall live again, but time that is past shall never return. Even God Himself cannot bring it back. The record of 1886—what we may call its character—is, therefore, fixed forever. As regarded ourselves, while it was passing by, we had it in our power to make its record either good or bad. Now it is utterly out of our power to do so. Is the record a good one ? Through all eternity it shall be so. Is the record a bad one ? Through all eternity it shall be so. Suppose a person working on a lump of clay. He can put it into any shape that pleases him. At length a wind passes over it and turns it into adamant.

Then no change can be made on its shape. So it was, and so it is with the year just ended. So it is, and so it shall be, with our lives, which are made up of years. "Time is the stuff of which life is made." While we are in this world, we can live either holy or wicked lives. But, when death comes, their record is made unchangeable. So, also, it is with our character and state. "It is appointed unto men once to die, but after this, the judgment." He who is righteous then, shall be righteous for ever. He who is wicked then, shall be wicked for ever. Then it is well with the righteous, and shall be so for ever. Then it is ill with the wicked, and shall be so for ever. As we are when we pass out of this world, we shall be when we stand before the judgment seat of Christ.

All our life long, we are dying. What we commonly call death, is merely the ending of life. Life is the burning of the candle. Death is the burning out of it. Hence the poet very truly says :

"The moment we begin to live,
We then begin to die."

Our days on the earth are, at the most, few. Our life here is, at the longest, short. What a solemn thought then it is that these few days, this short life, make eternity what it shall be with us! It is the germ in the nut which makes the tree which grows from it what it becomes—either an oak, an elm, a walnut or any other. The germ is itself very small—just like the point of a pin. The rest of the nut is nourishment for it. Immensely greater is the difference between the germ and the full-grown tree—for example, the oak—which springs from it. So it is with this life and the next—with time and eternity. The one is the germ, the other the tree. But infinitely greater is the difference between time and eternity. The longest part of the first which we can conceive is not even a moment in comparison with the second. Suppose two lines, one a million of miles long, the other—if it be possible to suppose it—though having a beginning, having no end. The length of the former would be absolutely nothing in comparison with that of the latter. If, then, it be a solemn thing to die, it is even more solemn to live, for—as we have already seen—our life decides what death shall be to us.

If we live a holy life, we do not need concern ourselves in the least about our death. We cannot but die well. If a person begin a picture properly, and continue his work on it in the same way, he will, in the nature of things, finish it properly. It would be utterly impossible for his picture to be a bad one. All, then, that he need concern himself about, is how he begins and goes on with it. So if we begin to live a holy life, and go on doing so, a happy death will be the result, even if we should, at the moment of it, have our minds occupied with lawful earthly things, or be in a state of utter unconsciousness.

APPENDIX XXIV.

I have spoken of time as distinct from eternity. We generally do so. The difference between the two is, however, really that between a part of a thing and the whole of it. Suppose a certain length measured on the line above mentioned. That distance is time. The measured line is simply a part of the endless one. So time is, in reality, a part of eternity. Yes, we are, in a certain sense, already in eternity. In this world we are on trial ; in the other—as I have already said—our character and state are fixed for ever. Hence we call our life in the first, time ; our life in the second, eternity. But, while it is quite correct thus to distinguish time and eternity from each other, it is still true that we are, in a certain sense, already in eternity. Our being shall never end. Though we die, we shall live again, and live for ever. We may take away our natural life, but we cannot put ourselves out of being. Seeing, then, that we shall live for ever according as we have lived here, either in happiness or misery, our wisdom is so to live here, that endless happiness shall be ours hereafter.

Our stay here is fast drawing to a close. It is utterly impossible for us to mark how quickly the present changes into the past. You have, no doubt, sometimes, when going on a railway train through a cutting in a soil in which were layers of stones, noticed that the rows of stones seemed only so many lines. That was because you went so quickly past each stone, that the image of no one had time to be fixed in your eye. The word " now " is a very short one. Yet a certain part of time passes away between our pronouncing the first part of it and the last. The present moment, however—which is so small that we cannot conceive it—is the only one which we can use. Both time past and time to come are out of our grasp. In that part of time which is like a pin's point, we sow what we shall reap in the other world.

Let us look back on the year just closed, and be *thankful*. Every day of it, God has loaded us with blessings. We cannot tell the number of blessings which we receive during a day. Much less can we tell the number of those which we receive during a year. Let us look back on the year just closed, and be *humble*. How imperfectly, at the best, we have performed the good resolutions which we made when it began ! How often, during it, we have sinned by doing what we should not have done, and by not doing what we should have done !

We have seen another year begin. To the goodness and power of God we owe it. This day last year, we looked forward to this day, but "shadows, clouds and darkness rested on it." We had no assurance that we should see it. We are like persons walking in a very thick fog. We see before us only step by step. How many of our fellow-beings have, during the past year, joined "the great congregation of the dead !" Yea, thousands have done so who never saw a New-Year. They came into the world after the year began, and left it before the year closed. Some of us have been called to mourn, during the past year, for friends removed by death. The writer lost three, one of them his mother, his nearest and dearest earthly friend. Shall we be on earth, the 1st of January, 1888 ? He alone can answer this question who has determined our days, and with whom is the number of our months. It is well for us that, as regards this life, the future is hid from us. It may be that He has written in the book of His decrees, opposite the names of some of the readers of this article, "This year thou shalt die." Some year will certainly come of which we shall see only a part. This year is that one to thousands. Why may it not be so to some of those who read these lines ? But, if we have lived aright, should next New-Year's day not find us on earth, it shall find us in glory.

. But how can we live aright? We can do so only by taking the Lord Jesus as our only Saviour, and following His example. This is like the painter beginning his work aright, and going on with it in the same way. We have seen that he cannot but finish it aright.

Reader, if thou have not begun to live as I have just described, begin *at once*. Thou hast great reason to thank the Lord for having spared thee to the present. The night of death cometh when thou shall not be able to work. What thy hand findeth to do, do it with thy might *now*.

If thou have begun to live as I have just described, happy art thou. This day, thou art "a year's march nearer home." Though this be the day of life with thee, and the night of death cometh ; it is as true that this is the night with thee, and the eternal day cometh. Be thou, then, steadfast, unmoveable, always abounding in the work of the Lord.

Reader, whatever be thy spiritual state, I wish thee in accordance therewith,

A HAPPY NEW YEAR.

Elder's Mills, Ont.   T. F.

I have already given a version of a grand old Latin hymn, the *Te Deum*. I shall now give one of another, the *Dies irae*, by Thomas de Celano, which, as it relates to the Last Judgment, is in harmony with this Appendix. In Michael Angelo's picture of the Last Judgment, in the Sistine Chapel, the Virgin Mary is represented as seated on His throne, beside the Lord Jesus. In this hymn, however, neither she, nor any other creature, is addressed :—

DIES IRAE ! DIES ILLA !

  1. The day of wrath ! that day of days !
   When earth shall vanish in a blaze,
   Oft burden of prophetic lays.

2. How men shall quake, o'ercome with fear,
   When the Judge shall with clouds appear
   To try all things by test severe !

3. Like thunder-peal, the trump of doom
   Sounds through the chambers of the tomb,
   Making before the throne all come.

4. Nature and death shall, with surprise
   O'erwhelmed, behold the dead arise,
   To stand before the dread assize.

5. The massive book unclosed behold !
   Wherein life's deeds are all enrolled,
   Which shall th' award to each one mould.

6. So when the Judge His seat has ta'en,
   Whate'er's been hid shall be made plain,
   Unsentenced there shall naught remain.

7. Then shall I say, Ah ! wretched me !
   To whom shall I for succour flee,
   When scarce is saved the just, ev'n he ? [1]

8. Thou King of awful majesty,
   Salvation's freely given by Thee,
   Save me, O Fount of piety !

9. Think on me, Jesus, I Thee pray,
   For I the cause am of Thy way, [2]
   Do not consume me in that day.

10. Weary, Thou'st at the well me sought, [3]
    By Thy cross, Thou'st me ransom brought,
    Let not so great love be for naught.

11. Thou judge of righteous decision,
    Bestow on me a free remission,
    Before shall come the great division.

12. As one accused, I deeply groan.
    I blush for all the sins I've done.
    Lord, spare a supplicating one.

(1) A reference to 1 Peter iv. 18. The word "scarce" is here used, not in the sense of incompleteness, but of difficulty.

(2) In the original, *Quod sum causa Tuae viae*. The meaning seems to be this : " Thou camest into the world to save sinners. I am one. Therefore, I am, in part, the cause of Thy coming."

(3) A reference to Christ meeting the woman of Samaria at Jacob's well. He came to it, to seek and to save that lost woman. The Good Shepherd seeks every one of His strayed sheep.

13. Thou to the harlot didst speak cheer. [1]
    Thou didst the dying thief's cry hear;
    To me, too, Thou say'st, Do not fear.

14. My prayers Thou justly mightest spurn;
    But, Lord, to me in mercy turn,
    Lest I in fire eternal burn.

15. With the sheep me associate,
    From the goats keep me separate,
    And at Thine own right hand me set.

16. When sentence 'gainst th' unjust is given,
    And into fierce flames they are driven,
    O call me with Thine own to heaven.

17. I'm dust and ashes, yet to Thee,
    With contrite heart I bow my knee.
    In my last hour watch over me.

18. O on that day of sorrow deep,
    When man awakes from the grave's sleep,
    To stand before the judgment-throne,
    Lord, be Thy sparing grace him shown!   T. F.

(1) In the original, *Qui Mariam absolvisti.* The Mary here spoken of, is Mary Magdalene, who is commonly supposed to have been, at one time, a harlot. For this opinion, there is not the slightest foundation. The fact that seven devils were cast out of her, is no proof whatever that she was a "sinner."

www.ingramcontent.com/pod-product-compliance
Lightning Source LLC
Chambersburg PA
CBHW020759230426
43666CB00007B/763